J.R.F. ALONSO is a lecturer in computer science at Swinburne Institute of Technology, Melbourne, Australia. He has been a Research Assistant at the Massachusetts Institute of Technology Computer Center and is a member of many professional computer, chemical, petroleum, and chemical engineering societies. In addition, he is the author of numerous technical articles.

SIMPLE

BASIC PROGRAMS FOR BUSINESS APPLICATIONS

J. R. F. Alonso

A SPECTRUM BOOK

Prentice-Hall, Inc. / Englewood Cliffs, New Jersey 07632

Library of Congress Cataloging in Publication Data

Alonso, J.R.F.
  SIMPLE, BASIC programs for business applications.

  (A Spectrum Book)
  Includes bibliographical references and index.
    1. Basic (Computer program language)
2. Business   Data processing. I. Title.
HF5548.5.B3A44   001.64'24   81-8518
ISBN 0 - 13 - 809897 - 2   AACR2
ISBN 0 - 13 - 809889 - 1 (pbk.)

This Spectrum Book can be made available to businesses and
organizations at a special discount when ordered in large quantities.
For more information contact: Prentice-Hall, Inc., General Book
Marketing, Special Sales Division, Englewood Cliffs, New Jersey
07632.

Prentice-Hall International, Inc., London
Prentice-Hall of Australia Pty. Limited, Sydney
Prentice-Hall of Canada, Ltd., Toronto
Prentice-Hall of India Private Limited, New Delhi
Prentice-Hall of Japan, Inc., Tokyo
Prentice-Hall of Southeast Asia Pte. Ltd., Singapore
Whitehall Books Limited, Wellington, New Zealand

To Patricia and Kenneth
who lived through the writing of this manual
and
to my parents—who wish they had.

CONTENTS

Miscellaneous Business Calculations 187

SECTION **III**

APPLYING SIMPLE

Most Common BASIC Instructions 237

FORTRAN-BASIC Conversion Tables

Cross References to Leading Statistics Textbooks

PREFACE

The SIMPLE programs in this book are well tested, require only a minimally technical background, and are flexible enough to apply to almost limitless situations. Tested for five years in the United States, Europe, and Australia, these comprehensive calculational programs are equally at home in a large computer system, in minicomputers, or in personal microsystems. No program requires more than 16K bytes of memory for execution. Since these programs are completely conversational, users can tackle realistic problems immediately, without going through the usual training in program package syntax or in job control language. Even though users can employ these programs without any knowledge of the BASIC computer language, a familiarity with it enables them to customize the programs for their particular applications. (Striking up an acquaintance with BASIC is, of course, generally a good idea, insofar as users then better understand the logic behind the programs.)

This manual, dealing with business applications, is only one of three volumes, the other two of which are:

- SIMPLE for Social Sciences
- SIMPLE for Engineering and Mathematics

All these programs are available in magnetic tape (Industry Standard, nine-track, EDCDIC, odd-parity, 800 bpi, 80 character records). The magnetic listings, containing the entire suite of programs, cost a total of $100, including air mail shipping expenses. Since some 200 pages of BASIC programs are involved, the purchase of these listings is strongly advised for academic, industrial, and all serious users.

To make this SIMPLE manual as useful as possible to as many readers as possible, it has been organized so as to apply to numerous individual situations:

- A section on BASIC brings readers along to the point that they can tailor the SIMPLE programs to their specific needs.

- The second section contains a suite of computer programs in SIMPLE, each of which contains:

    user instructions,

    —a sample problem,

    —references to other reading material,

    —an actual program listing, and

    —a sample run of the sample program.

    (What could be clearer?)

- The third section of the manual contains:

    —tables listing the most common BASIC instruction sets: TRS–80, HP–85, Apple II, and Commodore PET. These sets provide you with a bird's eye view of the principal syntax differences between common computers. (As they appear in this manual, the SIMPLE programs will run on almost any minicomputer or large computer system, as well as on home systems.)

    —FORTRAN-BASIC conversion tables, which are very seldom found in the open literature. With these tables, if you don't have BASIC in your system, you can convert the programs into FORTRAN.

    —cross-reference tables that relate the SIMPLE programs to the leading statistics textbooks—a tremendous aid to students.

No matter what your needs, no matter what your system, and no matter what your level of technical expertise—you can use SIMPLE programs.

Despite the testing and care taken in providing these programs, the inevitable bugs always lurk, ready to appear at the most inconvenient times. My apologies go out to any users who encounter them, along with the request to send any errors to the attention of the author. Rest assured that your suggestions and criticisms will be incorporated into future printings.

Good luck in your experience with SIMPLE!

J. R. F. Alonso

Melbourne, Australia

ACKNOWLEDGMENTS

The author wishes to acknowledge his gratitude to the following:

Mrs. Joan Champion, typist and guardian angel during the different writing stages of the work.

Prof. E. J. Henley, of the University of Houston, without whose invitation to spend the year 1977 at the University of Houston this work may have taken a little longer to develop.

Mr. K. Anderson of the Educational Technology Unit at Swinburne College of Technology, who provided both administrative support and a mental ping-pong partner.

Messrs. C. Scott and H. Yeo, Mathematics Department, Swinburne College, for their help in developing some programs and input formats.

Messrs. R. Stewart, R. Charest, G. Sutter and Prof. R. McClintock, of the University of Houston, and Prof. K. Bishop of the University of Kansas for their help in the installation and testing of SIMPLE in their own institutions.

Messrs. James L. Poirot and David N. Groves, authors, and Sterling Swift Publishing Company, publisher of the book *Computers and Mathematics* for their kind permission to use some of their material in Section I of this work, "A Basic Primer."

Last, but not least, the author thanks his students, whose enthusiasm, understanding and forebearance made the developing and testing of the programs a mutually rich and rewarding experience, in particular Messrs. W. Pizzey (AV2, AV3), R. Schorer (PCA), J. Garrioch (Some of the business routines) and J. Campbell (PFA) who had quite a bit to do with the writing of the programs in parentheses.

SIMPLE can be supplied in:

MAGNETIC TAPE MINI-REEL, INDUSTRY STANDARD, (9 track, 800 Bits per inch, Odd Parity; EBCDIC)

FROM **Sterling Swift Publishing Company**
P.O. Box 188
Manchaca, Texas 78652

SECTION

I

A BASIC PRIMER

Computers and computer programming developed into a commercially practical reality in the late forties and early fifties. Yet the machines, besides being ponderous, were diabolically difficult to program with the then available machine languages (strings of zeros and ones) or assembly languages (shorter acronymic word commands not unlike cabalistic incantations). To make things worse, programmers could communicate with their computers only through punched cards.

During the late fifties and early sixties, the punched-card-oriented FORTRAN, COBOL, and SNOBOL languages catered to the programming needs of scientific, business, and lexicographic computer users and practitioners. The SSP package was the standard computer subroutine library, and its use required a considerable knowledge not only of FORTRAN, but also of the mathematical techniques that it entails.

The late sixties saw the advent of BASIC—the first truly easy-to-use conversational programming language, which has since become the lingua franca of the micro- and minicomputer communities. The late sixties also saw the development of SPSS, IMSL, BMDP, FAKAD, and other statistical and mathematical subroutine libraries which were easier to use than SSP. These newer routines allowed users who were not skilled in programming to do large data set file handling with just a reasonable expenditure of learning effort. At the same time, they replaced the need for a deep knowledge of FORTRAN by an equally onerous set of syntax rules.

The seventies brought the development of the large time-sharing networks and the thousand-dollar microcomputer. This decade also saw the very active reevaluation and rationalization of programming methods and practices: "structured" or "top-down" programming and the PASCAL language, "bottom-up" languages like APL, and the standardization of the world's armed forces around the newer still ADA language and the 8080/8085 microprocessor and its associated assembly language. Despite all these disparate forces at work, it still seems safe to say that:

1. BASIC is here to stay as the principal language for minicomputers.
2. Educational interactive software is—and likely will continue to be—most commonly written in BASIC.
3. BASIC allows the greatest ease of modification of existing programs to fit the calculational, data, or format needs of particular applications.
4. Programs written in BASIC to cover the small data set area are not included in the large subroutine packages and are desperately needed by users of microcomputers, minicomputers, and educational computers.

BASIC AND SIMPLE

The SIMPLE suite of programs provides minicomputer and educational computer users with a comprehensive range of calculational facilities that up to now were not available in such easy-to-use and easy-to-install form. Because all programs listings are available, the programs can be easily modified to better suit a particular application. A sample problem supplied with every program shows unequivocally how it should be used and for what type of problem. The form of BASIC used is widely compatible, and the storage requirements (a maximum of 16K bytes) very modest.

As an adjunct to most common textbooks, the suite enables both teachers and students to solve dozens of problems in the time taken to solve just one by hand or by hand calculator. They can also tackle those larger, more realistic problems that they could not do manually but that do not justify the time and expense of a large package.

WHY STUDY COMPUTER PROGRAMMING?

A computer cannot think. Even though we often envision it as a large electronic brain, it simply does what users tell it to do. In other words, it merely carries out instructions. These instructions constitute a *program*. Translating a user's ideas and problem solutions into appropriate instructions is called *programming*. And the people who write out these programs are *programmers*. If all this is a little obvious to some readers, it serves to point out a somewhat less obvious fact: A computer will do nothing unless you instruct it to do something through a program. Hence the importance of knowing how to program a computer.

Learning to program is not very hard at all, since you needn't learn everything there is to know. Actually, a better name for this chapter might be "BASIC I Should Know to be Better Able to Take Advantage of SIMPLE." In this chapter, you should limit your objectives to the following:

1.   to modify an existing program so as to make its input requirements or output format more relevant to the problem that the program is being used to solve.
2.   to design and construct programs which solve "everyday" problems in several different disciplines.
3.   to construct programs that use a variety of instruction types.
4.   to document programs properly, supplying the needed flowcharts and program descriptions.

Of these four skills, the first is the primary reason for including this section of the manual. This section is designed to enable you to modify the input and output requirements of any SIMPLE program to better suit the specific requirements of your particular problem application.

Nonetheless, the chapter is quite comprehensive, and any reader who studies it with the help of a computer terminal or minicomputer will indeed become a competent programmer in the process. Study it remembering that programming knowledge comes in through the fingers, not through the eyes. Pencil, paper, and access to a computer are the only means of acquiring mastery of the BASIC language.

INTRODUCTION TO PROGRAMMING

The computer is a tool used to aid in the solution of a problem. It cannot be overemphasized that, as far as possible, a problem-solving approach should be language-independent. Only after a logical sequence of decisions and manipulations has been formulated should translation into any language begin.

The choice of the proper language to use in the solution of a problem is not always a simple one; literally hundreds of computer languages are now in use. FORTRAN, BASIC, COBOL, SNOBOL, APL, PL/I, and Assembly Language are some of the more common languages. The choice of BASIC as the language for developing SIMPLE is due to its simplicity, its widespread availability as a time-sharing and microcomputer language, and its prospects of future use that point well into the late eighties.

A program written in BASIC must be translated into the machine language of the computer (1's and 0's). This translation is accomplished by another program called a compiler (or interpreter for some languages). Errors in the program, detected during the process of translation, are called compiler or "syntax" errors. These errors are due to the programmer's use of an incorrect form of the language. After the program has been translated into machine language, the program may be executed. Errors occurring during execution are referred to as "logic" errors, for these errors are due to errors in the design of the problem solution. We will return to the topic of "debugging," i.e., the removal of errors (bugs) from a program, in later sections.

The knowledge of one programming language helps greatly in the learning of a new one, particularly if the two languages have similar characteristics. This chapter will end with a comparison of BASIC and FORTRAN, demonstrating the similarity of the two languages.

BEGINNING BASIC

The majority of the terminology and specific symbols used in this chapter are those associated with the Radio Shack TRS-80 microcomputer system. Commands used by different systems often vary, for a "standard" BASIC has not yet been accepted. Choice of the TRS-80 is based upon the author's conviction that the microcomputer is not only the computer system of tomorrow, but that of today. Very little in substance will be found different from other BASIC systems, and the variation in command names, etc., will be found in the users manual for the system being used.

There are three general categories of BASIC items: system commands, program statements, and functional or operational symbols. System commands such as RUN, LIST, etc., are those commands given to the computer as regards the handling and execution of the program. Program statements (PRINT, END, etc.) and operation symbols (*, −, +, etc.) are used in the actual coding of the BASIC program. We will first concentrate on writing simple programs and then study the system commands needed to run the program.

Since BASIC is primarily an interactive language, the computer terminal (or keyboard and video display) is the primary "interface" the programmer has with the computer system. The terminal is used for program generation as well as for data input and output.

The procedures for gaining access to a system for programming vary significantly from system to system. For microcomputer systems, for example, one simply turns on the power and hits the ENTER key. The system is then ready to accept commands. For time-sharing systems, the sign-on procedures are generally referred to as logging-on (and later logging-off). The use of certain passwords or code words is a typical method to control unauthorized access to a time-sharing system. The user's manual to the system being used is the only reliable source for such information.

There are relatively few formal procedures necessary to the writing of programs in BASIC. At least two, however, should be followed, even though these are not essential for all systems: every statement must have a number, say n, such that $1 \leq n \leq 9999$; the last statement in any program must be an END statement. For example:

100 END

ASSIGNMENT STATEMENTS

In order to store a number in the computer's memory, a storage position must be allocated for that number. This is accomplished by assigning a name to each number and referring to it by that name. Since we can change the value of the number stored in this allocated position, we use the term "variable" and say the variable is assigned a value. For example, we might use the variable C to denote a counter. To initialize or set C to the value 1, we would use the assignment statement:

10 LET C = 1

The compiler would allocate a storage position for C and upon execution of statement number 10, C would be assigned the value 1. Later in the program if the statement:

50 LET C = 2

were executed, the value of C would be changed to 2.

In BASIC, variables may be assigned names with a single alphabetic letter or with a letter followed by a digit. Thus B, Q, A, A1, A9, and Z2 are legal variable names in BASIC. Variable names may be longer than two characters but only the first two characters will be used by the computer to distinguish between variables. Thus VARIABLE, VAR, and VA will all be treated as the same variable. Examples of variable names that do not satisfy the above requirements, and thus are illegal, include A/ , #4, Z*, and 52.

The operations of addition, subtraction, multiplication, division, and exponentiation are denoted by $+$, $-$, $*$, $/$ and $\uparrow$, respectively. The exponentiation operation $\uparrow$, requires that the exponent be a one- or two-digit integer number or variable. These operations may be included in an assignment statement such as:

```
10 LET A = 4 + 7
20 LET B = A + 7
30 LET C = Q * A
40 LET V1 = V2/8
50 LET A = A - 7
```

The rules governing hierarchy of the arithmetic operation are the same as those in algebra. That is, exponentiation is performed first, then multiplications and divisions (left-to-right), and finally additions and subtractions (left-to-right). Thus:

10 LET A = 5 + 4 * 3

yields a value of 17 for A, whereas:

10 LET A = 5 * 4 + 3

leaves a value of 23. The following are further examples of assignment statements. Use the rules of operational hierarchy to check the results.

Statement	Result
10 LET A = 4 + 9/3	A = 7
10 LET A = 9 * 7 − 3	A = 60
10 LET A = 3 * 4 − 6/2	A = 9
10 LET A = 4 * 3↑2	A = 36
10 LET A = 4↑3 * 2	A = 128
10 LET A = 4↑3 * 2 + 4	A = 132

Parentheses may be used in assignment statements the same way as they are used in algebra, defining the order in which operations are to be performed. Thus:

10 LET A = 3 + 9/3

gives a result of A = 6, whereas:

10 LET A = (3 + 9) /3

gives A = 4. Other examples follow.

Statement	Result
10 LET A = 4/ (3 + 1)	A = 1
10 LET A = (9 + 3) / (4 + 2)	A = 2
10 LET A = 20 / 5 + 5	A = 9
10 LET A = 20 / (5 + 5)	A = 2
10 LET A = 5 * 6/ (3 + 2)	A = 6

The use of the LET in assignment statements is optional, so that the statements:

60 LET E = 70.1/5

and:

60 E = 70.1/5

are equivalent.

Variables that have been previously defined (either by other assignment statements or by input) may be used on the right hand side of the equality sign. For example:

100 A1 = 5
110 B = 3 + A1
120 C = 7 * A1 + B/A1 + A1↑B

are legal assignment statements. If A = 5, B = 7 and C = −9, the following results would be obtained:

Statement	Result
10 D = A + B	D = 12
10 D = A − B + C	D = −11
10 D = A↑2 + 4	D = 29
10 D = (A + B) * C	D = −108

Exercise 1

1. Which of the following variable names are illegal in BASIC?

    C1   A   BC   5A $1   Z21   A9

2. Write BASIC assignment statements for the following equations.

    (a) $P = (4)(5) + 7$

    (b) $A1 = 3X^2 + 2X + 1$

    (c) $C = \dfrac{4A - 5B^2}{A - 1}$

    (d) $C = 2.146X - \dfrac{3.12}{X} + \dfrac{2.74}{X}$

    (e) $C = (A - B)(A - C)\left\{4.1 - \left[\dfrac{A}{D}\right]^2\right\}$

    (f) $C5 = \dfrac{1 + 4.2A}{(A - B)(B - C)^2}$

DATA INPUT

Data input in BASIC may be accomplished by using either the READ or INPUT commands. The READ command requires that the data be placed in a DATA statement somewhere in the program. For example:

```
10 DATA 15
20 READ A
```

would allow the value 15 to be input to the variable A. The statements:

```
30 DATA 174, − 261, 14
40 READ A, B
50 READ C
```

upon execution give values of A = 174, B = − 261, and C = 14. We note that several numbers separated by commas may be placed in one DATA statement and that one READ statement may contain several variables separated by commas.

It should also be noted that the DATA statement is not an executed statement and may appear anywhere in the program. In general, however, it is best to place all DATA statements either at the beginning of a program or just ahead of the END statement.

In order for a READ statement to be successfully executed, there must be at least as many unused values still in DATA statements as the READ statement requires. Thus, if the following READ statement were used:

```
20 READ A, B, C
```

and only two values remained in the DATA statement(s), the computer would print something like:

```
OUT OF DATA IN 20
```

since a value for C was not available.

Any number of DATA statements may be used in a single program. These DATA statements simply set up a list of input values which will be read by one or more READ statements. The following are further examples of READ and DATA statements.

	Statements	Results after READ
a)	10 READ A, B, C 20 DATA 15, 25, 30	A = 15, B = 25, C = 30
b)	10 READ A, B, C 20 DATA 15, 30 30 DATA 25	A = 15, B = 30, C = 25
c)	10 DATA 30, 25 20 READ A 30 DATA 15 40 READ B, C	A = 30, B = 25, C = 15

Restore

The RESTORE statement allows you to reuse the same DATA lines by causing the next READ statement executed to start with the first item in the first DATA statement. Thus, in the following:

```
10 READ A
20 RESTORE
30 READ B
40 DATA 40
```

both A and B are assigned the value of 40.

Input

The command INPUT allows data to be supplied directly from the terminal during the actual execution of the BASIC program. For example, the execution of the statement:

```
30 INPUT A
```

would require that the input to A be typed in from the terminal (after the "?" is supplied by the computer). As in the case of the READ command, more than one value may be requested in one INPUT command:

```
40 INPUT A, B, C
```

would cause a question mark to be printed on the terminal, indicating a request for data. Data input such as

```
? 25, 10, 15
```

followed by "$\boxed{\text{ENTER}}$", would assign the listed values to A, B, and C. If fewer than or more than three numbers are typed in, an error message will be generated by the computer.

The INPUT statement allows interaction between the computer and the programmer during the execution of the program. This communication will be better demonstrated by examples in the next section.

Exercise 2

1. Prepare one DATA statement to satisfy each of the following.

    (a) 10 READ A, B
    (b) 10 READ A, B, C, D, E
    (c) 10 READ C2
    (d) 20 READ A, B, D
    (e) 30 READ Q, R, S1

2. Re-do the three problems (a), (b), and (c) in problem 1 using exactly two DATA statements for each problem.
3. How many DATA statements may a BASIC program contain?
4. May two or more READ statements located at different points in a BASIC program read values from the same DATA statement?
5. How many values does the computer expect to be typed in when the following command is executed?

   40 INPUT W1, W2, W3, W4

6. List the primary differences in the INPUT and READ commands.

DATA OUTPUT

Output is accomplished in BASIC by use of the PRINT command. Values of variables may be printed by listing the variable names in a PRINT statement. When variables are separated by commas, the values are printed in columns on the terminal, up to five values per line. Thus, assuming 5, 25, and -6 were the values assigned to A, C1, and D, respectively, the statement:

   70 PRINT A, C1, D

would produce output on the terminal:

Col.1	Col. 2	Col. 3	Col. 4	Col. 5
5	25	-6		

A PRINT statement containing more than five variables produces more than one printed output line on the terminal.

A semicolon may be used in place of a comma, causing the printed values to be printed closer together, separated only by one or two blanks.

English language or literal messages may also be printed by enclosing the message in quotation marks. These messages, including blanks and special characters, are printed exactly as prepared by the programmer. For example, the statements:

   10 PRINT "   CSCI 110"
   20 PRINT " SAMPLE PROGRAM"

would result in the following printed output.

```
    CSCI 110
SAMPLE PROGRAM
```

The statement:

30 PRINT "THE VALUE OF X IS" ;X; "THE VALUE OF Y IS" ;Y

illustrates the printing of messages and values of variables in the same PRINT statement. Assuming the value of X is 51.6 and the value of Y is −17.1, the following would be printed:

THE VALUE OF X IS 51.6   THE VALUE OF Y IS −17.1

Note the use of the semicolons and blanks in the messages for proper spacing in the output.

The final usage of the PRINT statement is having the computer print the results of a calculation defined within the PRINT statement. For example:

```
10 PRINT A − B
20 PRINT A + B, A − B, A · B, A/B
30 PRINT "SUM OF A AND B IS"; A + B
```

are legitimate uses of the PRINT statement. In statement 20, the results of the addition, subtraction, multiplication, and division of A and B are printed. If A has the value 5 and B the value 4, the following printout would result from the execution of the three PRINT statements above:

```
1
9           1           20          1.25
SUM OF A AND B IS 9
```

Using the READ, INPUT and PRINT for communication between computer and user, and using assignment statements for performing operations, we may now write the following program:

```
10 READ A, B, C
20 S1 = A + B
30 S2 = A + C
40 S3 = B + C
50 PRINT S1, S2, S3
60 DATA 10, 15, 20
70 END
```

S1, S2, and S3 represent the three possible sums of three input values A, B, and C. The following program accepts as input from the terminal two values, V1 and V2, and computes the sum, difference, product and quotient of the two:

```
100 INPUT V1, V2
110 S = V1 + V2
120 D = V1 − V2
130 P = V1 * V2
140 Q = V1/V2
150 PRINT S, D, P, Q
160 END
```

Meaningful statements can easily be supplied to the user when this program is executed, by modifying the program to read:

```
90 PRINT "INPUT THE VALUES V1 AND V2";
100 INPUT V1, V2
110 S = V1 + V2
120 D = V1 − V2
130 P = V1 * V2
140 Q = V1/V2
150 PRINT "THE SUM IS"; S
160 PRINT "THE DIFFERENCE IS"; D
170 PRINT "THE PRODUCT IS"; P
180 PRINT "THE QUOTIENT IS"; Q
190 END
```

As a final example in this section, consider the following sequence:

```
10 DATA 15, 20, 5
20 READ A, B, C
30 LET R = A − B + 2 * C
40 PRINT "INPUT VALUES ARE: A = ";A; "B = ";B; "C = ";C
50 PRINT "RESULT R = ";R
60 END
```

Upon execution of the above program, the following output would be obtained:

```
INPUT VALUES ARE: A = 15 B = 20 C = 5
RESULT R = 5
```

If statements 10 and 20 above were replaced with the following:

```
10 PRINT "INPUT THE VALUES FOR A, B, AND C"
20 INPUT A, B, C
```

the program output would be the following:

```
INPUT THE VALUES FOR A, B, AND C
?15, 20, 5
INPUT VALUES ARE: A = 15 B = 20 C = 5
RESULT R = 5
```

As stated in the previous section, the INPUT command allows for conversation between programmer or user and the computer. The underlined numbers 15, 20, and 5 had to be input to the program during the actual running of the program.

Exercise 3

1. Assume the following values for A, B, C, D, E, and F respectively: (10, −5, 14, 7, 2, 25). What would be the printed output for the following?

   (a) 10 PRINT A, B, C
   (b) 10 PRINT A; B; C
   (c) 10 PRINT A, B; C; A
   (d) 10 PRINT A, B, C, D, E, F
   (e) 10 PRINT A; B; C; D; E; F
   (f) 10 PRINT "SUM OF B AND F"; B + F
   (g) 10 PRINT A * D, A + B + C, F/B, C + E
   (h) 10 PRINT A * B − C + D * E, 5 * A + 4

2. Write PRINT statements which will print the values of A and B, and the sum of A and B:

   (a) on one line at standard column positions
   (b) on one line as close together as possible
   (c) on separate lines with no messages
   (d) on separate lines with appropriate messages

3. Prepare PRINT statements to print on separate lines your name, class, date and teacher's name. Center the output assuming you have 64 spaces per line.

SYSTEM COMMANDS—THE FIRST PROGRAM

The input, output and assignment statements we have now examined are all program statements. In fact, simple BASIC programs may now be written. Before we can execute such programs, however, we must study certain system commands. System commands are special commands to the computer giving instructions on what to do with our programs. It should be remembered that these commands are not instructions used in the problem solution.

System commands are always dependent on the particular system being used, with the command names sometimes differing. However, the command functions included here are common to most systems.

After having logged-in, giving the necessary password, or simply turning on the system if a microcomputer is being used, the system responds with:

">", "?", or "READY".

This informs the programmer that the system is ready to accept BASIC program statements or system commands.

Assuming a BASIC program is to be written, the program statements when entered are placed in a temporary working area inside the computer's memory. Any program to be executed must be present in this working area. Moreover, only one program at a time is allowed in this area.

RUN

Consider the example program of the previous section. After the READY is supplied by the system, we enter the commands:

```
10 DATA 15, 20, 5
20 READ A, B, C
30 LET R = A − B + 2 * C
40 PRINT "INPUT VALUES ARE: A = ";A; "B = ";B; "C = ";C
50 PRINT "RESULT R = ";R
60 END
```

The program has now been completely entered into the memory and is now ready to be executed. Thus we issue the system command:

```
RUN
```

The program is then executed yielding the appropriate output:

```
INPUT VALUES ARE: A = 15 B = 20 C = 5
RESULT R = 5
```

Modifying the Program

Lines of code in a program in memory may be easily modified. For example, assume that the following line has been entered:

```
20 A = B * C
```

Suppose that we now decide that the operation should be addition rather than multiplication. We only have to reenter the line, using the same line number. That is, entering:

```
20 A = B + C
```

now changes the line in memory.

Lines of code may also be inserted into a program by using the appropriate line number. For example, assume we have entered the two lines:

```
10 INPUT A
20 C = A + B
```

Now assume that we find that the statement:

```
INPUT B
```

must be inserted between lines 10 and 20. We accomplish this feat by simply typing:

```
15 INPUT B
```

By using a line number between the two (10 and 20), we perform an "insert." The sequence of instructions then appears as

```
10 INPUT A
15 INPUT B
20 C = A + B
```

Consider again the program

```
10 DATA 15, 20, 5
20 READ A, B, C
30 LET R = C − B + 2 * C
40 PRINT "INPUT VALUES ARE: A = ";A; "B = ";B; "C = ";C
50 PRINT "RESULT R = ";R
60 END
```

Assume that we wish to run this program with a new set of data, say 7, 9, and − 4 for A, B, and C respectively. This may be accomplished by entering:

```
10 DATA 7, 9, − 4
```

The previous DATA statement has been replaced, and we are now ready to run the program by typing RUN.

LIST

Now assume that we wish to insert a new statement right before the END statement. This may be accomplished by entering, say:

```
55 PRINT "PROGRAM COMPLETE"
```

The system automatically places all statements in ascending line number order. Now to get a complete listing of the program, we type:

```
LIST
```

This system command causes the entire program in the temporary area to be listed:

```
10 DATA 7, 9, − 4
20 READ A, B, C
30 LET R = A − B + 2 * C
40 PRINT "INPUT VALUES ARE: A = ";A; "B = ";B; "C = ";C
50 PRINT "RESULT R = ";R
55 PRINT "PROGRAM COMPLETE"
60 END
```

The advantage and necessity of the use of line numbers in BASIC should now be seen, as well as the advantage of initially using line numbers that are multiples of ten. Insertion of new statements and correction or replacement of existing statements are easily accomplished.

AUTO

A rather handy system command available on some systems allows for the automatic line numbering of a program. All the programmer has to do is issue the command

AUTO (line number), (increment)

where (line number) is the beginning line number desired and (increment) is the increment between lines. From that point on the system displays the line number and all the programmer has to do is enter the program statement. Each time the ENTER key is hit, the computer advances to the next line number. The following example illustrates the function of AUTO:

Command	to use line numbers
AUTO 5, 5	5, 10, 15, 20, . . .
AUTO 100, 20	100, 120, 140, 160, . . .
AUTO	10, 20, 30, 40, . . .
AUTO 50	50, 60, 70, 80

Note that when (line number) and (increment) are omitted, the value 10 is used. To turn off the AUTO function, hit the BREAK key.

DELETE

DELETE N-M deletes all lines of a program in memory that are between (and including) those numbered N and M. For example:

DELETE 20-30

deletes all lines with numbers greater than or equal to 20 and less than or equal to 30. If the following sequence of statements were in memory:

```
10 DATA 5
20 READ A
30 PRINT A
40 END
```

and if we issue the commands:

```
DELETE 20, 30
LIST
```

the following would be printed:

```
10 DATA 5
40 END
```

Two other variations of DELETE may be used. For example:

```
DELETE 50
```

deletes only line number 50:

```
DELETE - 100
```

deletes all program lines up to and including 100.

SAVING A PROGRAM ON A MICROCOMPUTER SYSTEM

Once a program has been debugged, a programmer may wish to retain that program for running at a later date. On most microcomputer systems, programs are stored on cassette tapes. Variations of command names are common from system to system. However, the following demonstrates the usage of cassette storage.

CSAVE

Assume that you have a program that is currently in the temporary working area of memory. The cassette recorder must be properly connected, cassette loaded, and in the Record mode. The command:

```
CSAVE "SAMPLE"
```

where SAMPLE is the name to be given the program, is entered. The program stored on tape will then bear the specified file name. However, only the first letter of the file name is used by CSAVE (and CLOAD) so files on the same tape must start with different alpha-numeric characters.

CLOAD

The system command:

    CLOAD "SAMPLE"

loads the program named SAMPLE from cassette tape into memory. The cassette recorder must be in Play mode before the command CLOAD is issued. CLOAD automatically clears out the previously stored program in memory.

NEW

Once a program has been saved on tape (or when you wish to start a new program), memory may be cleared or erased, by issuing the system command:

    NEW

The system is now ready for a new program to be entered.

SUMMARY OF SYSTEM COMMANDS INTRODUCED

As a point of review, the following system commands have been introduced so far:

RUN	Causes the computer to execute the program stored in memory
LIST	Instructs the computer to display all program lines presently stored in memory
AUTO	Turns on an automatic line numbering function
DELETE	Erases program lines from memory
CSAVE	Stores the program in memory on a cassette tape
CLOAD	Loads a BASIC program stored on a cassette tape into memory
NEW	Erases all program lines in memory

Exercise 4

1. Place the following sample program on your computer system and use each of the following (or equivalent) system commands: RUN, LIST, DELETE, CSAVE, CLOAD, AUTO and NEW.

```
10 PRINT "INPUT VALUE OF A";
20 INPUT A
30 PRINT "INPUT VALUE OF B";
40 INPUT B
50 C = A + B
60 PRINT "SUM IS "; C
70 END
```

2. What is the difference between program statements and system commands?
3. (a) Write a program to input two numbers A and B, using the READ command. Then find and output the product and quotient of A and B. Use appropriate messages with your output.
    (b) Save the program in (a) on your tape (or library). Then modify the program so that the INPUT statement is used instead of the READ statement.

CONTROL STATEMENTS AND LOOPS

As was seen in the previous chapter on flowcharting, many problem solutions require the use of "decision" or "control" statements. These control statements not only allow us to make decisions, but also allow loops, another important programming topic, to be set up.

GO TO Statements

The statement:

```
GO TO N
```

allows for an unconditional branch or jump to statement number N. The example:

```
50 GO TO 100
```

would cause the program to execute statement number 100 immediately after 50. GO TO statements are most often used in BASIC in conjunction with decisions accomplished by the IF command. However, the following example shows the use of a GO TO in a program that has an "infinite loop":

```
10 S = 0
20 INPUT A
30 S = S + A
40 PRINT "SUM IS"; S
50 GO TO 20
60 END
```

Note that the GO TO statement forces a return to statement 20 where a new value for A is requested.

Excessive uses of GO TO's should be avoided in program design, since they often make the program logic complicated and difficult to follow.

IF (expression) (action)

The IF statement, with its several variations, represents the most powerful BASIC language instruction relating to decision making. The first IF statement considered:

    IF (expression) (action)

instructs the computer to test the (expression). If the (expression) is "True," the (action) will be accomplished. If the (expression) is "False," the control will jump to the next program line. As an example, consider:

    100 IF A > 0 LET B = A + 5

If the value of A is greater than 0, then B is set to A + 5.

Other examples follow:

    110 IF A < 0 PRINT   "VALUE NEGATIVE"
    120 IF A + B < = 0   GO TO 500
    130 IF I > 5   A = B * I

The relational symbols = , < , > , < = , > = , and < > mean equals, less than, greater than, less than or equals, greater than or equals and not equal, respectively. All of these symbols may be used in the (expression) of the IF.

The logical operators of AND and OR may be used to join several relational expressions. For example:

    100 IF A < 0 OR A > 10   B = 50

sets B to 50 if A is less than 0 or if A is greater than 10. While:

    100 IF A > 0 AND B > 0   C = A + B

sets C to the sum of A plus B only if both A and B are greater than 0.

The following is an example program that inputs two values, A and B, and prints out the larger of the two. If the values are equal, we simply print out that value as the larger:

```
10 PRINT "INPUT A, B";
20 INPUT A, B
30 IF A > = B   PRINT "LARGER VALUE IS"; A
40 IF B > A   PRINT "LARGER VALUE IS"; B
50 END
```

IF (expression) THEN (action or line number)

Another variation of the IF statement utilizes the THEN statement. All of the examples in the previous section could be rewritten inserting the THEN before the (action). Thus:

```
110 IF A > 0   THEN PRINT "VALUE NEGATIVE"
120 IF A + B < = 0   THEN GO TO 500
130 IF I > 0   THEN A = B * I
```

are legitimate uses of the THEN. Using the THEN in an IF statement generally clarifies the logic and is often less confusing. Thus we encourage the usage of the IF . . . THEN . . . combinations.

There are two situations when the THEN must be included with the IF, when specifying a branch and when utilizing the ELSE statement. We may specify a branch to a line number by, say:

```
120 IF A + B < = 0   THEN 500
```

which has the same meaning as:

```
110 IF A + B < = 0   THEN GO TO 500.
```

The following program, similar to the one in the previous section, finds the larger of two numbers:

```
10 PRINT "INPUT A, B"
20 INPUT A, B
30 IF A > B   THEN 60
40 L = B
50 GO TO 70
60 L = A
70 PRINT "LARGEST VALUE IS" ;L
80 END
```

Note the use of the GO TO statement and the use of the temporary storage variable L.

As another example of usage of the IF statement, consider the problem of computing the mean or average of 10 numbers. Notice the necessity of a counter I and a variable S to retain the sum of the values:

```
10 PRINT "PROGRAM TO COMPUTE THE"
20 PRINT "MEAN OF 10 NUMBERS"
30 S = 0
40 I = 0
50 I = I + 1
60 PRINT "INPUT NUMBER";
70 INPUT A
80 S = S + A
90 IF I < > 10 THEN 50
100 M = S/10
110 PRINT "MEAN IS";M
120 END
```

Entering A Program

Many errors (bugs) in a program, whether caused by typing or logic, are detected by the computer. Appropriate error messages are then given, allowing the programmer to correct the statements before re-running the program. Figures 1 through 3 show a typical attempt at running the "MEAN" program of the previous section.

In Figure 1, the first error detected by the computer is the absence of a line number for the statement:

```
S = 0
```

This error is easily corrected by retyping the line:

```
30 S = 0
```

When the RUN command is given, an additional error is noted by the system. The correction for this error is shown in Figure 2, along with a new listing and run.

A different type of error and one which is not "caught" by the computer is evident in Figure 2. Data input is accomplished, but for only 5 values of A rather than the 10 desired. This logic error must be found by the programmer without diagnostic messages from the computer. Upon examination, one sees that statement 50 is in error.

Figure 3 shows the correct version of the program, along with a sample run.

```
10 PRINT "PROGRAM TO COMPUTE THE"
20 PRINT "MEAN OF 10 NUMBERS"
S = 0
READY
>
30 S = 0
40 I − 0
50 I = I + A
60 PRINT "INPUT NUMBER" ;
```

```
70 INPUT A
80 S = S + A
90 IF I < > 10 THEN 50
100 M = S/10
110 PRINT "MEAN IS" ;M
120 END
RUN
PROGRAM TO COMPUTE THE
MEAN OF 10 NUMBERS
?SN ERROR IN 40
```

Figure 1.   **Run 1 for the example.**

```
40 I = 0
LIST
10 PRINT "PROGRAM TO COMPUTE THE"
20 PRINT "MEAN OF 10 NUMBERS"
30 S = 0
40 I = 0
50 I = I + A
60 PRINT "INPUT NUMBER" ;
70 INPUT A
80 S = S + A
90 IF I < > 10 THEN 50
100 M = S/10
110 PRINT" MEAN IS" ;M
120 END
RUN
PROGRAM TO COMPUTE THE MEAN OF 10 NUMBERS
INPUT NUMBER ? 2
INPUT NUMBER ? 4
INPUT NUMBER ? – 2
INPUT NUMBER ? 6
INPUT NUMBER ? 5
MEAN IS 1.5
```

Figure 2.   **Run 2 for the example.**

IF (expression) THEN (action or line number)
ELSE (action or line number)

Including an ELSE statement with the IF--THEN-- specifies an alternative action in case the IF test fails (when no ELSE statement is used, control falls through to the next program line after a test fails):

```
100 IF A > 0 THEN C = A ELSE B = A
```

```
50 I = I + 1
LIST
10 PRINT "PROGRAM TO COMPUTE THE"
20 PRINT "MEAN OF 10 NUMBERS"
30 S = 0
40 I = 0
50 I = I + 1
60 PRINT "INPUT NUMBER" ;
70 INPUT A
80 S = S + A
90 IF I < > 10 THEN 50
100 M = S/10
110 PRINT "MEAN IS" ;M
120 END
RUN
PROGRAM TO COMPUTE THE MEAN OF 10 NUMBERS
INPUT NUMBER ? 2
INPUT NUMBER ? 4
INPUT NUMBER ? – 2
INPUT NUMBER ? 6
INPUT NUMBER ? 5
INPUT NUMBER ? 7
INPUT NUMBER ?  – 2
INPUT NUMBER ? 14
INPUT NUMBER ? 12
INPUT NUMBER ? 3
MEAN IS 4.9
```

Figure 3.   **Run 3 for the example.**

specifies that if A is greater than 0, C is set to A. If A is less than or equal to 0, B is set to A.

Once again we write the program which finds the larger of A and B.

```
10 PRINT "INPUT A, B";
20 INPUT A, B
30 IF A > B THEN L = A ELSE L = B
40 PRINT "LARGER VALUE IS"; L
50 END
```

FOR—NEXT

The loop set up in Figure 3 corresponds to the following flowchart and program segment:

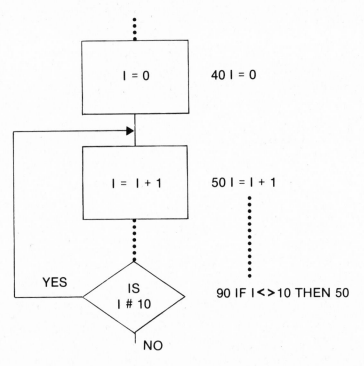

A more concise BASIC statement, the FOR statement, is specifically designed for looping. The two statements:

50 FOR I = 1 to 10

.

.

.

90 NEXT I

accomplish the looping sequence, executing the statements between 50 and 90 ten times. The general form for the FOR statement is:

100 FOR J = *p* to *q* STEP *r*

.

.

.

200 NEXT J

where *p* is the initial value assigned to J,
          q is the upper limit for J,
     and *r* is the amount by which the counter J is to
          be incremented
The step size *r* is optional and is 1 if not specified.

Simply speaking, the FOR—NEXT statement allows for (a) the initializing of a counter, (b) the incrementing of a counter by a prescribed step value, and (c) the testing to see if the counter has surpassed a specified value.

Consider the following example:

500 FOR K = 2 TO 100 STEP 2
.
.
.
750 NEXT K
760 FOR Q = 5 TO −5 STEP −.1
.
.
.
800 NEXT Q

In the first loop 500-750, since the step value is 2, K takes on the values 2, 4, 6, . . ., 100. In the loop 760-800, Q goes from 5 to −5 in steps of −.1.

In the FOR—NEXT statement, the initial value, upper limit and step size may be constants, variables or expressions. The first time the FOR statement is executed, the three values are evaluated and the values saved. Changing of these values inside the loop should be avoided, for then the loop will not operate normally.

The following flowchart demonstrates a nested loop, that is, a loop within a loop.

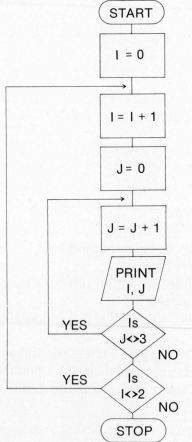

A BASIC program using FOR—NEXT statements for this problem would be:

```
10 FOR I = 1 TO 2
20 FOR J = 1 TO 3
30 PRINT I, J
40 NEXT J
50 NEXT I
60 END
```

Output would be:

```
1    1
1    2
1    3
2    1
2    2
2    3
```

Note that the inner loop variable varies the fastest and starts back over for each new value of the outer loop variable.

Exercise 5

1. Which relational symbols may be used in an IF statement and what do they mean?
2. Rewrite the program in Figure 4.3 using the FOR statement in place of the IF.
3. Use the IF statement in place of the FOR statement in the following segments

    ```
    (a) FOR J = 1 TO 50
          .
          .
          .
        NEXT J
    (b) FOR W = 10 TO 100 STEP 10
          .
          .
          .
        NEXT W
    (c) FOR J1 = 2 TO −1 STEP −.5
          .
          .
          .
        NEXT J1
    (d) FOR I = 1 TO 10
        FOR J = 1 TO 10
          .
          .
          .
        NEXT J
        NEXT I
    ```

DEBUGGING

In the previous section, examples of "typical" programming errors were given. It is almost inevitable that such errors occur in a program, although we all cross-our-fingers and hope for a successful run on the first trial.

In order to improve the chances of a successful first trial run or at least to minimize the number of debug runs, the programmer should go through the program step-by-step as if he/she is the computer. By performing the operations exactly as the program specifies, using a paper and pencil to compute results, many of the obvious logic errors in a program can be eliminated. This not only saves computer time, but also saves programmer debug time.

When developing a new program, it is a good programming practice to "echo" or print out the data that was input to the program. This always helps to assure the programmer that the desired input in fact did get read in and used as the programmer intended. Simple test data should be used for debug runs so that the results are easily obtained and compared to the program output.

When logic errors have occurred and cannot be easily located, PRINT statements can be inserted throughout the program, printing values of variables or intermediate results of data computation. This quite often allows the programmer to narrow-down the possible problem area in the program. After the errors are found and removed these PRINT statements may be deleted.

After the program has run successfully on the simple test data, more complex sets of test data should be used to "exercise" the program to be as sure as possible that the program will run for all possible cases.

Typing errors, errors caused in use of incorrect forms for the BASIC statements (syntax errors), and simple logic errors can usually be corrected immediately for a new try at running the program. For those errors which are not so obvious, the programmer should CSAVE the program as described in a previous section, log off and then take the necessary time to think about the problem.

Some systems have system commands that allow for system supplied debugging aids. One of these type commands is the command:

TRON

TRON turns on a "trace" function that lets you follow the program flow for execution analysis. Each time the program advances to a new program line, that line number will be displayed inside a pair of brackets. For example, consider the following program entered in memory:

```
10 PRINT "START"
20 FOR I = 1 TO 2
30 NEXT I
40 PRINT "END"
50 END
```

Typing the system commands:

```
TRON
RUN
```

would produce the following output:

```
<10> START
< 20 ><30> <30> <40> END
<50>
```

One turns off the trace function by issuing the command:

```
TROFF
```

TRON and TROFF represent rather unique system commands, for they may be used inside BASIC programs to help tell when a given line (or set of lines) is executed. For example:

```
100 TRON
110 A = B + C
120 TROFF
```

would enable the programmer to tell each time statement 110 is executed.

LIBRARY FUNCTIONS

The BASIC language has available several frequently used mathematical functions. The square root function:

```
SQR(X)
```

for example, computes the square root of the argument X, if the argument is non-negative. The argument is enclosed within parentheses and may be either a number or variable. The supplied function may be used within statements in many of the same ways variables are used. The following are examples of the usage of SQR:

```
40 A = SQR(49)
50 B = A + 2 * SQR(A + 9)
60 PRINT A, B, SQR(25)
```

The function ABS(X) computes the absolute value of the argument X while INT(X) computes the greatest integer less than or equal to the argument. The statements:

```
80 A = ABS( – 14.2)
90 B = INT(A)
```

would result in the value 14.2 for A and 14 for B.

The function LOG(X) computes the logarithm to the base *e* of the non-negative argument. SIN(X), COS(X), and TAN(X) compute the trigonometric functional values of the argument X, where X is in radians.

Once again, study of the reference manuals of the system being used is necessary to determine the functions available on that system.

EXAMPLE PROGRAMS

Before studying additional features of BASIC, the following example programs will help clarify the material discussed so far.

Finding The Largest of a Set of Numbers

Assume that a set of N positive numbers, where N is a variable to be input, is to be read in, with the program to find the largest of these numbers. A flowchart for the solution of this problem follows.

The variable L will contain the largest of the numbers, and since all numbers are positive, it may be initially set to 0. The following BASIC program corresponds to the above flowchart:

```
10 PRINT "INPUT THE NUMBER OF DATA ITEMS"
20 INPUT N
30 L = 0
40 FOR I = 1 TO N
50 PRINT "INPUT VALUE NUMBER"; I
60 INPUT A
70 IF L< A THEN L = A
80 NEXT I
90 PRINT "THE LARGEST VALUE IS"; L
100 END
```

If we are unable to assume that there is at least one positive number in our set, the above program would not work. For instance, if the numbers – 10, – 6, – 4 were read in, the largest number is – 4. However, the program would print out 0 as the largest value. Can you modify the flowchart and program so that it would work for the case of all negative numbers?

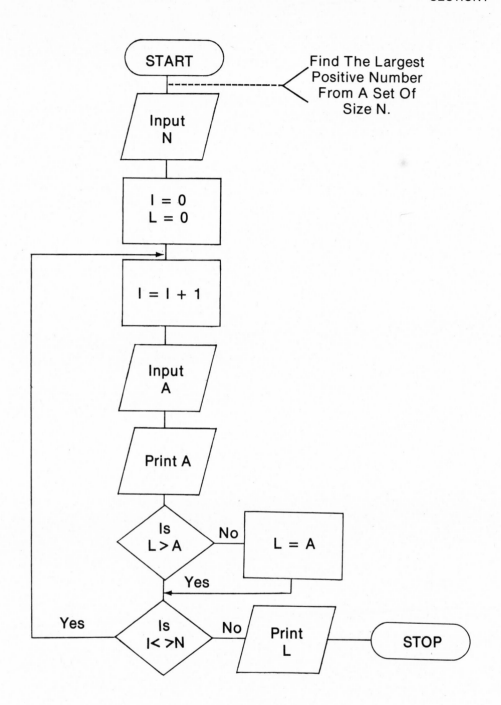

Calculating The Hypotenuse of a Right Triangle

The hypotenuse of a right triangle with sides A and B, is defined as:

$$H = \sqrt{A^2 + B^2}$$

Assume that we wish to be able to read in the lengths of the sides, A and B, of a variable number of triangles, without specifying the number of triangles beforehand. Since we know that the length of the side must be positive, we can use a data check to terminate the loop. That is, we simply check the sign of A; if it is negative, we terminate the program. This technique of termination is quite useful, particularly when we know the range of values our input data is to have. The following is a flowchart of this problem's solution:

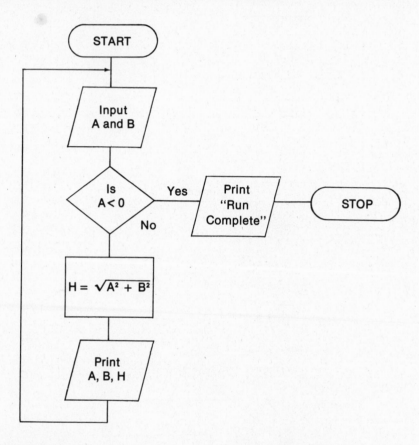

A BASIC program corresponding to the above flowchart follows:

```
 10 PRINT "THIS PROGRAM COMPUTES THE HYPOTENUSE
    OF A RIGHT TRIANGLE"
 20 PRINT "INPUT A NEGATIVE VALUE FOR A WHEN YOU
    WISH TO STOP"
 30 PRINT "INPUT VALUES FOR A AND B"
 40 INPUT A, B
 50 IF A< 0 THEN 90
 60 H = SQR (A↑2 + B↑2)
 70 PRINT "SIDE A = "; A; "SIDE B = "; B; "HYPOTENUSE =
    "; H
 80 GO TO 30
 90 PRINT "RUN COMPLETE"
100 END
```

Exercise 6

1. Enter the two example programs on your system and run them with appropriate data.
2. Modify the example program that finds the largest positive number so that it will work for any set of numbers.

STRING VARIABLES

The variables discussed so far have been numeric in nature. When we referred to the variable A, we assumed that A had been previously defined or input as a number. Most BASIC systems allow for alphanumeric (alphabetic or numeric) variables; these variables are assigned "values" which are in fact a *string* of alphanumeric characters. String variable names are distinguished from numeric variables by appending a $ character. Thus A$, A1$, and X2$ are legitimate string variable names.

Each string may contain up to 255 characters and may be input to a program just as numeric constants are input. They may also be initialized by assignment statements such as:

```
40 N$ = THIS IS A SAMPLE
50 Q$ = QUESTION NUMBER 1
60 L$ = LAST NAME
```

Examples of input and output follow:

```
10 DATA NOW IS , THE TIME
20 DATA " FOR ALL GOOD PEOPLE"
30 READ F$
40 READ G$, H$
50 PRINT F$; G$; H$
60 END
```

The resulting line of output would be:

    NOW IS THE TIME FOR ALL GOOD PEOPLE

String variables may generally be input without quotes; however, to input a string constant containing commas, colons or leading blanks (as in the example above), the string must be enclosed in quotes. For example, to input the last name and first name of an individual, with a comma separating the two names, the following would be used:

```
10 DATA "DOE,JOHN"
20 READ N$
```

If an INPUT command were used, the user would type:

? "DOE, JOHN"

Use of the INPUT command implies that the string variable is to be input during execution of the program. Thus the segment:

```
10 PRINT "PLEASE INPUT YOUR FIRST NAME"
20 INPUT F$
30 PRINT "HELLO";F$;", I HOPE YOU ARE HAVING A
   GOOD DAY"
```

upon execution would request the name of the program user (say Jeff) and upon receipt of the input name, Jeff, would type:

HELLO JEFF, I HOPE YOU ARE HAVING A GOOD DAY

Once string variables have been initialized, one may use them in IF statements such as:

```
200 IF A$ = B$ THEN 400
210 IF A$ < B$ THEN 500
220 IF A$ = "STOP" THEN 700
```

String variables are equal if the corresponding character in each variable is the same. When inequalities are used, the following relationships are assumed:

$$0 < 1 < 2 .. < 9 < A < B < .. < Z$$

Thus if:

A\$ = "SANDY"
and B\$ = "RANDY"

then A$ is not equal to B$ but B$ < A$ since R < S.

Some systems allow for various types of string operations such as concatenation (stringing together), string length determination, etc. We summarize these operations in the appendix for the TRS-80 and for other systems, for those wishing to pursue string operations.

We close this section with an additional warning about BASIC system "compatibility." String operations are perhaps the most unstandardized of all operations and commands, and so reference to the computer system manuals is a necessity.

Exercise 7

1. Examine the documentation on your computer system and list the limitations, restrictions, and options for string data input, output and operations.

2. Write a program which reads in a person's name, last name first, and prints out the name, last name last.

Exercise 8

3. Write a program which carries on a simple conversation with a user. The program should ask for the person's name, age, etc., and print out the input data along with appropriate comments.

SUBSCRIPTS

The importance of subscripted variables was discussed in the previous chapter on flowcharting. The BASIC language allows variables to be subscripted as long as certain conventions are followed. First the subscript must be a positive integer value. Next subscripted variables must be defined in a dimension statement, DIM. The DIM statement not only informs the system which of the variables will be subscripted, but also gives the maximum size of the subscript. Thus:

```
10 DIM A(50), Q1(100)
```

defines two subscripted variables A and Q1, having a maximum number of elements of 50 and 100, respectively.

The following statements are examples of subscripted variable usage:

```
20 A(1) = 50
30 B = A(I) + A(I + 1)
40 C = A(I − 5) * A(7)
```

Note that arithmetic operations may be performed within parentheses as long as the result is a positive integer.

The following simple program reads in a set of numbers of size N (where N must be less than 100) and computes the average:

```
10 DIM A(100)
20 PRINT "INPUT THE NUMBER OF DATA ELEMENTS, N";
30 INPUT N
40 PRINT "NOW INPUT THE DATA"
50 FOR I = 1 TO N
60 INPUT A(I)
70 NEXT I
80 S = 0
90 FOR I = 1 TO N
100 S = S + A(I)
110 NEXT I
120 A1 = S/N
130 PRINT "THE AVERAGE IS"; A1
140 END
```

Of course the sum could have been computed with only one of the above loops; we did wish to illustrate, however, the fact that the values of the subscripted variable remain available to the user and are accessed by simply supplying the correct subscript.

Ordering a set of numbers in numerical sequence is an important application problem and requires the use of subscripts.

If one has had exposure to matrix algebra in previous mathematics coursework, several BASIC matrix statements (MAT statements) would be of interest. The MAT statements allow for such matrix operations as addition, multiplication, transposition, etc., and are extremely useful when working with matrices. Reference to the system manuals is advised if such operations are of interest. SIMPLE programs MLR, NLAEMM, PR, and ACA provide examples of the use of MAT statements.

SUBROUTINES

The library function SQR(X) is a complete program that, when executed, computes the square root of the supplied argument, X. The SQR function may be called several times in a user's program, each time causing the SQR routine to be executed. If a programmer has a set of programming code which is to be executed in more than one location in the program, this code may be duplicated or the programmer may write the code as a subroutine. Subroutines are utilized in much the same fashion as are the library functions.

Two BASIC system commands are necessary for subroutine usage, GOSUB and RETURN. The statement:

```
100 GOSUB 2000
```

causes an unconditional branch to a subroutine. This subroutine is defined starting at location 2000. The GOSUB statement not only causes the branch to 2000 to occur (for "GO TO 2000" could be used for this) but also sets a linking procedure such that when a RETURN statement in the subroutine is encountered, the program returns to the statement immediately following the GOSUB.

As an example of subroutine usage, assume that a sequence of instructions, with different line numbers of course, must be executed three times in a program. Thus, the program might appear:

```
          .
          .
          .
100 IF A > B THEN 130
110 C = B - A
120 GO TO 140
130 C = A - B
140 ------
```

```
        .
        .
        .
420 IF A > B THEN 450
430 C = B − A
440 GO TO 460
450 C = A − B
460 ------
        .
        .
        .
700 IF A > B THEN 730
710 C = B − A
720 GO TO 740
730 C = A − B
740 ------
        .
        .
        .
```

Using a subroutine, the program would be as follows:

```
        .
        .
        .
100 GOSUB 900
        .
        .
420 GOSUB 900
        .
        .
700 GOSUB 900
        .
        .
900 IF A > B THEN 930
910 C = B − A
920 GO TO 940
930 C = A − B
940 RETURN
```

Remember that the subroutine returns to the statement number immediately following the executed GOSUB.

PROGRAM DOCUMENTATION

The beginning programmer is primarily concerned with the "debugging" of the computer program. Once the syntax and logic errors have been removed and a successfully running program obtained, one is tempted immediately to move on to the solution of the next problem. When working in business or industry however, the running program would be used, possibly over-and-over again by many different people. Some might even wish to modify the program. The efficient usage and modification of a program is possible only if that program has been well documented.

Minimum requirements for a properly documented program are as follows:

> A description of what the program is to do
>
> At least one flowchart (two for a complex program: one general, one more detailed)
>
> A program listing, which should include:
>> Name of the programmer
>>
>> Name and time of course
>>
>> Assignment number (and problem number, if applicable)
>>
>> An abstract of what the program is to do
>>
>> A list of variables used and a functional description of each
>>
>> Comment statements well placed to aid in analysis
>
> Sample data
>
> Sample run
>
> Comments, if any

The instructions "Write a program . . ." should be interpreted as "Write all the proper documentation to a program . . ." The next section contains an example of a well documented program.

In the chapter on flowcharting, the importance of explanatory comments within a program was discussed. Such comments are equally important within a BASIC program and may be included by use of the REM (remark) statement. Thus the statements

```
10 REM THIS PROGRAM COMPUTES
20 REM THE MEAN OF A SET OF
30 REM NUMBERS
```

are not executed by the system and only serve as documentation within the program listing.

DOCUMENTATION EXAMPLE

Program Description

This program will compute the final grade for students in a class of any size. Input consists of the class size and a set of test grades, homework grades and a final exam grade where the number of test grades and homework grades are also input variables. The program allows the teacher to assign weights to each test, the homework average, and final exams, for computation of the final grade.

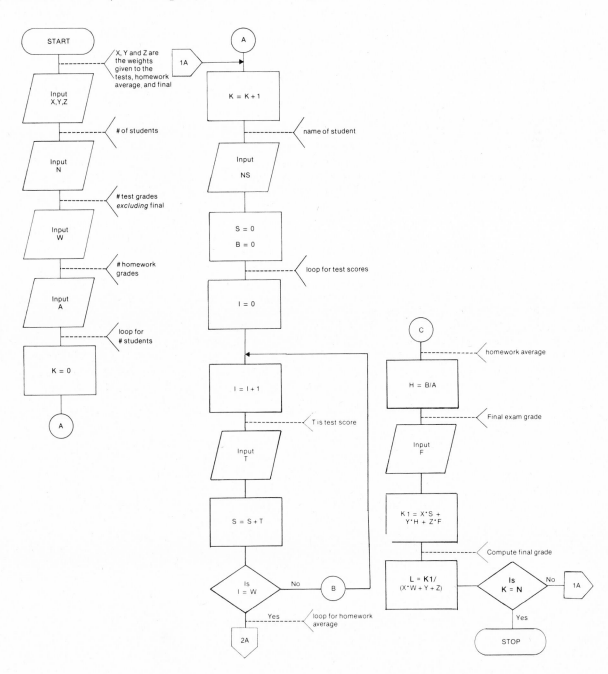

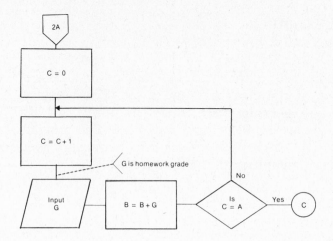

Program Listing

```
10 PRINT"CHARLENE WOOD"
11 PRINT"MATH 4358"
12 PRINT "9:30-11:00  DR. POIROT"
13 PRINT "ASSIGNMENT—WRITE A DOCUMENTED PROGRAM OF THE GENERAL"
14 PRINT"              FORM OF PROBLEM NUMBER 7, EXERCISE 4.2"
15 PRINT
20 PRINT"THIS PROGRAM WILL CALCULATE THE FINAL GRADE AVERAGE"
21 PRINT"OF EACH INDIVIDUAL IN THE CLASS."
22 PRINT"* * * * * * * * * * * * * * * * * * * * * * * * * * * * * * * * * * * * * * * * * * * *"
23 PRINT
24 REM**FUNCTIONAL DESCRIPTION OF VARIABLES**
25 REM X = HOW MANY TIMES THE TEST SCORES WILL COUNT IN THE
26 REM      FINAL AVERAGE
27 REM Y = HOW MANY TIMES THE HOMEWORK AVERAGE WILL COUNT IN
28 REM      THE FINAL AVERAGE
29 REM Z = HOW MANY TIMES THE FINAL EXAM WILL COUNT IN THE
30 REM      FINAL AVERAGE
31 REM N = NUMBER OF STUDENTS IN THE CLASS
32 REM W = NUMBER OF TESTS
33 REM A = NUMBER OF HOMEWORK GRADES
34 REM A$ = STUDENTS NAME
35 REM T = TEST SCORE
36 REM G = HOMEWORK GRADE
37 REM H = HOMEWORK AVERAGE
38 REM F = FINAL EXAM SCORE
39 REM L = FINAL GRADE
43 PRINT"HOW DO YOU WANT THE SCORES TO COUNT?"
44 PRINT"TEST = ","HOMEWORK AVERAGE = ","FINAL EXAM = "
45 INPUT X,Y,Z
50 PRINT"HOW MANY STUDENTS IN THE CLASS?"
60 INPUT N
70 PRINT"HOW MANY TESTS GRADES EXCLUDING THE FINAL?"
80 INPUT W
90 PRINT"HOW MANY HOMEWORK GRADES?"
100 INPUT A
105 FOR K = 1 TO N
110 PRINT"WHAT IS THE STUDENTS NAME?"
120 INPUT A$
130 S = B = 0
150 FOR I = 1 TO W
160 PRINT"INPUT TEST NUMBER",I
170 INPUT T
175 REM**SUM OF TESTS**
180 S = S + T
190 NEXT I
```

```
200 REM**CALCULATE HOMEWORK AVERAGE**
205 FOR C = 1 TO A
210 PRINT"INPUT HOMEWORK GRADE NUMBER", C
220 INPUT G
225 REM**SUM OF HOMEWORK GRADES**
230 B = B + G
235 NEXT C
240 H = B/A
250 PRINT A$"'S HOMEWORK AVERAGE IS" H
255 PRINT
260 PRINT"INPUT THE FINAL EXAM SCORE"
270 INPUT F
280 REM**CALCULATE THE FINAL GRADE**
285 L = (X*S + Y*H + Z*F)/(X*W + Y + Z)
290 PRINT A$"'S FINAL GRADE IS" L
295 PRINT"***********************************************"
300 NEXT K
310 END
```

Sample Data

Class size = 2

Number of tests = 2

Number of homework grades = 3

Weights: Each test will count once, homework average once and
final exam twice.

Student: Pam

Test grades = 90, 85

Homework grades = 90, 98, 75

Final Exam Grade = 95

Student: Jeff

Test Grades = 95, 87

Homework grades = 90, 60, 70

Final Exam Grade = 93

Sample Run

```
CHARLENE WOOD
MATH 4358
9:30-11:00 DR. POIROT
ASSIGNMENT—WRITE A DOCUMENTED PROGRAM OF THE GENERAL
            FORM OF PROBLEM NUMBER 7, EXERCISE 4.2

THIS PROGRAM WILL CALCULATE THE FINAL GRADE AVERAGE
OF EACH INDIVIDUAL IN THE CLASS.
****************************************************
HOW DO YOU WANT THE SCORES TO COUNT?
TEST =      HOMEWORK AVERAGE =      FINAL EXAM =
 ?1,1,2
HOW MANY STUDENTS IN THE CLASS?
 ?2
HOW MANY TESTS GRADES EXCLUDING THE FINAL?
 ?2
HOW MANY HOMEWORK GRADES?
 ?3
WHAT IS THE STUDENTS NAME?
 ?PAM
INPUT TEST NUMBER            1
 ?90
```

```
INPUT TEST NUMBER              2
 ?85
INPUT HOMEWORK GRADE NUMBER  1
 ?90
INPUT HOMEWORK GRADE NUMBER  2
 ?98
INPUT HOMEWORK GRADE NUMBER  3
 ?75
PAM'S HOMEWORK AVERAGE IS 87.6667

INPUT THE FINAL EXAM SCORE
 ?95
PAM'S FINAL GRADE IS 90.5333
*******************************************************
WHAT IS THE STUDENTS NAME?
 ?JEFF
INPUT TEST NUMBER              1
 ?95
INPUT TEST NUMBER              2
 87
INPUT HOMEWORK GRADE NUMBER  1
 ?90
INPUT HOMEWORK GRADE NUMBER  2
 ?60
INPUT HOMEWORK GRADE NUMBER  3
 ?70
JEFF'S HOMEWORK AVERAGE IS 73.3333

INPUT THE FINAL EXAM SCORE
 ?93
JEFF'S FINAL GRADE IS 88.2667
*******************************************************
```

ADDITIONAL FEATURES OF BASIC

With the system commands and program statements introduced so far, almost any programming problem can be solved. There are, however, many additional features, some unique to specific systems, that one may utilize. We do not attempt here to discuss all of these features. Instead we summarize all commands and statements of the TRS-80, Apple II, Commodore CBM and Hewlett Packard 85 in an appendix. It is hoped that those programmers desiring to utilize these special features may gain sufficient information by referring to these summaries and system reference manuals.

The summaries are reprinted, with permission, from the four computer manufacturers.

The programs in SIMPLE have been run with little or no modification on microcomputers, minicomputers, and large systems. A representative sampling follows:

PDP 11	Data General ECLIPSE
HP 2000	SIGMA
UNIVAC 1108	IBM
DEC 10	Apple II

ADDITIONAL EXERCISES
IN BASIC PROGRAMMING

1. Write a program to read a list of numbers and print them out in two columns:
   (a)   as close together as possible;
   (b)   as far apart as possible;
   (c)   somewhere in between.
2. Write a program that will generate the first ten positive integers, calculate their squares, and print out in columns headed "Number," "Square," "Sum of Squares."
3. Write a program that will generate the first ten integers, compute their square roots, print out the number and its square root in appropriately labeled columns.
4. Write a program to add up the squares of odd numbers from 101 to 201, inclusive.
5. Write a program to compute $(X * Y)^2$ without using either the operator ↑ or ∗, if X and Y are both integers.

Exercise 9

Write a program to generate the first n terms in each sequence. The output should print the current value of n and the value of the nth term.

(1) $1(2), 2(3)(4), 3(4)(5)(6), 4(5)(6)(7)(8),..., k(k + 1)...(2k)$

(2) $(1 + \frac{1}{1}), (1 + \frac{1}{1})(1 + \frac{1}{2}), (1 + \frac{1}{1})(1 + \frac{1}{2})(1 + \frac{1}{3}),...$

(3) $4(1 - \frac{1}{3^2}), 4(1 - \frac{1}{3^2})(1 - \frac{1}{5^2}), 4(1 - \frac{1}{3^2})(1 - \frac{1}{5^2})(1 - \frac{1}{7^2}), ...$

(4) $\frac{1}{2}, \frac{1}{3}, \frac{1}{5}, \frac{1}{7}, \frac{1}{11}, \frac{1}{13},..., \frac{1}{p_k}$, where p_k is the kth prime.

(5) $e_k = (1 + \frac{1}{k})^k$

(6) $1, 1, 2, 3, 5, 8, 13, 21, ..., F_n, ...,$ the Fibonacci series.

(7) $1, 2, 6, 24, 120, 720, ..., n!, ...,$ factorial n

(6) 1, 1, 2, 3, 5, 8, 13, 21, ..., F_n, ..., the Fibonacci series.

(7) 1, 2, 6, 24, 120, 720, ..., $n!$, ..., factorial n

Exercise 10

Write a program to compute the sum of each series. Each partial sum should be printed, with the number of terms being used in the sum. Include a limit as to the number of iterations to be allowed. Choose a suitable variable for the left-hand side, identifying it in the program.

(1) $e^x = 1 + x + \dfrac{x^2}{2!} + \dfrac{x^3}{3!} + ...,$ given x

(2) $e^{-x} = 1 - x + \dfrac{x^2}{2!} - \dfrac{x^3}{3!} + ...,$ given x

(3) $\ln x = (x - 1) - \dfrac{1}{2}(x - 1)^2 + \dfrac{1}{3}(x - 1)^3$

$- \dfrac{1}{4}(x - 1)^4 + ...,$ given $x > 0$

(4) $\sin x = x - \dfrac{x^3}{3!} + \dfrac{x^5}{5!} - ...,$ given x

(5) $\cos x = 1 - \dfrac{x^2}{2!} + \dfrac{x^4}{4!} - ...,$ given x

(6) $\tan x = \dfrac{2}{\pi - 2x} - \dfrac{2}{\pi + 2x} + \dfrac{2}{3\pi - 2x} - \dfrac{2}{3\pi + 2x} + \dfrac{2}{5\pi - 2x}$

$- \dfrac{2}{5\pi + 2x} + ...,$ for $x = \dfrac{(2n + 1)\pi}{2}, n \geq 1$

(7) $\sin^{-1} x = x + \dfrac{1}{2(3)} x^3 + \dfrac{1(3)}{2(4)(5)} x^5 + \dfrac{(3)(5)}{2(4)(6)(7)} x^7 + ...$ for $x^2 < 1$

(8) $\tan^{-1} x = x - \dfrac{1}{3} x^3 + \dfrac{1}{5} x^5 - \dfrac{1}{7} x^7 + ...,$ for $x^2 < 1$

(9) $\tan^{-1} x = \dfrac{1}{2} - \dfrac{1}{x} + \dfrac{1}{3x^2} - \dfrac{1}{5x^2} + ...,$ for $x^2 > 1$

(10) $J_0(x) = 1 - \dfrac{x^2}{2(2)} + \dfrac{x^4}{2^2(4^2)} - \dfrac{x^6}{2^2(4^2)(6^2)} + ...$ given x

(11) $J_1(x) = \dfrac{x}{2} - \dfrac{x^3}{2^2(4)} + \dfrac{x^5}{2^2(4^2 6)} - \dfrac{x^7}{2^2(4^2)(6^2)(8)} + ...$ given x

(12) Evaluate (8) above for $x = 1$, showing partial sums as before.

(13) Write a program to determine and print the maximum M for a set of input values a, b, c, d.

More Exercises

1. Write a program which will compute the ratio R of two successive numbers in the Fibonacci series (see Problem 6, Exercise 9 above), taking the ratio or each number to its predecessor. Also compute the value of $(2R - 1)^2$ for each value of R.

2. Write a program to read a four-digit number; print out the number; print out the number of times the digit 7 (or some other digit) appears in the number.

3. Write a program to locate perfect numbers.

4. Write a program to determine if a set of three given points is on a straight line. The input data are the coordinates of the three points. Call these (A1,A2), (B1,B2) and (C1,C2). [Note: this can be done without subscripted variables or arrays.]

5. Write a program to compute the volume of the following ''plumb-bob,'' for input values of r, a, and b.

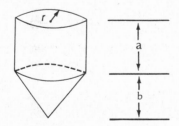

6. Write a program to determine and print the maximum m for a set of input values a, b, c, d, without using MAX operations.

7. The symbol $_nP_r$ denotes the number of permutations of r objects taken from a set of n objects, where $_nP_r$ is given by:

$$_nP_r = n(n-1)(n-2)\dots)n-r+1)$$

Write a program which will compute and print out n, r, and $_nP_r$, with input of n and r. Show how an alteration could be made (and then implement it) to compute $_nP_r$ for an input n and a range of r from 1 to n, printing out each result. See program P in SIMPLE for one way of tackling this problem.

8. On a time-sharing system, write a program to print out a symbol timed in any number of seconds, using as a time base the internal system clock (which gives minutes only).

9. Write a program to compute and print all solutions of $a \cdot \sin^2 x + b \cdot \sin x + c = 0$ in the interval $0 \le x \le 2\pi$. Input data are the values of a, b, and c.

10. Write a program to convert numbers from any one to any other of the forms:
    decimal
    octal
    binary
    BCD

11. Write a program to evaluate a real polynomial for various values of the variable, such as

$$5x^3 - 3x^2 + 7x - 23, \text{ for } x \in \{1, 3, 10, 12\}$$

Output should give the polynomial, the value being used for the variable, and the resultant value of the polynominal. See program PE in SIMPLE for one way of tackling this problem. Study the difference between SIMPLE programs PE and PRE.

APPENDIX A
Answers to Miscellaneous Exercises

Exercise 1

(1) BC, 5A, $1, Z21
(2) a) 10 LET P = 4 * 5 + 7
    c) 20 LET C = (4 * A −5 * B ** 2)/(A − 1)
    e) 15 LET C = (A − B) * (A − C) * (4.1 − (A/D)** 2)

Exercise 2

(1) a) 100 DATA 5, 10
    c) 100 DATA 30, 70, −5, 0, 60, 4, 7
(2) a) 100 DATA 5
       100 DATA 10
    c) 100 DATA 30
       110 DATA 70, −5, 0, 60, 4, 7
(3) Unlimited
(5) 4

Exercise 3

(1) a) 10   −5   14
　　c) 10   −5 14   10
　　e) 10 −5 14 7 2 25
　　g) 70   19   −5   16

(2) a) 10   PRINT   A,B,A + B
　　c) 10 PRINT A
　　　 20 PRINT B
　　　 30 PRINT A+B

Exercise 5

(1) a) > greater than
　　b) < less than
　　c) = equal to
　　d) < > # not equal to
　　e) > = greater than or equal to
　　f) < = less than or equal to

(3) a) 10   J = 0
　　　 20   J = J + 1
　　　　　 .
　　　　　 .
　　　　　 .
　　　 90 IF J # 50 THEN 20
　　　 100 END

　　c) 10   J1 = 2.5
　　　 20   J1 = J1 − .5
　　　　　 .
　　　　　 .
　　　　　 .
　　　 90   IF J1 # −1 THEN 20
　　　 100 END

Exercise 10

(1)

```
10 INPUT X,N
20 LET K = E = 1
30 FORI = 1 TON
40 LET K = K*1
50 LET E = E + X↑I/K
60 NEXT I
70 PRINT E, EXP(X)
80 STOP
90 END
```

(13)

```
10 INPUT A(1),A(2),A(3),A(4)
20 LET M = A(1)
30 FORI = 2 TO 4
40 IF A(I)<=M, THEN 60
50 LET M =A(I)
60 NEXT I
70 PRINT M
80 STOP
90 END
```

SECTION

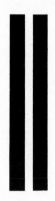

COMPUTER PROGRAM SUITES

TERMINAL OPERATING INSTRUCTIONS

You are about to write a BASIC main program that will sequentially call any number of BASIC calculation programs from the SIMPLE suite of programs stored in the memory files of the computer. But you don't need to know this. All you have to do is to follow the instructions ...

PANIC INSTRUCTIONS

Should the terminal go berserk--infinite loops often make terminals act overenthusiastically--do not wait for the terminal to type READY. Instead, just simultaneously press the control key and the C key. The terminal will stop and type READY. Then you type RUN%PANIC.

PROTOCOL FORMALITIES

1. Overcome your fear, sit yourself in front of the time-share computer terminal, and carry on.

2. Turn the main terminal switch to the position marked ON.

3. Type _____. Friendly, aren't you? Be careful of the difference between the letter O and the numeral Ø. Now press the key labeled RETURN.

4. The computer will now type some usually uninformative and unexciting material. Read it, just in case.

5. The computer now types _____.

6. You immediately type _____ (your account number) and press the RETURN key.

7. The computer now requests your password.

8. You type the password: _____. Notice that the computer does not print your password (it is secret, you know). Press the RETURN key again.

9. The computer prints one other unexciting message and your log-in time. Then it types _____.

10. Now to tell the computer that you want to run the SIMPLE suite of programs, type RUN%SIMPLE. Then press the RETURN key. From now on, these instructions will omit the press RETURN advice. After every command entered on the keyboard from now on, press the return key. (Instead of the % sign between RUN and SIMPLE, some computer installations may use a # or a $--or no character at all. Check with your computer center for advice on the system you are using.)

You are in business!! Easy, wasn't it? You can begin your serious business now that the accounting and protocol formalities are over.

LOGGING OUT

Now you are in the hands of SIMPLE. Follow his (her, its?) advice. But remember, when you are finished for the day you must log out, otherwise your computer user's privileges may be withdrawn. To log out of the system at anytime,

1. Wait until the computer types READY.

2. Then type _____ .

3. The computer replies _____.

4. You type _____ .

The computer will then type some other messages and even roll the paper to a convenient cutting position. You now tear off your masterpiece and show it to your lecturer, before you frame it as the record of perhaps your first computer interactive encounter with SIMPLE. Thank you for your patience. This sequence of instructions will shortly become second nature, and you will be able to use SIMPLE without referring to them.

In response to the RUN%SIMPLE command, the computer will type or display the following:

```
RUN SIMPLE
HELLO SIMPLE AT YOUR SERVICE.  PLEASE TURN TO CONDENSED USERS INSTRUCTION
MANUAL.  DECIDE WHICH PROGRAM YOU WISH TO USE FOR THE PROBLEM AT HAND AND
AFTER THE TERMINAL TYPES
          READY
YOU TYPE THE COMPUTER PROGRAM CALL NAME PRECEDED BY THE WORD RUN%
FOR EXAMPLE, TO RUN THE SINGLE VARIABLE STATISTICS PROGRAM YOU TYPE
          RUN%SVS
OR TO RUN THE CATALOG OF ALL AVAILABLE ROUTINES YOU TYPE
          RUN%CAT
NOW WAIT FOR THE READY MESSAGE TO APPEAR BEFORE YOU TYPE YOUR FIRST COMMAND
STOP AT LINE 20

READY
```

THINGS TO WATCH FOR
IN IMPLEMENTATION

1. Some machines, such as Honeywell, use a single quote (') instead of a double quote (") for string.

2. Delimiter on (PRINT) statements: a single text editor command takes the form

   This command will change the supplied program accordingly. The syntax of this command varies for different machines.

3. The "computed go to" statement: on (variable) go to (stmt#), (stmt#), (stmt#) in some machines, for example, HP2000 system, takes the form GO TO J OF (stmt#),(stmt#)

4. MAT statements may be slightly different in format.

A diagnostic in easily comprehensible English will be given by the compiler or interpreter at execution time. The whole system can be up and running usually within 2 or 3 hours of arrival of the program tape.

PROBABILITY
CALCULATIONS

RUN#F
FACTORIAL

Factorial of an integer M is defined as M! = M* (M - 1) * (M - 2)* ....*2*1. This program calculates the factorial of an integer M < 34. An integer M $\geq$ 34 will produce an overflow condition message to be printed out. Notice as a matter of interest that:

$$1! = 1 \text{ by definition.}$$
$$0! = 1 \text{ by definition.}$$

INPUT REQUIREMENTS

Value of M. M must be less than 34 otherwise machine will overflow.

PROGRAM OUTPUT

Value of M!

REFERENCES

Any standard textbook on algebra or combinatory theory.

SAMPLE PROGRAM

Calculate factorial of seven (7!)

$$7 \times 6 \times 5 \times 4 \times 3 \times 2 \times 1 = 5040 = 7!$$

```
RUN
F
THIS PROGRAM COMPUTES THE VALUE OF M-FACTORIAL (M!),0<M,M IS INTEGER
M MUST BE LESS THAN 34, OTHERWISE OVERFLOW OCCURS
VALUE OF M=? 7
THE VALUE OF  7 -FACTORIAL IS 5040
CALCULATIONS COMPLETED

Ready


Ready

LIST
F
100 PRINT"THIS PROGRAM COMPUTES THE VALUE OF M-FACTORIAL (M!),0<M,M IS INTEGER"
110 PRINT"M MUST BE LESS THAN 34, OTHERWISE OVERFLOW OCCURS"
120 INPUT"VALUE OF M=";M
130 L=M
140 F1=M
150 FOR I=1 TO M-1 STEP 1
160 L=L-1
170 F1=F1*L
180 NEXT I
190 PRINT"THE VALUE OF "; M;"-FACTORIAL IS";F1
200 REM _ SHOULD ANY RUNNING DIFFICULTIES ARISE, PLEASE BRING THEM
210 REM _ TO THE ATTENTION OF THE AUTHOR, JOSE ALONSO, SWINBURNE
220 REM _ COLLEGE OF TECHNOLOGY
230 PRINT"CALCULATIONS COMPLETED"
240 END

Ready
```

RUN#P
PERMUTATIONS

This program calculates the number of possible subsets each containing N objects which can be formed from a larger set of M objects. Permutations are normally denoted by:

$$_mP_n$$

and are calculated as follows:

$$_mP_n = \frac{M!}{(M-N)!} = M*(M-1)*(M-2)*...*(M-N+1)$$

given M,N are integers, $0 < M < N$. (Different references use other notations, namely $(M)_n$ or $P(M,N)$ or P_n^m.) Notice as a matter of interest that:

$$_mP_o = 1$$

$$_mP_1 = M$$

$$_mP_m = M!$$

If M = 4, N = 3, and the objects in question are called A, B, C, and D, the following subsets are all considered <u>different</u> and thus counted as different permutations, (ABC), (ACB), (CBA), (BCA), (BAC), and so on.

INPUT REQUIREMENTS

Integer values of M and N.

PROGRAM OUTPUT

M, N and $_mP_n$.

REFERENCES

Any standard textbook in combinatory theory or probability theory.

SAMPLE PROGRAM

Calculate

$$_7P_3 = \frac{7!}{(7-3)!} = \frac{7 \times 6 \times 5 \times 4 \times 3 \times 3 \times 1}{4 \times 3 \times 2 \times 1} = 210$$

```
RUN
P
THIS PROGRAM COMPUTES THE NUMBER OF POSSIBLE PERMUTATIONS OF
M DISTINCT OBJECTS IN GROUPS OF N OBJECTS EACH. O<N<M BOTH INTEGER
NUMBER OF DISTINCT OBJECTS, M=? 7
NUMBER OF OBJECTS IN EACH GROUP; N=? 3
THE PERMUTATIONS OF  7 OBJECTS IN GROUPS OF  3 EACH ARE= 210
CALCULATIONS COMPLETED

Ready
```

Ready

```
LIST
P
100 PRINT"THIS PROGRAM COMPUTES THE NUMBER OF POSSIBLE PERMUTATIONS OF"
110 PRINT"M DISTINCT OBJECTS IN GROUPS OF N OBJECTS EACH. O<N<M BOTH INTEGER"
120 INPUT"NUMBER OF DISTINCT OBJECTS, M=";M
130 INPUT"NUMBER OF OBJECTS IN EACH GROUP; N=";N
140 LET N1=M-N+1
150 LET M1=M
160 FOR I=M-1 TO N1 STEP -1
170 LET M1=M1*I
180 NEXT I
190 PRINT"THE PERMUTATIONS OF ";M;"OBJECTS IN GROUPS OF ";N;"EACH ARE=";M1
200 REM _ SHOULD ANY RUNNING DIFFICULTIES ARISE, PLEASE BRING THEM
210 REM _ TO THE ATTENTION OF THE AUTHOR, JOSE ALONSO, SWINBURNE
220 REM _ COLLEGE OF TECHNOLOGY
230 PRINT"CALCULATIONS COMPLETED"
240 END
```

Ready

RUN#C
COMBINATIONS

This program calculates the number of possible subsets each containing N objects which can be formed from a larger set of M objects. Combinations are normally designed by:

$$_mC_n$$

and are calculated as follows:

$$_mC_n = \frac{M!}{(M - N)!N!} = \frac{M*(M - 1)*(M - 2)*...*(M - N + 1)}{1*2...*N}$$

given M,N are integers, $0 < M < N$. A value of $N \geq 34$ may not be used, because an overflow condition will occur. Similarly for $(M - N) \geq 34$.

Notice as a matter of interest that $_mC_n$ is also called the binomial coefficient. (Different references use different notations namely $C(M,N)$ or C_n^m or $\binom{M}{N}$.)

$$_mC_1 = {_mC_{m-1}} = M$$

$$_mC_0 = {_mC_m} = 1$$

$$_mC_n = {_mC_{m-n}}$$

If M = 4, N = 3, and the objects in question are called A, B, C, D, the following subsets are all considered <u>equal</u> and thus counted as one and the same combination: (ABC), (ACB), (CBA), (BCA), (BAC), and so on.

INPUT REQUIREMENTS

Integer value for M and N.

PROGRAM OUTPUT

M, N, and $_mC_n$.

REFERENCES

Any standard textbook on combinatory theory or probability theory.

SAMPLE PROGRAM

Calculate

$$_7C_3 = \frac{7 \times 6 \times 5 \times 4 \times 3 \times 2 \times 1}{(4 \times 3 \times 2 \times 1)(4 \times 3 \times 2 \times 1)} = 35$$

```
RUN
C
THIS PROGRAM COMPUTES THE NUMBER OF POSSIBLE COMBINATIONS
OF M OBJECTS IN SETS OF N OBJECTS EACH WITHOUT REGARD TO ORDER
O<N<M<34 BOTH M AND N INTEGER
TOTAL NUMBER OF OBJECTS M=? 7
NUMBER OF OBJECTS IN EACH SET=? 3
THE COMBINATIONS OF  7  OBJECTS IN GROUPS OF  3 OBJECTS TAKING
ORDER INTO ACCOUNT ARE  35
CALCULATIONS COMPLETED

Ready
```

```
Ready

LIST
C
1 REM - PROGRAM C
100 PRINT"THIS PROGRAM COMPUTES THE NUMBER OF POSSIBLE COMBINATIONS"
110 PRINT"OF M OBJECTS IN SETS OF N OBJECTS EACH WITHOUT REGARD TO ORDER"
120 PRINT"0<N<M<34 BOTH M AND N INTEGER"
130 INPUT"TOTAL NUMBER OF OBJECTS M=";M
140 INPUT"NUMBER OF OBJECTS IN EACH SET=";N
150 REM - CALCULATE M FACTORIAL
160 LET F1=M
170 LET L1=M
180 FOR I=1 TO M-1 STEP 1
190 L1=L1-1
200 F1=F1*L1
210 NEXT I
220 REM - M FACTORIAL HAS NOW BEEN CALCULATED
230 REM - CALCULATE (M-N) FACTORIAL
240 LET F2=M-N
250 LET L2=M-N
260 FOR I=1 TO M-N-1 STEP 1
270 L2=L2-1
280 F2=F2*L2
290 NEXT I
300 REM - (M-N) FACTORIAL HAS NOW BEEN CALCULATED
310 REM - CALCULATE N FACTORIAL
320 LET F3=N
330 LET L3=N
340 FOR I=1 TO N-1 STEP 1
350 L3=L3-1
360 F3=F3*L3
370 NEXT I
380 REM - N FACTORIAL HAS NOW BEEN CALCULATED
390 F4=F1/(F2*F3)
400 PRINT"THE COMBINATIONS OF ";M;" OBJECTS IN GROUPS OF ";N;"OBJECTS TAKING "
410 PRINT"ORDER INTO ACCOUNT ARE ";F4
420 REM _ SHOULD ANY RUNNING DIFFICULTIES ARISE, PLEASE BRING THEM TO
430 REM _ THE ATTENTION OF THE AUTHOR, JOSE ALONSO, SWINBURNE COLLEGE
440 REM _ OF TECHNOLOGY
450 PRINT"CALCULATIONS COMPLETED"
460 END

Ready
```

61

RUN#BF
BAYES FORMULA

This is a useful formula for computing probability of various events $E_1, E_2, \ldots, E_i, \ldots, E_n$ which have resulted in the event A occurring. If

1. the probabilities of occurrence of the events E_i are known and are denoted by $P(E_i)$,

2. if the conditional probabilities of occurrence of event A due to the occurrence of event E_i are known and denoted by $P(\frac{A}{E_i})$,

then the conditional probability $P(\frac{E_r}{A})$ of any one event E_r given A is:

$$P(\frac{E_r}{A}) = \frac{P(E_r)\ P(\frac{A}{E_r})}{\sum\limits_{i=1}^{n} P(E_i)\ P(\frac{A}{E_i})}$$

given r = 1,2,3, ... or n. (It should be mentioned on passing that much controversy has arisen over the interpretation of this formula.)

INPUT REQUIREMENTS

n Pairs of $P(E_i)$ and $P(\frac{A}{E_i})$ values.

PROGRAM OUTPUT

Four columns of n values each, as follows:

i	$P(E_i)$	$P(\frac{A}{E_i})$	$(P\frac{E_i}{A})$

REFERENCES

1. Original Paper: Bayes, T., Biometrika, vol. 46 (1958)m, p. 293-315.

2. Application to Bridge Games: Waugh, E. F., and Waugh, F. V., Jnl. Am. Stats. Assn., vol. 48 (1953), p. 79-87.

3. Clear Exposition: Parzen, E., Modern Probability Theory and Its Application, John Wiley and Sons, 1960, Chapter 3, Section 4, p. 113-124.

SAMPLE PROGRAM

The probability that one person, found in the street at random, has cancer is 0.004. Assume that this one person is tested for cancer and that the test has a 0.96 probability of detecting cancer if the person does have cancer. Conversely, if the person does not have cancer, the probability of its not being found is 0.912088.

The program calculates that the probability of a person walking in the street being found to have cancer by the test is 0.0879121 if the unfortunate person happens to have cancer.

```
RUN
BF
THIS PROGRAM COMPUTES THE VALUE OF BAYES' FORMULA FOR ALL N VALUES OF
P(E(I)/A) GIVEN N PAIRS OF VALUES P(E(I)),P(A/E(I))) WHERE 1<I<N
NUMBER OF PAIRS OF P(E(I)),P(A/(E(I))) VALUES TO BE ENTERED=? 2
ENTER NOW THE INFORMATION FOR PAIR OF VALUES NUMBER 1
ENTER VALUE OF P(E( 1 )) =
? .96
ENTER VALUE OF P(A/E( 1 )) =
? .004
ENTER NOW THE INFORMATION FOR PAIR OF VALUES NUMBER 2
ENTER VALUE OF P(E( 2 )) =
? .04
ENTER VALUE OF P(A/E( 2 )) =
? .996
I               P(E(I))        P(A/E(I))        P(E(I)/A)
 1                .96            .004          .879121E-1
 2                .04            .996          .912088
CALCULATIONS COMPLETED

Ready




Ready

LIST
BF
100 DIM E(25),A4(25),E4(25)
110 PRINT"THIS PROGRAM COMPUTES THE VALUE OF BAYES' FORMULA FOR ALL N VALUES OF"
120 PRINT"P(E(I)/A) GIVEN N PAIRS OF VALUES P(E(I)),P(A/E(I))) WHERE 1<I<N"
130 INPUT"NUMBER OF PAIRS OF P(E(I)),P(A/(E(I))) VALUES TO BE ENTERED=";N
140 FOR I1=1 TO N STEP 1
150 PRINT"ENTER NOW THE INFORMATION FOR PAIR OF VALUES NUMBER";I1
160 PRINT"ENTER VALUE OF P(E(";I1;")) ="
170 INPUT E(I1)
180 PRINT"ENTER VALUE OF P(A/E(";I1;")) ="
190 INPUT A4(I1)
200 NEXT I1
210 LET S=0
220 FOR I=1 TO N STEP 1
230 LET S=S+(E(I)*A4(I))
240 NEXT I
250 PRINT"I              P(E(I))        P(A/E(I))        P(E(I)/A)"
260 FOR I=1 TO N STEP 1
270 LET E4(I)=(E(I)*A4(I))/S
280 PRINT I,E(I),A4(I),E4(I)
290 NEXT I
300 REM _ SHOULD ANY RUNNING DIFFICULTIES ARISE, PLEASE BRING THEM
310 REM _ TO THE ATTENTION OF THE AUTHOR, JOSE ALONSO, SWINBURNE
320 REM _ COLLEGE OF TECHNOLOGY
330 PRINT"CALCULATIONS COMPLETED"
340 END

Ready
```

RUN#PNR
PROBABILITY OF NO REPETITION IN A SAMPLE

The well known "repeated birthday" problem led to the popularity of this formula: What is the probability of two people having the same birthday in a room with N persons? This problem is solved with this program for N equal to the number of people in the room and M equal to 365 days to "choose" from in the year. The probability of no repetitions (that is, no two people may have the same birthday) is given by:

$$P_{NR} = (1 - \frac{1}{M}) * (1 - \frac{2}{M}) * ... * (1 - \frac{N-1}{M})$$

given M, N are integers, M > N > 1. The probability of repetition is, of course:

$$P_R = 1 - P_{NR}$$

INPUT REQUIREMENTS

Integers M and N.

PROGRAM OUTPUT

M, N, PNR, PR = $(1 - P_{NR})$.

REFERENCES

Parzen, E., <u>Modern Probability Theory and Its Application</u>, John Wiley and Sons, 1960, Chapter 2, p. 44.

SAMPLE PROGRAM

What are the chances of 2 people having the same birthday among a group of 51 people? 0.974432. Staggering, isn't it!

```
RUN
PNR
THIS PROGRAM COMPUTES THE PROBABILITY P THAT THERE ARE NO REPETITIONS
IN A SAMPLE OF SIZE N DRAWN WITH REPLACEMENT FROM A POPULATION OF SIZE M
NATURALLY M>N>1
NUMBER OF OBJECTS IN TOTAL POPULATION, M=? 365
NUMBER OF CHOSEN OBJECTS (REPLACED AFTER EACH CHOICE) N=? 51
THE PROBABILITY OF NO REPETITION DRAWING WITH REPLACEMENT N DIFFERENT
OBJECTS FROM A SAMPLE OF SIZE M IS P= .025568
THE PROBABILITY OF A REPETITION OCCURRING IS (1-P)= .974432
CALCULATIONS COMPLETED

Ready
```

```
Ready

LIST
PNR
100 PRINT"THIS PROGRAM COMPUTES THE PROBABILITY P THAT THERE ARE NO REPETITIONS"
110 PRINT"IN A SAMPLE OF SIZE N DRAWN WITH REPLACEMENT FROM A POPULATION OF SIZE M"
120 PRINT"NATURALLY M>N>1"
130 INPUT"NUMBER OF OBJECTS IN TOTAL POPULATION, M=";M
140 INPUT"NUMBER OF CHOSEN OBJECTS (REPLACED AFTER EACH CHOICE) N=";N
150 LET P=1
160 FOR I=1 TO N-1 STEP 1
170 LET P=P*(1-(I/M))
180 NEXT I
190 LET P2=1-P
200 REM - PROBABILITY OF OCCURRENCE IS (1-P)
210 PRINT"THE PROBABILITY OF NO REPETITION DRAWING WITH REPLACEMENT N DIFFERENT"
220 PRINT"OBJECTS FROM A SAMPLE OF SIZE M IS P=";P
230 PRINT"THE PROBABILITY OF A REPETITION OCCURRING IS (1-P)=";P2
240 REM _ SHOULD ANY RUNNING DIFFICULTIES ARISE PLEASE BRING THEM
250 REM _ TO THE ATTENTION OF THE AUTHOR, JOSE ALONSO, SWINBURNE
260 REM _ COLLEGE OF TECHNOLOGY
270 PRINT"CALCULATIONS COMPLETED"
280 END

Ready
```

ONE INDEPENDENT
VARIABLE STATISTICS

RUN#SVS
SINGLE VARIABLE STATISTICS

This program calculates, for a given set of N data points x_1, x_2, ..., x_N the following statistical parameters:

Standard deviation

$$S = \sqrt{\frac{\Sigma x_i^2 - N \bar{x}^2}{N - 1}}$$

Standard error

$$S_{\bar{x}} = \frac{S}{\sqrt{N}}$$

Arithmetic mean

$$\bar{x} = \frac{\Sigma x_i}{N}$$

Geometric mean

$$G = (x_1 \cdot x_2 \cdot x_3 \ldots x_n)^{\frac{1}{N}}$$

Harmonic mean

$$H = \frac{n}{\frac{1}{x_1} + \frac{1}{x_2} + \ldots + \frac{1}{x_n}}$$

Quadratic mean

$$Q = \frac{(x_1^2 + x_2^2 + \ldots + x_n^2)^{\frac{1}{2}}}{n}$$

Moments:

First moment

$$m_1 = \frac{\Sigma x_i}{n} \qquad \text{about the origin}$$

Second moment

$$m_2 = \frac{\Sigma (x_i - \bar{x})^2}{n} \qquad \text{about the mean}$$

Third moment

$$m_3 = \frac{\Sigma (x_i - \bar{x})^3}{n} \qquad \text{about the mean}$$

Fourth moment

$$m_4 = \frac{\Sigma (x_i - \bar{x})^4}{n} \qquad \text{about the mean}$$

Coefficient of skewness

$$\gamma_1 = \frac{m_3}{m_2^{1.5}}$$

Coefficient of kurtosis

$$\gamma_2 = \frac{m_4}{m_2^2}$$

Unbiased second moment

$$= \frac{\Sigma (x_i - \bar{x})^2}{N - 1} \qquad \text{about the mean}$$

Coefficient of variation

$$= \frac{S}{\bar{x}}$$

INPUT REQUIREMENTS

Integer N, N values of x_i.

PROGRAM OUTPUT

All calculated statistical parameters listed above.

REFERENCES

Burington, R. S. and May, D. C., <u>Handbook of Probability and Statistics with Tables</u>, Handbook Publishers, Inc., Sanduski, Ohio, 1958.

SAMPLE PROGRAM

Calculate the usual measures of dispersion for the values: 3, 5, 7, 9, 11, 13, 15. The values may be input in any order with identical results.

```
RUN
SVS
THIS PROGRAM COMPUTES THE MOST COMMON  SINGLE VARIABLE X STATISTICS
OF A SET OF NUMBERS
NUMBER OF DATA VALUES COMPRISING YOUR DATA=? 7
ENTER NOW YOUR SET OF DATA VALUES SEPARATED BY COMMAS
? 3,5,7,9,11,13,15
THE MEAN OR FIRST MOMENT ABOUT THE ORIGIN OF THE DATA SET IS= 9
THE UNBIASED SECOND MOMENT ABOUT THE MEAN IS= 18.6667
THE SECOND MOMENT ABOUT THE MEAN IS= 16
THE HARMONIC MEAN OF THE DATA SET IS= 6.85065
THE QUADRATIC MEAN, RMS VALUE, OR SECOND MOMENT ABOUT THE ORIGIN OF THE DATA IS= 9.84886
THE GEOMETRIC MEAN, OR THE ARITHMETIC MEAN OF THE LOG OF THE  DATA SET IS= 7.96123
NOTICE THAT THE GEOMETRIC MEAN MAY BE PRINTED AS ZERO IF THERE ARE NEGATIVE VALUES IN THE DATA SET
THE STANDARD DEVIATION OF THE SAMPLE IS= 4.32049
THE THIRD MOMENT ABOUT THE MEAN IS= 0
THE FOURTH MOMENT ABOUT THE MEAN IS= 448
THE COEFFICIENT OF SKEWNESS IS= 0
THE COEFFICIENT OF KURTOSIS IS= 1.75
THE STANDARD ERROR OF THE SAMPLE IS= 1.63299
CALCULATIONS COMPLETED

Ready
```

```
Ready

LIST
SVS
100 DIM X(200)
110 PRINT"THIS PROGRAM COMPUTES THE MOST COMMON  SINGLE VARIABLE X STATISTICS"
120 PRINT"OF A SET OF NUMBERS"
130 INPUT "NUMBER OF DATA VALUES COMPRISING YOUR DATA=";N
140 PRINT"ENTER NOW YOUR SET OF DATA VALUES SEPARATED BY COMMAS":MAT INPUT X(N)
150 REM - CALCULATE FIRST MOMENT ABOUT ZERO, THE ORIGIN
160 LET Y1=0
170 LET M=1
180 FOR I=1 TO N STEP 1
190 LET Y1=Y1+X(I)
200 NEXT I
210 LET Y1=Y1/N
220 REM - CALCULATE SECOND MOMENT ABOUT THE MEAN
230 LET Y3=0
240 LET Y4=0
250 LET Y2=0
260 LET Q=0
270 LET H=0
280 LET G=1
290 FOR I=1 TO N STEP 1
300 LET Q=Q+X(I)**2
310 LET H=H+(1/X(I))
320 LET G=G*X(I)
330 LET Y2=Y2+(X(I)-Y1)**2
340 LET Y3=Y3+(X(I)-Y1)**3
350 LET Y4=Y4+(X(I)-Y1)**4
360 NEXT I
370 LET Q=(Q/N)**.5
380 LET H=N/H
390 LET G=G**(1/N)
400 LET Y2=Y2/N
410 LET Y3=Y3/N
420 LET Y4=Y4/N
430 LET C5=Y3/(Y2**1.5)
440 LET C8=Y4/(Y2*Y2)
450 LET V1=Y2*N/(N-1)
460 PRINT"THE MEAN OR FIRST MOMENT ABOUT THE ORIGIN OF THE DATA SET IS=";Y1
470 PRINT"THE UNBIASED SECOND MOMENT ABOUT THE MEAN IS=";V1
480 PRINT"THE SECOND MOMENT ABOUT THE MEAN IS=";Y2
490 PRINT "THE HARMONIC MEAN OF THE DATA SET IS=";H
500 PRINT "THE QUADRATIC MEAN, RMS VALUE, OR SECOND MOMENT ABOUT THE ORIGIN OF THE
    DATA IS=";Q
510 PRINT "THE GEOMETRIC MEAN, OR THE ARITHMETIC MEAN OF THE LOG OF THE  DATA SET IS=";G
520 PRINT "NOTICE THAT THE GEOMETRIC MEAN MAY BE PRINTED AS ZERO IF THERE ARE NEGATIVE
    VALUES IN THE DATA SET"
530 LET S1=V1**0.5
540 PRINT"THE STANDARD DEVIATION OF THE SAMPLE IS=";S1
550 PRINT"THE THIRD MOMENT ABOUT THE MEAN IS=";Y3
560 PRINT"THE FOURTH MOMENT ABOUT THE MEAN IS=";Y4
570 PRINT"THE COEFFICIENT OF SKEWNESS IS=";C5
580 PRINT"THE COEFFICIENT OF KURTOSIS IS=";C8
590 LET S2=S1/(N**0.5)
600 PRINT"THE STANDARD ERROR OF THE SAMPLE IS=";S2
610 REM _ SHOULD ANY RUNNING DIFFICULTIES ARISE, PLEASE BRING THEM TO
620 REM _ THE ATTENTION OF THE AUTHOR, JOSE ALONSO, SWINBURNE COLLEGE
630 REM _ OF TECHNOLOGY
640 PRINT"CALCULATIONS COMPLETED"
650 END

Ready
```

RUN#MA
MOVING AVERAGE

This program calculates moving averages of order M for a set of N numbers x_i by the application of the algorithm:

$$\frac{x_1 + x_2 + \ldots + x_M}{M}, \quad \frac{x_2 + x_3 + \ldots x_M + 1}{M}, \ldots$$

Moving averages are very useful in trend analysis for data smoothing purposes.

INPUT REQUIREMENTS

Integers M and N, and N values of x_i.

PROGRAM OUTPUT

Three columns of index i, original x_i values, and moving averages of desired order.

REFERENCES

Any standard statistics textbook.

SAMPLE PROGRAM

Printout above is self-explanatory. Notice it is a "right-hand" average.

```
RUN
MA
THIS PROGRAM COMPUTES THE MOVING AVERAGE OF ORDER M OF A SET OF N DATA VALUES
NUMBER OF DATA VALUES TO BE ENTERED, N=? 12
ORDER OF MOVING AVERAGE DESIRED, M=? 3
ENTER NOW SET OF N DATA VALUES SEPARATED BY COMMAS? 1,2,3,4,5,6,7,8,9,10,11,12
I               X(I)            MOVING AVERAGE OF ORDER 3
 1               1               0
 2               2               0
 3               3               2
 4               4               3
 5               5               4
 6               6               5
 7               7               6
 8               8               7
 9               9               8
10              10               9
11              11              10
12              12              11
CALCULATIONS COMPLETED

Ready
```

Ready

```
LIST
MA
100 DIM X(200), X2(200)
110 PRINT"THIS PROGRAM COMPUTES THE MOVING AVERAGE OF ORDER M OF A SET OF N DATA VALUES"
120 INPUT"NUMBER OF DATA VALUES TO BE ENTERED, N=";N
130 INPUT"ORDER OF MOVING AVERAGE DESIRED, M=";M
140 INPUT"ENTER NOW SET OF N DATA VALUES SEPARATED BY COMMAS":MAT INPUT X(N)
150 LET S1=0.0
160 FOR I=1 TO M STEP 1
170 LET S1=S1+X(I)/M
180 NEXT I
190 X2(M)=S1
200 FOR I=M+1 TO N STEP 1
210 X2(I)=X2(I-1)+X(I)/M-X(I-M)/M
220 NEXT I
230 PRINT"I              X(I)            MOVING AVERAGE OF ORDER";M
240 FOR I=1 TO N STEP 1
250 PRINT I,X(I),X2(I)
260 NEXT I
270 REM _ SHOULD ANY RUNNING DIFFICULTIES ARISE, PLEASE BRING THEM TO
280 REM _ THE ATTENTION OF THE AUTHOR, JOSE ALONSO, SWINBURNE COLLEGE
290 REM _ OF TECHNOLOGY
300 PRINT"CALCULATIONS COMPLETED"
310 END
```

Ready

RUN#SS
STANDARDIZED SCORES

This program produces, from a set of N data values x_i, two sets of N values each:

y_i with mean equal to 0 and standard deviation equal to 1.

z_i with a specified mean equal to μ and specified standard deviation equal to σ. The output has the following format:

Data Value	Original Data Values	Standardized Scores with Mean = 0 and Standard Deviation = 1	Standardized Scores with Mean = μ and Standard Deviation = σ
i	x	y_i	z_i
1	37	-0.50	60.1
2	92	-0.30	40.7
.	.	.	.
.	.	.	.
.	.	.	.
N	54	+0.32	90.2

Where: $\bar{x}$ = calculated

s_{x_i} = calculated

$\bar{y}$ = 0

s_{y_i} = 1

μ = given mean

σ = given standard deviation

The desired values of μ and σ have, of course, to be provided as input data. The values of $\bar{x}$ and s are calculated by the program. The values of $\bar{y}$ = 0 and s_{y_i} = 1 are preprogrammed specifications.

Notice as a matter of interest that $z_i = \mu + \sigma y_i$ for i = 1,2...N.

INPUT REQUIREMENTS

Number of data value to be entered: N;N data values x_i; μ and σ for z.

PROGRAM OUTPUT

Four columns of N values each i, x_i, y_i, z_i, as defined above, and the respective means and standard deviations of x_i, y_i, z_i.

REFERENCES

Any standard textbook on elementary statistics.

SAMPLE PROGRAM

The printout is self-explanatory.

X_i are the original grades of a group of students in a class. These grades X_i are somewhat low. So the teacher has the computer recalculate them centered about 75 with a spread of 15 (that is, from 60 to 90) about 75. Z_i array is the result of these calculations. Y_i column shows the grades with mean of zero and spread of 1 about zero.

```
RUN
SS
THIS PROGRAM CALCULATES TWO SETS OF STANDARDIZED SCORES
Y(I) OF MEAN ZERO AND STANDARD DEVIATION ONE
Z(I) OF MEAN MU    AND STANDARD DEVIATION SIGMA
GIVEN VALUES OF MU AND SIGMA, AND N DATA POINTS X(I)
DESIRED MEAN VALUE OF Z(I) ARRAY, MU=? 75
DESIRED STANDARD DEVIATION OF Z(I) ARRAY, SIGMA=? 15
NUMBER OF DATA VALUES X(I) TO BE ENTERED, N=? 12
ENTER NOW N DATA VALUES SEPARATED BY COMMAS? 38,75,46,49,65,37,71,65,45,65,49,71
I              X(I)              Y(I)              Z(I)
 1              38             -1.34077           54.8884
 2              75              1.36515           95.4773
 3              46              -.755709          63.6644
 4              49              -.53631           66.9554
 5              65               .63382           84.5073
 6              37             -1.41391           53.7914
 7              71              1.07262           91.0893
 8              65               .63382           84.5073
 9              45              -.828843          62.5674
10              65               .63382           84.5073
11              49              -.53631           66.9554
12              71              1.07262           91.0893
CALCULATIONS COMPLETED

Ready




Ready

LIST
SS
100 DIM X(200),Y(200),Z(200)
110 PRINT"THIS PROGRAM CALCULATES TWO SETS OF STANDARDIZED SCORES"
120 PRINT"Y(I) OF MEAN ZERO AND STANDARD DEVIATION ONE"
130 PRINT"Z(I) OF MEAN MU    AND STANDARD DEVIATION SIGMA"
140 PRINT"GIVEN VALUES OF MU AND SIGMA, AND N DATA POINTS X(I)"
150 INPUT"DESIRED MEAN VALUE OF Z(I) ARRAY, MU=";M2
160 INPUT"DESIRED STANDARD DEVIATION OF Z(I) ARRAY, SIGMA=";S2
170 INPUT"NUMBER OF DATA VALUES X(I) TO BE ENTERED, N=";N
180 INPUT"ENTER NOW N DATA VALUES SEPARATED BY COMMAS":MAT INPUT X(N)
190 REM - CALCULATE MEAN
200 LET Y1=0
210 FOR I=1 TO N STEP 1
220 LET Y1=Y1+X(I)/N
230 NEXT I
240 REM -CALCULATE STANDARD DEVIATION
250 LET Y2=0
260 FOR I=1 TO N STEP 1
270 Y2=Y2+((X(I)-Y1)**2/(N-1))
280 NEXT I
290 LET S1=Y2**.5
300 REM - CALCULATE Y(I) AND Z(I) AND PRINT OUTPUT
310 PRINT"I               X(I)           Y(I)            Z(I)"
320 FOR I=1 TO N STEP 1
330 Y(I)=(X(I)-Y1)/S1
340 Z(I)=M2+S2*Y(I)
350 PRINT I,X(I),Y(I),Z(I)
360 NEXT I
370 REM _ SHOULD ANY RUNNING DIFFICULTIES ARISE PLEASE BRING THEM
380 REM _ TO THE ATTENTION OF THE AUTHOR, JOSE ALONSO, SWINBURNE
390 REM _ COLLEGE OF TECHNOLOGY, LTD.
400 PRINT"CALCULATIONS COMPLETED"
410 END

Ready
```

RUN#GM
GENERALIZED MEAN

This program calculates the generalized mean of order M according to the equation:

$$\text{Generalized mean} = \frac{1}{N} \left[\sum_{i=1}^{N} x_i^M \right]^{\frac{1}{M}}$$

for a given set of N values of x_i for values of M from 1 to 10.

Notice as a matter of interest that:

    if M = 1, the generalized mean becomes the arithmetic mean.

    if M = -1, the generalized mean becomes the harmonic mean.

INPUT REQUIREMENTS

Integer N, and N values of x_i.

PROGRAM OUTPUT

Calculated value of generalized mean of desired order M.

REFERENCES

Any standard textbook of statistics.

SAMPLE PROGRAM

The printout is self-explanatory

```
RUN
GM
THIS PROGRAM CALCULATES THE GENERALIZED MEAN OF ORDER M OF A SET OF
N DATA VALUES X(I), FOR VALUES OF M FROM 1 TO 10
NUMBER OF DATA VALUES X(I) TO BE ENTERED, N=? 20
ENTER NOW THE N DATA VALUES, SEPARATED BY COMMAS? 1,3,5,2,4,6,3,5,7,4,6,8,5,7,9,6,8,10,7,9,
THE MEAN OF ORDER  1   IS = 5.75
THE MEAN OF ORDER  2   IS = 6.22495
THE MEAN OF ORDER  3   IS = 6.59045
THE MEAN OF ORDER  4   IS = 6.88614
THE MEAN OF ORDER  5   IS = 7.13306
THE MEAN OF ORDER  6   IS = 7.34356
THE MEAN OF ORDER  7   IS = 7.52565
THE MEAN OF ORDER  8   IS = 7.68491
THE MEAN OF ORDER  9   IS = 7.82546
THE MEAN OF ORDER  10  IS = 7.95046
CALCULATIONS COMPLETED

Ready
```

```
Ready

LIST
GM
100 DIM X(200)
110 PRINT"THIS PROGRAM CALCULATES THE GENERALIZED MEAN OF ORDER M OF A SET OF"
120 PRINT"N DATA VALUES X(I), FOR VALUES OF M FROM 1 TO 10"
130 INPUT"NUMBER OF DATA VALUES X(I) TO BE ENTERED, N=";N
140 INPUT"ENTER NOW THE N DATA VALUES, SEPARATED BY COMMAS":MAT INPUT X(N)
150 FOR J=1 TO 10 STEP 1
160 M=J
170 LET M1=0
180 FOR I=1 TO N STEP 1
190 LET M1=(M1+(X(I)**M)/N)
200 NEXT I
210 LET T1=1/M
220 LET M1=M1**T1
230 PRINT"THE MEAN OF ORDER ";M;" IS =";M1
240 NEXT J
250 REM _ SHOULD ANY RUNNING DIFFICULTIES ARISE, PLEASE BRING THEM TO
260 REM _ THE ATTENTION OF THE AUTHOR, JOSE ALONSO, SWINBURNE COLLEGE
270 REM _ OF TECHNOLOGY LTD.
280 PRINT"CALCULATIONS COMPLETED"
290 END

Ready
```

RUN#FH
FREQUENCY HISTOGRAM

Given a set of N observations x_i, this program calculates a frequency histogram and a cumulative frequency histogram.

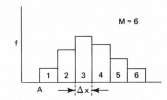 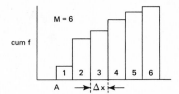

given   A = the lower limit of the histogram
     ΔX = the interval size desired
      M = the number of intervals

<u>Caveat:</u> Please ensure that the smallest and the largest values of the observations fall within A and $(A + M\Delta X)$!!

PROGRAM RESTRICTIONS

N < 300, M < 20.

PROGRAM OUTPUT

Interval limits, corresponding frequencies, and cumulative frequencies.

REFERENCES

Burington, R. S. and May, D. C., <u>Handbook of Probality and Statistics with Tables</u>, Handbook Publishers, Inc., Sanduski, Ohio, 1958, Chapter III.

SAMPLE PROGRAM

The printout is self-explanatory. Notice that the mean, s^2, s, and skewness values are calculated from the histogram, not from the original data!

```
RUN
FH
THIS PROGRAM PRODUCES A FREQUENCY HISTOGRAM FOR A GIVEN SET OF OBSERVATIONS
AND CALCULATES FROM THE HISTOGRAM THE MEAN, VARIANCE
ENTER NUMBER OF OBSERVATIONS, N=? 20
ENTER DESIRED NUMBER OF HISTOGRAM INTERVALS, NH=? 4
ENTER DESIRED WIDTH OF INTERVAL, DELTA X=? 6
ENTER DESIRED LOWER LIMIT OF FIRST INTERVAL, A=? 0
ENTER NOW, SEPARATED BY COMMAS, THE 20 OBSERVATION VALUES
PLEASE ENSURE THAT YOUR VALUES DO NOT FALL OUTSIDE THE LOWER AND UPPER
VALUES OF YOUR OVERALL INTERVAL'S RANGE
? 1,2,3,4,5,6,7,8,9,20,19,18,17,16,15,14,10,11,12,13
INTERVAL RANGE                FREQUENCY    CUMULATIVE
FROM          TO              VALUE        FREQUENCY
 .001          6               6            6
 6.001        12               6           12
 12.001       18               6           18
 18.001       24               2           20
MEAN          S-SQUARED        S            SKEWNESS
 10.2          34.56           5.87878      .229637
STANDARD DEVIATION OF THE MEAN IS= 1.31453
THE LATTER 5 PARAMETERS ARE CALCULATED FROM THE HISTOGRAM
NOT FROM THE RAW DATA VALUES!!!!!!!!
CALCULATIONS COMPLETED

Ready
```

```
Ready

LIST
FH
1 DIM X(300),X3(21),Y(21),F(21),F3(21)
10 PRINT"THIS PROGRAM PRODUCES A FREQUENCY HISTOGRAM FOR A GIVEN SET OF OBSERVATIONS"
11 PRINT"AND CALCULATES FROM THE HISTOGRAM THE MEAN, VARIANCE"
12 INPUT"ENTER NUMBER OF OBSERVATIONS, N=";N
14 INPUT"ENTER DESIRED NUMBER OF HISTOGRAM INTERVALS, NH=";N3
16 INPUT"ENTER DESIRED WIDTH OF INTERVAL, DELTA X=";W3
18 INPUT"ENTER DESIRED LOWER LIMIT OF FIRST INTERVAL, A=";X3(1)
20 PRINT"ENTER NOW, SEPARATED BY COMMAS, THE";N;"OBSERVATION VALUES"
26 PRINT"PLEASE ENSURE THAT YOUR VALUES DO NOT FALL OUTSIDE THE LOWER AND UPPER"
27 PRINT"VALUES OF YOUR OVERALL INTERVAL'S RANGE"
31 N3=N3+1
32 MAT INPUT X(N)
40 FOR K=1 TO N3 STEP 1
45 F(K)=0.0
46 NEXT K
47 FOR K=2 TO N3 STEP 1
50 X3(K)=X3(K-1)+W3
55 NEXT K
60 F8=0.0
86 FOR I=1 TO N STEP 1
88 K=1
89 IF(X(I)-X3(N3))>0 THEN GO TO 115
90 IF(X(I)-X3(K))<0 THEN 100
92 IF(X(I)-X3(K))=0 THEN 100
94 K=K+1
96 GO TO 90
100 F(K-1)=F(K-1)+1.0
110 F8=F8+1.0
115 NEXT I
120 PRINT"INTERVAL RANGE                FREQUENCY      CUMULATIVE"
125 PRINT"FROM             TO           VALUE          FREQUENCY"
130 L=N3-1
135 S9=0.0
140 S6=0.0
145 S3=0.0
146 C4=0
150 FOR K=1 TO L STEP 1
153 C4=C4+F(K)
155 PRINT X3(K)+.001,X3(K+1),F(K),C4
160 Y(K)=.5*(X3(K)+X3(K+1))
165 S9=F(K)*Y(K)+S9
170 S6=F(K)*Y(K)**2+S6
175 S3=F(K)*Y(K)**3+S3
180 NEXT K
190 S9=S9/F8
195 S6=S6/F8
200 S3=S3/F8
210 V5=S6-S9**2
220 IF(V5<0) GO TO 1000
225 S1=V5**(.5)
230 S7=S3-3*S6*S9+2*S9**3
235 S8=S7/(S1**3)
240 PRINT"MEAN            S-SQUARED       S              SKEWNESS"
245 PRINT S9,V5,S1,S8
250 W1=(V5/N)**0.5
260 PRINT"STANDARD DEVIATION OF THE MEAN IS=";W1
265 PRINT"THE LATTER 5 PARAMETERS ARE CALCULATED FROM THE HISTOGRAM"
266 PRINT"NOT FROM THE RAW DATA VALUES!!!!!!!"
999 GO TO 1010
1000 PRINT"DATA ERROR, NEGATIVE SQUARE ROOT CAN NOT BE CALCULATED"
1010 PRINT"CALCULATIONS COMPLETED"
1020 END

Ready
```

DISCRETE
DISTRIBUTION FUNCTIONS

RUN#BD
BINOMIAL DISTRIBUTION

This program calculates values of the binomial distribution

$$f(x) = \frac{n!}{x! \ (n-x)!} \ p^x \ (1-p)^{n-x}$$

given $x = 0, 1, 2, \ldots n; \ 0 \leq p \leq 1$.
   n = Number of independent trials.
   p = probability of success in a single trial.

x_1, x_2, and x_3 indicate that the user wants the binomial distribution function calculated from a value of x_1 to a value of x_2 in steps of x_3, where x_1, x_2, and x_3 are integers.

The program also calculates the left-hand cumulative binomial distribution:

$$F(x) = \sum_{k=0}^{x} f(k) \ \text{for each value of x.}$$

The mean m and the variance δ^2 of the distribution are also calculated.

INPUT REQUIREMENTS

Integers n, p, x_1, x_2, x_3.

PROGRAM OUTPUT

Two columns of numbers as follows:

Argument	Distribution	"Left-Hand" Integral of Distribution
x_1	$f(x_1)$	$F(x_2)$
$x_1 + x_3$	$f(x_1 + x_3)$	$F(x_1 + x_3)$
$x_1 + 2x_3$	$f(x_1 + 2x_3)$	$F(x_1 + 2x_3)$
.	.	.
.	.	.
.	.	.
x_2	$f(x_2)$	$F(x_2)$

REFERENCES

Any standard textbook in statistics

SAMPLE PROGRAM

```
RUN
BD
THIS PROGRAM CALCULATES VALUES OF THE BINOMIAL DISTRIBUTION
AND OF THE CUMULATIVE BINOMIAL DISTRIBUTION FOR VALUES OF X
FROM X1 TO X2 IN STEPS OF X3, GIVEN VALUES OF THE PROBABILITY OF
SUCCESS P AND THE INTEGER N
ENTER VALUE OF THE PROBABILITY OF SUCCESS P=? .6
ENTER INTEGER VALUE N=? 5
ENTER INITIAL VALUE OF X, X1=? 0
ENTER FINAL VALUE OF X, X2=? 4
ENTER STEP SIZE OF X, X3=? 1
 X              BINOMIAL(X)    CUMULATIVE BINOMIAL(X)
 0                 .01024        .01024
 1                 .0768         .08704
 2                 .2304         .31744
 3                 .3456         .66304
 4                 .2592         .92224
THE MEAN OF THE DISTRIBUTION IS= 3
THE VARIANCE OF THE DISTRIBUTION IS= 1.2
CALCULATIONS COMPLETED

Ready
```

```
Ready

LIST
BD
100 PRINT"THIS PROGRAM CALCULATES VALUES OF THE BINOMIAL DISTRIBUTION"
110 PRINT"AND OF THE CUMULATIVE BINOMIAL DISTRIBUTION FOR VALUES OF X"
120 PRINT"FROM X1 TO X2 IN STEPS OF X3, GIVEN VALUES OF THE PROBABILITY OF "
130 PRINT"SUCCESS P AND THE INTEGER N"
140 INPUT"ENTER VALUE OF THE PROBABILITY OF SUCCESS P=";P
150 INPUT"ENTER INTEGER VALUE N=";N9
160 INPUT"ENTER INITIAL VALUE OF X, X1=";K1
170 INPUT"ENTER FINAL VALUE OF X, X2=";K2
180 INPUT"ENTER STEP SIZE OF X, X3=";K3
190 LET L1=K1+1
200 LET L2=K2+1
210 IF K1==K2 OR K3==0 OR K1>K2 OR K3<0 THEN 340 ELSE 220
220 PRINT" X              BINOMIAL(X)    CUMULATIVE BINOMIAL(X)
230 FOR I=L1 TO L2 STEP K3
240 LET J=I-1
250 DIM P1(100),F(100)
260 F(0)=(1-P)**N9
270 P1(0)=F(0)
280 FOR X=0 TO I-1 STEP 1
290 F(X+1)=(P*(N9-X)/((X+1)*(1-P)))*F(X)
300 P1(X+1)=P1(X)+F(X+1)
310 NEXT X
320 PRINT J,F(J),P1(J)
330 IF K1==K2 OR K3==0 OR K1>K2 OR K3<0 THEN 340 ELSE 360
340 PRINT"ERROR IN INPUT"
350 CHAIN"PANIC.BAS"10
360 NEXT I
370 PRINT"THE MEAN OF THE DISTRIBUTION IS=" N9*P
380 PRINT"THE VARIANCE OF THE DISTRIBUTION IS=" N9*P*(1-P)
390 PRINT"CALCULATIONS COMPLETED"
400 REM _ SHOULD ANY RUNNING DIFFICULTIES ARISE, PLEASE BRING THEM TO
410 REM _ THE ATTENTION OF THE AUTHOR, JOSE ALONSO, SWINBURNE COLLEGE
420 REM _ OF TECHNOLOGY LTD
430 END

Ready
```

RUN#PD
POISSON DISTRIBUTION

This program calculates values of the Poisson distribution:

$$f(x) = \frac{\tau^x\, e^{-\tau}}{x!}$$

given $x = 0, 1, 2, \ldots$ from a value of x_1 to a value of x_2 in steps of x_3.
τ = mean of distribution

The values x_1, x_2, x_3, are integers. The program also calculates $F(x)$, the "left-hand" cumulative distribution at each value of x.

The Poisson distribution is a special case of the binomial distribution: If $p \rightarrow 0$, then binomial $\rightarrow$ Poisson. It is calculationally expedient to use the Poisson distribution formula in cases where n is very large, provided p is very small. In such case $\tau = n \cdot p$.

INPUT REQUIREMENTS

Real value of τ and integer of x_1, x_2, x_3. Some textbooks use λ (lambda) instead of τ (tau).

PROGRAM OUTPUT

Three columns of numbers as follows:

Argument	Distribution	"Left-Hand" Integral of Distribution
x_1	$f(x_1)$	$F(x_1)$
$x_1 + x_3$	$f(x_1 + x_3)$	$F(x_1 + x_3)$
$x_1 + 2x_3$	$f(x_1 + 2x_3)$	$F(x_1 + 2x_3)$
.	.	.
.	.	.
.	.	.
x_2	$f(x_2)$	$F(x_2)$

REFERENCES

Any standard textbook in statistics.

SAMPLE PROGRAM

```
RUN
PD
THIS PROGRAM COMPUTES VALUES OF THE POISSON DISTRIBUTION
FOR VALUES OF X FROM X1 TO X2 IN STEPS OF X3
VALUE OF DECIMAL NUMBER LAMBDA IN POISSON DISTRIBUTION=? 2.7
ENTER VALUE OF X1=? 0
ENTER VALUE OF X2=? 10
ENTER VALUE OF STEP SIZE X3=? 1
X              POISSON(X)     CUM POISSON(X)
 0             .672055E-1     .24866
 1             .181455        .493624
 2             .244964        .714092
 3             .220468        .862908
 4             .148816        .943268
 5             .803605E-1     .97943
 6             .361622E-1     .993379
 7             .139483E-1     .998086
 8             .470755E-2     .999498
 9             .141226E-2     .99988
10             .381311E-3     0
CALCULATIONS COMPLETED

Ready




Ready

LIST
PD
100 PRINT "THIS PROGRAM COMPUTES VALUES OF THE POISSON DISTRIBUTION"
110 PRINT"FOR VALUES OF X FROM X1 TO X2 IN STEPS OF X3"
120 INPUT "VALUE OF DECIMAL NUMBER LAMBDA IN POISSON DISTRIBUTION=";L
130 INPUT"ENTER VALUE OF X1=";K1
140 INPUT"ENTER VALUE OF X2=";K2
150 INPUT"ENTER VALUE OF STEP SIZE X3=";K3
160   IF K1==K2 OR K3==0 OR K1>K2 OR K3<0 THEN CHAIN"#PANIC.BAS"10 ELSE 170
170 LET L1=K1+1
180 LET L2=K2+1
190 PRINT"X                POISSON(X)       CUM POISSON(X)"
200 FOR I=L1 TO L2 STEP K3
210 LET J=I-1
220 REM - COMPUTE FACTORIAL
230 LET F8=1
240 IF J==0 THEN 290
250 FOR I2=1 TO J STEP 1
260 LET F8=F8*I2
270 NEXT I2
280 REM - COMPUTE POISSON DISTRIBUTION
290 LET P=L**J*EXP(-L)/F8
300 DIM P1(100),X(100)
310 F(0)=EXP(-L)
320 P1(0)=F(0)
330 FOR X=0 TO K2-1 STEP1
340 F(X+1)=(L/(X+1))*F(X)
350 P1(X+1)=P1(X)+F(X+1)
360 NEXT X
370 PRINT J,P,P1(I)
380 NEXT I
390 PRINT"CALCULATIONS COMPLETED"
400 END

Ready
```

CONTINUOUS
DISTRIBUTION FUNCTIONS

RUN#KMD
KHRGIAN AND MAZIN DISTRIBUTION

This program calculates values of the frequency f (bell shape) and cumulative F (sigmoidal shape) Khrgian and Mazin distribution.

$$\text{Frequency} = Ax^2\,e^{-Bx}$$

given values of f_0, the value of the frequency corresponding to x_0, the most common value of the independent variable x, for values of x from x_1 to x_2 in steps of x_3.

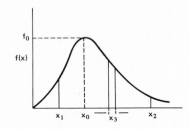 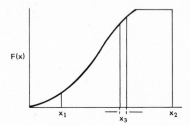

PROGRAM RESTRICTIONS

None.

INPUT REQUIREMENTS

Real values of f_0, x_0, x_1, x_2, and x_3.

PROGRAM OUTPUT

Table of values of x_i, $f(x_i)$, $F(x_i)$.

REFERENCES

Tverskoi, P. N., Atmospheric Physics, Israel Technical Translation Service, NASA (from the Russian).

SAMPLE PROGRAM

This, strictly speaking, a curve fitting program, to test whether the K - M distribution is a good fit to some data with a most common value (not mean value) of 50 and with a histogram frequency of 0.2 associated with the most common value of 50.

The original data (not required by the KMD program) can be compared to the calculated (density) data with program CSUEF followed by CSD.

```
RUN
KMD
THIS PROGRAM CALCULATES VALUES OF THE FREQUENCY(BELL SHAPE)
AND CUMULATIVE(SIGMOIDAL SHAPE) KHRGIAN AND MAZIN DISTRIBUTION
FREQUENCY=A*X**2 * EXP(-B*X)
GIVEN VALUES OF NO, THE VALUE OF THE FREQUENCY
CORRESPONDING TO XO, THE MOST COMMON VALUE OF THE INEPENDENT
VARIABLE X
FOR VALUES OF X FROM X1 TO X2 IN STEPS OF X3
ENTER VALUE OF NO=
? .2
ENTER VALUE OF DO=
? 50
ENTER VALUE OF X1=
? 5
ENTER VALUE OF X2=
? 150
ENTER VALUE OF X3=
? 10
```

X	DENSITY AT X	CUMULATIVE FROM ZERO TO X
5	.121172E-1	.212479E-1
15	.731017E-1	.427633
25	.136115	1.48558
35	.178832	3.08029
45	.19816	4.98351
55	.198426	6.9798
65	.185773	8.90905
75	.165791	10.671
85	.142744	12.2148
95	.119523	13.5254
105	.978732E-1	14.6106
115	.786978E-1	15.4912
125	.062326	16.1939
135	.487303E-1	16.747
145	.376834E-1	17.1771

```
CALCULATED DISTRIBUTION IS
 .000592 X**2 EXP(- .04 X)
CALCULATION COMPLETED

Ready



Ready

LIST
KMD
00100 PRINT"THIS PROGRAM CALCULATES VALUES OF THE FREQUENCY(BELL SHAPE)"
00110 PRINT"AND CUMULATIVE(SIGMOIDAL SHAPE) KHRGIAN AND MAZIN DISTRIBUTION"
00120 PRINT"FREQUENCY=A*X**2 * EXP(-B*X)"
00130 PRINT"GIVEN VALUES OF NO, THE VALUE OF THE FREQUENCY"
00140 PRINT"CORRESPONDING TO XO, THE MOST COMMON VALUE OF THE INEPENDENT"
00150 PRINT"VARIABLE X"
00160 PRINT"FOR VALUES OF X FROM X1 TO X2 IN STEPS OF X3"
00170 PRINT"ENTER VALUE OF NO="
00171 INPUT NO
00180 PRINT"ENTER VALUE OF DO="
00181 INPUT DO
00190 A=7.4*NO/DO**2
00200 B=2/DO
00210 S=-A*2/(B**3)
00220 PRINT"ENTER VALUE OF X1="
221 INPUT X1
00230 PRINT"ENTER VALUE OF X2="
00231 INPUT X2
00240 PRINT"ENTER VALUE OF X3="
00241 INPUT X3
00250 PRINT"X                    DENSITY          CUMULATIVE"
00260 PRINT"                     AT X             FROM ZERO TO X"
00270 FOR X=X1 TO X2 STEP X3
00280 F1=(A*(X**2))*EXP(-B*X)
00290 I1=-A*EXP(-B*X)*((2/(B**3))+(2*X/(B**2))+((X**2)/B))-S
00300 PRINT X, F1, I1
00310 NEXT X
00320 PRINT"CALCULATED DISTRIBUTION IS"
00330 PRINTA;"X**2 EXP(-";B;"X)"
00340 PRINT"CALCULATION COMPLETED"
00350 END

Ready
```

RUN#ED
EXPONENTIAL DISTRIBUTION

This program calculates values of the exponential distribution function

$$f(x) = \frac{1}{m} e^{-\frac{x}{m}}$$

given a value of a mean m, for values of x from x_1 to x_2 in steps of x_3. The program also calculates the value of the integral from zero to x of f(x), namely:

$$f(x) = 1 - e^{-\frac{x}{m}}$$

INPUT REQUIREMENTS

Values of mean m and real values of x_1, x_2, and x_3.

PROGRAM OUTPUT

Values of f(x) from x1 to x2 in steps of x3. Number of values printed equal the result of the fixed point calculation

$$\frac{(x_2 - x_1)}{x_3}$$

REFERENCES

Any standard textbook on statistics.

SAMPLE PROGRAM

```
RUN
ED
THIS PROGRAM CALCULATES VALUES OF THE EXPONENTIAL DISTRIBUTION FUNCTION
     F(X)=(1/M)*EXP(-(X/M))
THE PROGRAM ALSO CALCULATES THE LEFT HAND TAIL INTEGRAL AREA
THAT IS, THE AREA FROM ZERO TO X
FOR POSITIVE REAL VALUES OF X FROM X1 TO X2 IN STEPS OF X3
GIVEN VALUES OF THE MEAN M AND OF X1,X2,X3
ENTER VALUE OF MEAN M=? 45
ENTER VALUE OF X1=? 5
ENTER VALUE OF X2=? 100
ENTER VALUE OF X3=? 10
F( 5 )= .198853E-1 INT OF F( 5 ) FROM ZERO TO  5 = .105161
F( 15 )= .159229E-1 INT OF F( 15 ) FROM ZERO TO  15 = .283469
F( 25 )= .127501E-1 INT OF F( 25 ) FROM ZERO TO  25 = .426247
F( 35 )= .102095E-1 INT OF F( 35 ) FROM ZERO TO  35 = .540574
F( 45 )= .81751E-2 INT OF F( 45 ) FROM ZERO TO  45 = .632121
F( 55 )= .654611E-2 INT OF F( 55 ) FROM ZERO TO  55 = .705425
F( 65 )= .524171E-2 INT OF F( 65 ) FROM ZERO TO  65 = .764123
F( 75 )= .419724E-2 INT OF F( 75 ) FROM ZERO TO  75 = .811124
F( 85 )= .336088E-2 INT OF F( 85 ) FROM ZERO TO  85 = .84876
F( 95 )= .269119E-2 INT OF F( 95 ) FROM ZERO TO  95 = .878897
CALCULATIONS COMPLETED

Ready
```

```
Ready

LIST
ED
100 PRINT"THIS PROGRAM CALCULATES VALUES OF THE EXPONENTIAL DISTRIBUTION FUNCTION"
110 PRINT"      F(X)=(1/M)*EXP(-(X/M))"
120 PRINT"THE PROGRAM ALSO CALCULATES THE LEFT HAND TAIL INTEGRAL AREA"
130 PRINT"THAT IS, THE AREA FROM ZERO TO X"
140 PRINT"FOR POSITIVE REAL VALUES OF X FROM X1 TO X2 IN STEPS OF X3"
150 PRINT"GIVEN VALUES OF THE MEAN M AND OF X1,X2,X3"
160 INPUT"ENTER VALUE OF MEAN M=";M
170 INPUT"ENTER VALUE OF X1=";X1
180 INPUT"ENTER VALUE OF X2=";X2
190 INPUT"ENTER VALUE OF X3=";X3
200 FOR X=X1 TO X2 STEP X3
210 F=(1/M)*EXP(-(X/M))
220 I1=1-EXP(-(1/M)*X)
230 PRINT"F(";X;")=";F;"INT OF F(";X;") FROM ZERO TO ";X;"=";I1
240 NEXT X
250 PRINT"CALCULATIONS COMPLETED"
260 REM _ SHOULD RUNNING DIFFICULTIES BE ENCOUNTERED, PLEASE BRING THEM
270 REM _ TO THE ATTENTION OF THE AUTHOR, JOSE ALONSO, SWINBURNE COLLEGE
280 REM _ OF TECHNOLOGY
290 END

Ready
```

RUN#ND
NORMAL (GAUSSIAN) DISTRIBUTION

This program calculates the probability density function

$$f(x) = \frac{1}{\sqrt{2\pi}} e^{-\frac{x^2}{2}}$$

and the right tail area

$$F(x) = \frac{1}{\sqrt{2\pi}} \int_x^\infty e^{-\frac{t^2}{2}} dt$$

for real values of x from x_1 to x_2 in steps of x_3.

For every value of x, the program calculates both $f(x)$ and $f(-x)$ and both $F(x)$ and $F(-x)$. So only positive real values need be entered. Negative values simply result in double calculation printout time.

If you desire only one value, enter $x_1 = x_2$ = desired argument. Enter also $x_3 = 0$.

INPUT REQUIREMENTS

Values of x_1, x_2, x_3.

PROGRAM OUTPUT

Values of $f(x)$, $Q-(x)$, $f(-x)$, $Q(-x)$. The number of calculated values is the result of the fixed point calculation

$$\frac{(x_2 - x_1)}{x_3}$$

REFERENCES

Abramowitz, M., and Stegun, I., <u>Handbook of Mathematical Functions</u>, National Bureau of Standards, 1968, p. 932, item 26.2.17.

SAMPLE PROGRAM

```
RUN
ND
THIS PROGRAM CALCULATES THE PROBABILITY DENSITY FUNCTION FOR A
STANDARD NORMAL OR GAUSSIAN VARIABLE
   F(X)=(1/(2*PI)**.5)(EXP(-(X**2)/(2)))
FOR VALUES OF X FROM X1 TO X2 IN STEPS OF X3
THIS PROGRAM ALSO EVALUATES THE UPPER TAIL AREA
   Q(X)=INTEGRAL OF F(X) FROM X TO INFINITY
ENTER VALUE OF X1=? 0
ENTER VALUE OF X2=? 10
ENTER VALUE OF X3=? 2
F( 0 )= .398942      Q( 0 )= .5
F(- 0 )= .398942      Q(- 0 )= .5
F( 2 )= .053991      Q( 2 )= .02275
F(- 2 )= .053991      Q(- 2 )= .97725
F( 4 )= .13383E-3      Q( 4 )= .31686E-4
F(- 4 )= .13383E-3      Q(- 4 )= .999968
F( 6 )= .607589E-8      Q( 6 )= .990122E-9
F(- 6 )= .607589E-8      Q(- 6 )= 1
F( 8 )= .505228E-14      Q( 8 )= .628472E-15
F(- 8 )= .505228E-14      Q(- 8 )= 1
F( 10 )= .76946E-22      Q( 10 )= .777033E-23
F(- 10 )= .76946E-22      Q(- 10 )= 1
CALCULATIONS COMPLETED

Ready

Ready

LIST
ND
100 PRINT"THIS PROGRAM CALCULATES THE PROBABILITY DENSITY FUNCTION FOR A"
110 PRINT"STANDARD NORMAL OR GAUSSIAN VARIABLE"
120 PRINT"   F(X)=(1/(2*PI)**.5)(EXP(-(X**2)/(2)))"
130 PRINT"FOR VALUES OF X FROM X1 TO X2 IN STEPS OF X3"
140 PRINT"THIS PROGRAM ALSO EVALUATES THE UPPER TAIL AREA"
150 PRINT"   Q(X)=INTEGRAL OF F(X) FROM X TO INFINITY
160 INPUT"ENTER VALUE OF X1=";X1
170 INPUT"ENTER VALUE OF X2=";X2
180 INPUT"ENTER VALUE OF X3=";X3
190 FOR X=X1 TO X2 STEP X3
200 X=ABS(X)
210 F=1/(2*3.141592654)**0.5
220 F=F*EXP(-(X**2/2))
230 B1=0.31938153
240 B2=-.356563782
250 B3=1.781477937
260 B4=-1.821255978
270 B5=1.330274429
280 R=0.2316419
290 T=1/(1+R*X)
300 Q=B1*T+B2*T**2+B3*T**3+B4*T**4+B5*T**5
310 Q=Q*F
320 PRINT"F(";X;")=";F;"      Q(";X;")=";Q
330 PRINT"F(-";X;")=";F;"      Q(-";X;")=";1-Q
340 IF X1==X2 OR X3==0 THEN 370 ELSE 350
350 NEXT X
360 GO TO 380
370 PRINT"ONLY ONE VALUE OF X WAS REQUESTED"
380 PRINT"CALCULATIONS COMPLETED"
390 REM - SHOULD ANY RUNNING DIFFICULTIES DEVELOP, PLEASE BRING THEM TO
400 REM - THE ATTENTION OF THE AUTHOR, JOSE ALONSO, SWINBURNE COLLEGE
410 REM - OF TECHNOLOGY LTD.
420 END

Ready
```

RUN#IND
INVERSE NORMAL DISTRIBUTION

Given a value of $0 < A \leq 0.5$, this program calculates the value of x such that the upper tail area:

$$A = \frac{1}{\sqrt{2\pi}} \int_X^\infty e - \frac{t^2}{2} \, dt$$

It is of interest that:

    f(-x) = f(x)
    A(-x) = 1 - A(x)

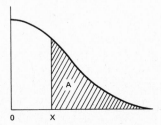

PROGRAM RESTRICTIONS

$0 < A < 0.5$.

INPUT REQUIREMENTS

Real value of A.

REFERENCES

Abramowitz, M., and Stegun, I., <u>Handbook of Mathematical Functions</u>, National Bureau of Standards, 1964, p. 933, item #26.2.23.

SAMPLE PROGRAM

```
RUN
IND
THIS PROGRAM CALCULATES THE INVERSE NORMAL DISTRIBUTION
VALUE X, GIVEN A VALUE OF THE UPPER RIGHT TAIL AREA A
BETWEEN ZERO AND 0.5
ENTER VALUE OF UPPER RIGHT TAIL AREA, A=? .3
THE VALUE OF X CORRESPONDING TO A RIGHT TAIL AREA OF .3 IS .521632
CALCULATIONS COMPLETED

Ready

Ready

LIST
IND
100 PRINT"THIS PROGRAM CALCULATES THE INVERSE NORMAL DISTRIBUTION"
110 PRINT"VALUE X, GIVEN A VALUE OF THE UPPER RIGHT TAIL AREA A"
120 PRINT"BETWEEN ZERO AND 0.5"
130 INPUT"ENTER VALUE OF UPPER RIGHT TAIL AREA, A=";A
140 T=(LOG(1/(A*A)))**0.5
150 A0=2.30753
160 A1=0.27061
170 B1=.99229
180 B2=.04481
190 X=T-((A0+A1*T)/(1+B1*T+B2*T*T))
200 PRINT"THE VALUE OF X CORRESPONDING TO A RIGHT TAIL AREA OF";A;"IS";X
210 PRINT"CALCULATIONS COMPLETED"
220 END

Ready
```

RUN#CSD
CHI-SQUARE DISTRIBUTION

This program calculates values of the Chi-square distribution F(x) and density function f(x) for real values of 0 < x < 22 and integer values of ν, the degrees of freedom.

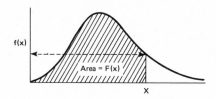

PROGRAM RESTRICTIONS

0 < x < 22.

INPUT REQUIREMENTS

Real value of x, integer value of ν.

PROGRAM OUTPUT

Values of f(x) and F(x).

REFERENCES

Abramowitz, M., and Stegun, I.A., Handbook of Mathematical Functions, National Bureau of Standards, 1968, p. 941, item #26.4.6.

SAMPLE PROGRAM

The printout should be self-explanatory. The values of argument X and degrees of freedom NU come from program CSEEF, CSUEF, CT, or similar calculations. This program CSD essentially reproduces the Chi-square tables in any standard handbook, but it is not restricted to the specific tabular values. You should learn what this program does in the context of the common tables by convincing yourself with a few examples from the common tables.

```
RUN
CSD
THIS PROGRAM EVALUATES VALUES OF THE CHI-SQUARE DISTRIBUTION
AND DENSITY FUNCTIONS FOR REAL VALUES OF 0<X<22 AND INTEGER
VALUES OF NU, THE DEGREES OF FREEDOM
ENTER VALUE OF NU=? 18
ENTER VALUE OF X=? 10.2
THE VALUE OF THE CHI-SQUARED DENSITY FUNCTION OF ARGUMENT X= 10.2
AND 18 DEGREES OF FREEDOM IS= .346026E-1
THE VALUE OF THE CHI-SQUARED CUMULATIVE DISTRIBUTION FOR THE SAME
PARAMETERS IS= .748172E-1
CALCULATIONS COMPLETED

Ready
```

```
Ready

LIST
CSD
100 PRINT"THIS PROGRAM EVALUATES VALUES OF THE CHI-SQUARE DISTRIBUTION"
110 PRINT"AND DENSITY FUNCTIONS FOR REAL VALUES OF 0<X<22 AND INTEGER"
120 PRINT"VALUES OF NU, THE DEGREES OF FREEDOM"
130 INPUT"ENTER VALUE OF NU=";N
140 INPUT"ENTER VALUE OF X=";X1
150 REM - CALCULATE GAMMA(N/2)
160 X=N/2
170 LET X5=X+5
180 G5=((2*3.141592654/X5)**0.5)*(X5**X5)
190 E5=-(X5-(1/(12*X5))+(1/(360*X5*X5*X5)))
200 E5=EXP(E5)
210 G5=G5*E5
220 G=G5/((X+4)*(X+3)*(X+2)*(X+1)*(X))
230 F1=X1**(X-1)
240 F2=(2**X)*G*EXP(X1/2)
250 F1=F1/F2
260 C=2*X1/N*F1
270 S1=1
280 FOR K=1 TO 50 STEP 1
290 S2=S1
300 S3=(X1**K)
310 S4=1
320 FOR J=1 TO K STEP 1
330 S4=S4*(N+2*J)
340 NEXT J
350 S1=S1+S3/S4
360 IF ABS(S1-S2)<5.0E-5 THEN 380
370 NEXT K
380 C=C*S1
390 PRINT"THE VALUE OF THE CHI-SQUARED DENSITY FUNCTION OF ARGUMENT X=";X1
400 PRINT"AND";N;"DEGREES OF FREEDOM IS=";F1
410 PRINT"THE VALUE OF THE CHI-SQUARED CUMULATIVE DISTRIBUTION FOR THE SAME"
420 PRINT"PARAMETERS IS=";C
430 PRINT"CALCULATIONS COMPLETED"
440 REM - SHOULD ANY RUNNING DIFFICULTIES DEVELOP, PLEASE REFER THEM
450 REM - TO THE AUTHOR, JOSE ALONSO, SWINBURNE COLLEGE OF TECHNOLOGY
460 END

Ready
```

RUN#FD
F DISTRIBUTION

The integral of the F frequency distribution function
(right-hand tail area) is evaluated as shown in the
graph to the right, given a real value of X (calculated
from an analysis of variance or similar procedure) and
integer values of the degrees of freedom m_1 and m_2.

The integral I(X) is defined as follows:

$$I(X) = \int_X^\infty \frac{\Gamma(\frac{m_1 + m_2}{2}) \; Y^{(\frac{m_1}{2} - 1)} (\frac{m_1}{m_2})^{(\frac{m_1}{2})}}{\Gamma(\frac{m_1}{2}) \; \Gamma(\frac{m_2}{2}) \; (1 + \frac{m_1}{m_2} Y)^{(\frac{m_1 + m_2}{2})}} \, dY$$

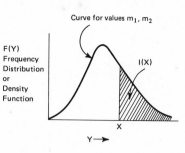

Curve for values m_1, m_2

F(Y) Frequency Distribution or Density Function

I(X)

X

Y →

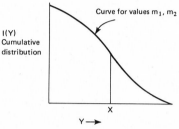

Curve for values m_1, m_2

I(Y) Cumulative distribution

X

Y →

PROGRAM RESTRICTIONS

None. I(X) is evaluated by power series from reference below.

INPUT REQUIREMENTS

Real value of X, and integer values of m_1 and m_2.

PROGRAM OUTPUT

Value of I(X)

REFERENCES

Abramowitz, M., and Stegun, I. A., Handbook of Mathematical Functions, National Bureau of Standards,
1968, pp. 496-497, items #26.6.4, 26.6.5, 26.6.6, and 26.6.8.

SAMPLE PROGRAM

```
RUN
FD
THIS PROGRAM EVALUATES THE RIGHT HAND TAIL AREA UNDER THE
F DISTRIBUTION DENSITY FUNCTION, GIVEN A REAL POSITIVE
VALUE OF X AND INTEGER VALUES OF M1 AND M2, THE DEGREES OF FREEDOM


ENTER VALUE OF ARGUMENT X = ? 2.8

ENTER VALUE OF M1 =          ? 35

ENTER VALUE OF M2 =          ? 19



F(X,M1,M2)=F( 2.8 , 35 , 19 ) = .993658E-2
VARIANCE= .247448
MEAN= 1.11765


CALCULATIONS COMPLETED

Ready
```

```
Ready

LIST
FD
50 REM PROGRAM FD
100 PRINT"THIS PROGRAM EVALUATES THE RIGHT HAND TAIL AREA UNDER THE"
110 PRINT"F DISTRIBUTION DENSITY FUNCTION, GIVEN A REAL POSITIVE"
120 PRINT"VALUE OF X AND INTEGER VALUES OF M1 AND M2, THE DEGREES OF FREEDOM"
130 PRINT
131 PRINT
140 INPUT "ENTER VALUE OF ARGUMENT X =",X
141 PRINT
150 INPUT "ENTER VALUE OF M1 =",M1
151 PRINT
160 INPUT "ENTER VALUE OF M2 =",M2
161 PRINT
162 PRINT
163 PRINT
170 C1=INT(M1/2)
180 C2=INT(M2/2)
190 IF (C1-M1/2)==0 GO TO 220
200 IF (C2-M2/2)==0 GO TO 250
210 GO TO 280
220 L=1
230 K=(M1-2)/2
240 GO TO 300
250 L=2
260 K=(M2-2)/2
270 GO TO 300
280 L=3
281 T3=ATN(((M1/M2)*X)**(1/2))
282 GO TO 1000
300 T=M2/(M2+M1*X)
320 P=1
330 FOR I=1 TO K STEP 1
340 ON L GO TO 350,430,510
350 N1=1
360 FOR J=1 TO I STEP 1
370 N1=N1*(M2+2*J-2)/(2*J)
390 NEXT J
400 P=P+N1*(1-T)**I
420 GO TO 530
430 N1=1
440 FOR J=1 TO I STEP 1
450 N1=N1*(M1+2*J-2)/(2*J)
470 NEXT J
480 P=P+N1*T**I
500 GO TO 530
510 N1=1
520 GO TO 530
530   REM NEXT SUM TERM
540 NEXT I
550 ON L GO TO 560,580,610
560 F=P*(T**(M2/2))
570 GO TO 610
580 F=1-((1-T)**(M1/2))*P
610 PRINT"F(X,M1,M2)=F(";X;",";M1;",";M2;") =";F
611 M7=M2/(M2-2)
612 IF M2<5 THEN 616
613 V7=2*(M2**2)*(M1+M2-2)
614 V7 = V7/(M1*((M2-2)**2)*(M2-4))
615 PRINT"VARIANCE=";V7
616 PRINT "MEAN=";M7
617 PRINT
618 PRINT
620 PRINT"CALCULATIONS COMPLETED"
621 GO TO 4000
1000 REM M1 AND M2 ARE BOTH ODD
```

```
1010 REM F=1-A+B3=1-C4+B3
1020 REM CALCULATE A
1030 IF M2=1 THEN 2100
1031 C4=COS (T3)
1036 FOR I2=M2-2 TO 3 STEP -2
1040 G3=1
1045 G6=1
1050 FOR I3=I2-1 TO 2 STEP -2
1055 G3=G3*I3
1060 G6=G6*(I3+1)
1065 NEXT I3
1070 C3=(G3/G6)*(COS(T3)**I2)
1071 C4=C4+C3
1075 NEXT I2
1085 C4=C4*SIN(T3)
1090 C4=C4+T3
1220 C4=(C4*2)/(3.14159)
2090 GO TO 2110
2100 C4=(2*T3)/(3.14159)
2110 REM CALCULATE B3
2120 IF M1=1 THEN 3200
2128 A5=1
2130 FOR I2=2 TO M1-3 STEP 2
2132 A4=1
2134 A2=1
2136 FOR I3=3 TO I2+1 STEP 2
2138 A4=A4*I3
2140 NEXT I3
2141 FOR I3=M2+1 TO M2+(I2-1) STEP 2
2142 A2=A2*I3
2143 NEXT I3
2144 A5=A5+(A2/A4)*(SIN(T3)**I2)
2152 NEXT I2
2182 A5=A5*SIN(T3)*(COS(T3)**M2)
2184 A5=A5*2/(3.14159**.5)
2186 REM CALCULATE TOP FACTORIAL A8
2187 A8=1
2188 FOR A7=1 TO (M2-1)/2 STEP 1
2190 A8=A8*A7
2196 NEXT A7
2200 REM CALCULATE BOTTOM FACTORIAL B2
2201 Z=((M2-2)/2)+6
2202 G5=((2*3.14159/Z)**.5)*(Z**Z)
2203 E5=-(Z-(1/(12*Z))+(1/(360*Z*Z*Z)))
2204 E5 = EXP(E5)
2205 G5=G5*E5
2206 Z=Z-5
2207 B2=G5/((Z+4)*(Z+3)*(Z+2)*(Z+1)*(Z))
2214 A5=A5*A8/B2
2220 B3=A5
2225 GO TO 3210
3200 B3=0
3210 REM CALCULATE F
3220 F=1-C4+B3
3230 GO TO 610
4000 END

Ready
```

RUN#RNG
RANDOM NUMBER GENERATOR

This program generates a set of N random numbers, given N.

PROGRAM RESTRICTIONS

This program utilizes a built-in BASIC routine.

INPUT REQUIREMENTS

Integer N, the number of random numbers desired.

PROGRAM OUTPUT

N random numbers.

REFERENCES

BASIC Reference Manual, PDP.11, Digital Equipment Corporation, Maynard, Mass., 1975.

SAMPLE PROGRAM

```
RUN
RNG
THIS PROGRAM CALCULATES RANDOM NUMBERS
ENTER NUMBER OF RANDOM NUMBERS DESIRED? 20
   21396    28378    77697    10780    65408    95422    83859    44353    11391
   69162    12451    52249     1436    38369    17291    58420    94898    43609
    7570    52938    CALCULATIONS COMPLETED

Ready


Ready

LIST
RNG
100 PRINT"THIS PROGRAM CALCULATES RANDOM NUMBERS"
110 RANDOMIZE
120 INPUT"ENTER NUMBER OF RANDOM NUMBERS DESIRED";N
130 FOR I=1 TO N STEP 1
140 PRINT INT(100000*RND(0)),
150 NEXT I
160 PRINT"CALCULATIONS COMPLETED"
170 END

Ready
```

RUN#TD
T DISTRIBUTION

Given a real positive value of x and an integer value of ν, the degrees of freedom associated with the value of x, this program calculates the area under the t distribution A, given by the expression:

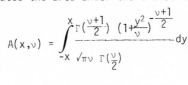

$$A(x,\nu) = \int_{-x}^{x} \frac{\Gamma(\frac{\nu+1}{2}) \ (1+\frac{y^2}{\nu})^{-\frac{\nu+1}{2}}}{\sqrt{\pi\nu} \ \Gamma(\frac{\nu}{2})} dy$$

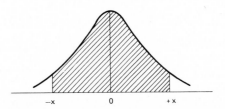

PROGRAM RESTRICTIONS

X > 0.

INPUT REQUIREMENTS

Real positive value of x, integer value of ν.

PROGRAM OUTPUT

Real value of A.

REFERENCES

Abramovitz, M., and Stegun, I., <u>Handbook of Mathematical Functions</u>, National Bureau of Standards, 1964, p. 948, items #26.7.4 and #26.7.3.

SAMPLE PROGRAM

```
RUN
TD
THIS PROGRAM CALCULATES THE VALUE OF THE INTEGRAL OF
THE T DISTRIBUTION FUNCTION FROM -X TO X GIVEN VALUES OF X
AND THE ASSOCIATED DEGREES OF FREEDOM NU
ENTER VALUE OF THE DEGREES OF FREEDOM, NU=? 3
ENTER VALUE OF ARGUMENT X=? 1.98
THE VALUE OF THE T DISTRIBUTION CORRESPONDING TO X= 1.98 WITH 3 DEGREES OF FREEDOM IS=
.857943
CALCULATIONS COMPLETED

Ready
```

Ready

```
LIST
TD
100 PRINT"THIS PROGRAM CALCULATES THE VALUE OF THE INTEGRAL OF "
110 PRINT"THE T DISTRIBUTION FUNCTION FROM -X TO X GIVEN VALUES OF X"
120 PRINT"AND THE ASSOCIATED DEGREES OF FREEDOM NU"
130INPUT"ENTER VALUE OF THE DEGREES OF FREEDOM, NU=";N
140INPUT"ENTER VALUE OF ARGUMENT X=";X
150 T=ATN(X/(N)**0.5)
160 N2=N/2
170 N1=INT(N2)
180 IF(N2-N1)>0 GO TO 500
190 REM EVEN DEGREES OF FREEDOM
200 S1=1
210 FOR I=2 TO (N-2) STEP 2
220 I1=1
230 FOR L=1 TO I STEP 2
240 I1=(I1*(L/(L+1)))
245 B7=L+1
250 NEXT L
255 I1=I1*(COS(T))**(B7)
260 S1=S1+I1
270 NEXT I
280 A=S1*SIN(T)
290 GO TO 990
500 REM ODD DEGREES OF FREEDOM
505 IF N>1 GO TO 530
510 A=2*T/3.141592
520 GO TO 990
530 S1=1
540 FOR I=3 TO N-1 STEP 2
550 I1=1
600 FOR L=2 TO I STEP 2
610 I1=(I1*L/(L+1))
615 B7=L
620 NEXT L
625 I1=I1*(COS(T))**B7
630 S1=S1+I1
800 NEXT I
810 A=S1*SIN(T)*COS(T)*2/3.141592+2*T/3.141592
990 PRINT"THE VALUE OF THE T DISTRIBUTION CORRESPONDING TO X=";X;"WITH";N;"DEGREES OF
    FREEDOM IS=";A
1000 PRINT"CALCULATIONS COMPLETED"
1010 END
```

Ready

SURVEY DATA
AND CONTINGENCY
TABLES

RUN#CT
CONTINGENCY TABLES
(SURVEY DATA ANALYSIS)

This program calculates a chi-squared statistic:

$$x^2 = \sum_{i=1}^{n} \sum_{j=1}^{k} \frac{(a_{ij} - e_{ij})}{e_{ij}}$$

where the expected matrix element e_{ij} is defined by:

$$e_{ij} = \frac{T_{Ri}}{T_{R+C}} \frac{T_{Cj}}{T_{R+C}} T_{R+C}$$

to test whether the column variable is statistically independent of the row variable for the values in the following contingency table.

	1	2 ... j ... k	Totals
1	a_{11}	$a_{12}...a_{1j}$ ... a_{1k}	T_{R1}
2	a_{21}	$a_{22}...a_{2j}$ ... a_{2k}	T_{R2}
.	.	. . .	.
.	.	. . .	.
.	.	. . .	.
i	a_{i1}	$a_{i2}...a_{ij}$ ... a_{ik}	T_{Ri}
.	.	. . .	.
.	.	. . .	.
.	.	. . .	.
N	a_{n1}	$a_{n2}...a_{nj}$ ... a_{nk}	T_{Rn}
Totals	T_{C1}	$T_{C2}...T_{Cj}$ ... T_{Ck}	T_{R+C}

given k = number of columns.
   n = number of rows.
   T_{Ri} = totals of row i.
   T_{Cj} = totals for column j.
   T_{R+C} = grand total.

If n = 2 or k = 2, Pearson's coefficient of contingency is also calculated:

$$C = \frac{x^2}{T_{R+C} + x^2}$$

If n = 2 and k = 2, Yates correction for continuity is incorporated into the chi-squared formulae as follows:

$$x^2 = \frac{(a_{11} + a_{12} + a_{21} + a_{22}) \, (|a_{11}a_{22} - a_{12}a_{21}| - \frac{1}{2}(a_{11} + a_{12} + a_{21} + a_{22}))^2}{(a_{11} + a_{12}) \, (a_{11} + a_{21}) \, (a_{21} + a_{22}) \, (a_{12} + a_{22})}$$

If n = 1 and k = 1, the user is requested to use the programs CSEEF and CSUEF.

INPUT REQUIREMENTS

Integers n and k, and (n x k) values of a_{ij}.

PROGRAM OUTPUT

(n x k) values of e_{ij} and values of χ^2 and corresponding degrees of freedom.

REFERENCES

Whitmore, G. A., Neter, J. and Wasserman, W., <u>Self Correcting Problems in Statistics</u>, Allyn and Bacon, Boston, 1970, p. 190.

SAMPLE PROGRAM

```
RUN
CT
THIS PROGRAM CALCULATES A CHI-SQUARED STATISTIC FOR AN N*K
CONTINGENCY TABLE TO TEST WHETHER THE COLUMN AND ROW VARIABLES
ARE STATISTICALLY INDEPENDENT
THE FOLLOWING EXPERIMENTAL DESIGN MATRIX IS REQUIRED:

      1      2    ...    J    ...    K      TOTALS
1     A11    A12  ...    A1J  ...    A1K    TR1
2     A21    A22  ...    A2J  ...    A2K    TR2

I     AI1    AI2  ...    AIJ  ...    AIK    TRI

N     AN1    AN2  ...    ANJ  ...    ANK    TRN

TOTALTC1     TC2  ...    TCJ  ...    TCK    T(C+R)

ENTER NUMBER OF COLUMNS,K=? 3
ENTER NUMBER OF ROWS,N=? 3
ENTER A( 1 , 1 )=
? 12
ENTER A( 1 , 2 )=
? 13
ENTER A( 1 , 3 )=
? 12
ENTER A( 2 , 1 )=
? 14
ENTER A( 2 , 2 )=
? 15
ENTER A( 2 , 3 )=
? 13
ENTER A( 3 , 1 )=
? 14
ENTER A( 3 , 2 )=
? 12
ENTER A( 3 , 3 )=
? 13
I             J          OBSERVED      EXPECTED      CHI SQ VALUE
  1           1          12            12.5424       .023454
  1           2          13            12.5424       .166971E-1
  1           3          12            11.9153       .602739E-3
  2           1          14            14.2373       .395481E-2
  2           2          15            14.2373       .408595E-1
  2           .3         13            13.5254       .204113E-1
  3           1          14            13.2203       .04598
  3           2          12            13.2203       .112647
  3           3          13            12.5593       .154624E-1
THE CHI-SQUARED TEST STATISTIC ASSOCIATED WITH THE A(I,J)
MATRIX IS= .280069 WITH 4 DEGREES OF FREEDOM
CALCULATIONS COMPLETED

Ready
```

```
Ready

LIST
CT
100 PRINT"THIS PROGRAM CALCULATES A CHI-SQUARED STATISTIC FOR AN N*K"
110 PRINT"CONTINGENCY TABLE TO TEST WHETHER THE COLUMN AND ROW VARIABLES"
120 PRINT"ARE STATISTICALLY INDEPENDENT"
130 PRINT"THE FOLLOWING EXPERIMENTAL DESIGN MATRIX IS REQUIRED:"
140 PRINT
150 PRINT"     1      2     ...     J     ...     K       TOTALS
160 PRINT"1    A11    A12   ...     A1J   ...     A1K     TR1
170 PRINT"2    A21    A22   ...     A2J   ...     A2K     TR2
180 PRINT
190 PRINT"I    AI1    AI2   ...     AIJ   ...     AIK     TRI
200 PRINT
210 PRINT"N    AN1    AN2   ...     ANJ   ...     ANK     TRN
220 PRINT
230 PRINT"TOTALTC1    TC2   ...     TCJ   ...     TCK     T(C+R)
240 PRINT
250   DIM A(30,30),C(30),R(30)
260INPUT"ENTER NUMBER OF COLUMNS,K=";K
270INPUT"ENTER NUMBER OF ROWS,N=";N
280 FOR I=1 TO N STEP 1
290 FOR J=1 TO K STEP 1
300 PRINT"ENTER A(";I;",";J;")="
310 INPUT A(I,J)
320 NEXT J
330 NEXT I
340 G1=0
350 FOR I=1 TO N STEP 1
360 R(I)=0
370 FOR J=1 TO K STEP 1
380 R(I)=R(I) + A(I,J)
390 NEXT J
400 G1=G1+R(I)
410 NEXT I
420 FOR J=1 TO K STEP 1
430 C(J)=0
440 FOR I=1 TO N STEP 1
450 C(J)=C(J) + A(I,J)
460 NEXT I
470 NEXT J
480 PRINT"I               J          OBSERVED    EXPECTED    CHI SQ VALUE"
490 C1=0
500 A2=A(1,1)
510 B2=A(1,2)
520 C2=A(2,1)
530 D2=A(2,2)
540 FOR I=1 TO N STEP 1
550 FOR J=1 TO K STEP 1
560 T1=(C(J)/G1)*(R(I)/G1)*G1
570 T6=A(I,J)
580 A(I,J)=(A(I,J)-T1)**2/T1
590 PRINT I,J,T6,T1,A(I,J)
600 C1=C1+A(I,J)
610 NEXT J
620 NEXT I
630 PRINT"THE CHI-SQUARED TEST STATISTIC ASSOCIATED WITH THE A(I,J)"
640 PRINT"MATRIX IS=";C1;"WITH";(K-1)*(N-1);"DEGREES OF FREEDOM"
650 IF(N=2) AND (K=2) THEN 720 ELSE 660
660 IF(N=2) AND (K>2) THEN 820 ELSE 670
670 IF(N>2) AND (K=2) THEN 820 ELSE 680
680 IF(N=1) OR  (K=1) THEN 870 ELSE 890
690 REM - SHOULD ANY COMPUTATIONAL TROUBLES DEVELOP, PLEASE REFER
700 REM - THEM TO THE AUTHOR, JOSE ALONSO, SWINBURNE COLLEGE OF
710 REM - TECHNOLOGY, LTD.
720 REM - 2X2 CONTINGENCY TABLE YATES CORRECTION
730 P1=A2+B2+C2+D2
```

```
740 P2=ABS(A2*D2-B2*C2)
750 P3=-0.5*(A2+B2+C2+D2)
760 P4=(P2+P3)**2
770 P5=P1*P4
780 P6=(A2+B2)*(A2+C2)*(C2+D2)*(B2+D2)
790 C2=P5/P6
800 PRINT"CHI-SQUARED RECALCULATED USING YATES CONTINUITY CORRECTION=";C2
810 GO TO 890
820 REM 2*K OR K*2 CONTINGENCY TABLE PEARSON'S COEFFICIENT CALCULATION
830 C2=C1
840 C1=(C2/(G1+C2))**0.5
850 PRINT"PEARSON'S COEFFICIENT OF CONTINGENCY ASSOCIATED WITH THIS A(";N;",";K;")
    MATRIX IS =";C1
860 GO TO 890
870 REM - 1*K OR K*1 CONTINGENCY TABLE CALCULATION
880 PRINT"PLEASE USE PROGRAMS CSEEF OR CSUEF"
890 PRINT"CALCULATIONS COMPLETED"
900 END

Ready
```

The sample problem above corresponds to the following feasible set of survey results:

Number of People Interviewed Who Mix Cakes from ...	Family income per annum ...		
	$j = 1$ <10,000	$j = 2$ <10,000 < income < 15,000	$j = 3$ >15,000
$i = 1$ Flour, eggs, milk	12	$a_{1,2} = 13$	12
$i = 2$ Add milk and egg mixture	14	$a_{2,2} = 15$	13
$i = 3$ Add egg-only mixture	14	$a_{3,2} = 12$	13

This program should be followed by program CSD (Chi Square Distribution) with arguments $x = 0.280069$ and degrees of freedom 4.

NONPARAMETRIC
STATISTICS

RUN#MWS
MANN-WHITNEY STATISTICS

This program calculates a Mann-Whitney test statistic C, to check whether there is a difference between two populations from which two samples of N1 and N2 elements respectively are taken. C is given by the expression:

$$C = (N1)(N2) + \frac{(N1)(N1+1)}{2} - \sum_{i=1}^{N1} r_i$$

where r_i are the ranks associated with the complete set comprising the N1 values of sample 1 and the N2 values of sample 2. If N1 > 8 and N2 > 8, then the statistic:

$$z = \frac{C - \frac{(N1)(N2)}{2}}{\sqrt{\frac{(N1)(N2)(N1 + N2 + 1)}{12}}}$$

has approximately a standard normal distribution.

If N1 < 8 and N2 < 8, special tables from Owen (see references) should be used.

PROGRAM RESTRICTIONS

N1 > 8, N2 > 8.

INPUT REQUIREMENTS

Integer values N1 and N2, N1 values of sample 1, N2 values of sample 2.

PROGRAM OUTPUT

Values of C and z.

REFERENCES

Freund, J. E., <u>Mathematical Statistics</u>, Prentice-Hall, New York, 1962.
Winer, B. J., <u>Statistical Principles in Experimental Design</u>, McGraw-Hill, New York, 1971.
Owen, D. B., <u>Handbook of Statistical Tables</u>, Addison-Wesley, New York, 1962.

SAMPLE PROGRAM

Two samples are available in this example with 9 and 10 elements respectively:

First: sample values of the observed variable 15,23,32,43,16,12,23,43,45

Second: sample values of the observed variables 12,23,34,34,45,54,43,32,21,34

```
RUN
MWS
THIS PROGRAM CALCULATES A MANN-WHITNEY TEST STATISTIC TO CHECK WHETHER
THERE IS A DIFFERENCE BETWEEN TWO POPULATIONS FROM WHICH
TWO SAMPLES OF N1 AND N2 ELEMENTS RESPECTIVELY ARE TAKEN
PROVIDED THAT BOTH N1 AND N2 ARE GREATER THAN EIGHT
THIS CALCULATION PROCEDURE DOES NOT APPLY TO SMALLER SAMPLES
ENTER NUMBER OF ELEMENTS IN SAMPLE 1, N1=? 9
ENTER NUMBER OF ELEMENTS IN SAMPLE 2, N2=? 10
ENTER NOW N1 VALUES OF ELEMENTS IN SAMPLE 1, SEPARATED BY COMMAS? 15,23,32,43,16,12,23,43,45
ENTER NOW N2 VALUES OF ELEMENTS IN SAMPLE 2, SEPARATED BY COMMAS? 12,23,34,34,45,54,43,32,
21,34
THE CALCULATED MANN-WHITNEY TEST STATISTIC IS= 57
THE CALCULATED Z TEST STATISTIC IS= .979796
CALCULATIONS COMPLETED

Ready
```

```
Ready

LIST
MWS
10 DIM X(100),Y(100),R(200),X1(200)
15 PRINT"THIS PROGRAM CALCULATES A MANN-WHITNEY TEST STATISTIC TO CHECK WHETHER"
16 PRINT"THERE IS A DIFFERENCE BETWEEN TWO POPULATIONS FROM WHICH"
17 PRINT"TWO SAMPLES OF N1 AND N2 ELEMENTS RESPECTIVELY ARE TAKEN"
18 PRINT"PROVIDED THAT BOTH N1 AND N2 ARE GREATER THAN EIGHT"
19 PRINT"THIS CALCULATION PROCEDURE DOES NOT APPLY TO SMALLER SAMPLES"
20 INPUT"ENTER NUMBER OF ELEMENTS IN SAMPLE 1, N1=";N1
40 INPUT"ENTER NUMBER OF ELEMENTS IN SAMPLE 2, N2=";N2
60 INPUT"ENTER NOW N1 VALUES OF ELEMENTS IN SAMPLE 1, SEPARATED BY COMMAS":MAT INPUT X(N1)
80 INPUT"ENTER NOW N2 VALUES OF ELEMENTS IN SAMPLE 2, SEPARATED BY COMMAS":MAT INPUT Y(N2)
110 FOR I=1 TO N1 STEP 1
120 X1(I)=X(I)
125 R(I)=I
130 NEXT I
140 FOR I=1 TO N2 STEP 1
150 X1(I+N1)=Y(I)
155 R(I+N1)=I+N1
160 NEXT I
170 FOR I=1 TO N1+N2 STEP 1
180 FOR J=I TO N1+N2 STEP 1
190 IF (X1(I)-X1(J))>0 THEN 200 ELSE 230
200 J1=X1(I)
205 X1(I)=X1(J)
210 X1(J)=J1
220 J4=R(J)
221 R(J)=R(I)
222 R(I)=J4
230 NEXT J
300 NEXT I
310 FOR I=1 TO N1+N2 STEP 1
312 J=R(I)
313 X1(J)=I
314 NEXT I
319 S1=0
320 FOR I=1 TO N1 STEP 1
325 S1=S1+X1(I)
330 NEXT I
390 U=N1*N2+(N1*(N1+1)/2)-S1
400 Z1=U-(N1*N2/2)
420 Z2=(N1*N2*(N1+N2+1)/12)**0.5
430 Z=Z1/Z2
440 PRINT"THE CALCULATED MANN-WHITNEY TEST STATISTIC IS=";U
450 PRINT"THE CALCULATED Z TEST STATISTIC IS=";Z
455 PRINT"CALCULATIONS COMPLETED"
500 END

Ready
```

RUN#SRCC
SPEARMAN'S RANK CORRELATION COEFFICIENT

This program calculates Spearman's rank correlation coefficient C for N pairs of observations (x_i, y_i) and generates the following table of values:

i	x_i	Rank of x_i j_i	y_i	Rank of y_i k_i
—	—	—	—	—
—	—	—	—	—
—	—	—	—	—

A value of C = 1 indicates total agreement in order of ranks. A value of C = -1 indicates total agreement in the opposite order of ranks.

C is given by the expression:

$$C = 1 - \frac{6 \sum_{i=1}^{i=N} (j_i - k_i)^2}{N(N^2 - 1)}$$

PROGRAM RESTRICTIONS

x and y are random variables and independent. $N \geq 100$.

INPUT REQUIREMENTS

Integer value of N, and N pairs of (x_i, y_i).

PROGRAM OUTPUT

Table of values above, and value of real C.

REFERENCES

Any standard textbook on statistics.

SAMPLE PROGRAM

This printout should be self-explanatory.

```
RUN
SRCC
THIS PROGRAM CALCULATES SPEARMAN'S RANK CORRELATION COEFFICIENT FOR
N PAIRS OF OBSERVATIONS (X(I),Y(I))
ENTER NUMBER OF PAIRS OF OBSERVATIONS, N=? 23
ENTER NOW, SEPARATED BY COMMAS,  23 PAIRS OF OBSERVATIONS
ENTER ONE PAIR OF OBSERVATIONS? 12,13
ENTER ONE PAIR OF OBSERVATIONS? 23,34
ENTER ONE PAIR OF OBSERVATIONS? 12,13
ENTER ONE PAIR OF OBSERVATIONS? 34,34
ENTER ONE PAIR OF OBSERVATIONS? 45,34
ENTER ONE PAIR OF OBSERVATIONS? 45,56,
ENTER ONE PAIR OF OBSERVATIONS? 34,35
ENTER ONE PAIR OF OBSERVATIONS? 43,56
ENTER ONE PAIR OF OBSERVATIONS? 23,45
ENTER ONE PAIR OF OBSERVATIONS? 24,24
ENTER ONE PAIR OF OBSERVATIONS? 31,41
ENTER ONE PAIR OF OBSERVATIONS? 15,23
ENTER ONE PAIR OF OBSERVATIONS? 31,32
ENTER ONE PAIR OF OBSERVATIONS? 61,68
```

```
ENTER ONE PAIR OF OBSERVATIONS? 67,65
ENTER ONE PAIR OF OBSERVATIONS? 58,54
ENTER ONE PAIR OF OBSERVATIONS? 34,64
ENTER ONE PAIR OF OBSERVATIONS? 25,72
ENTER ONE PAIR OF OBSERVATIONS? 45,52
ENTER ONE PAIR OF OBSERVATIONS? 79,89
ENTER ONE PAIR OF OBSERVATIONS? 65,67
ENTER ONE PAIR OF OBSERVATIONS? 65,23
ENTER ONE PAIR OF OBSERVATIONS? 23,34
THE CALCULATED SPEARMAN'S CORRELATION COEFFICIENT IS= .671937
THE RANKED RESULTS FOLLOW
```

I	X(I)	RANK OF X(I)	Y(I)	RANK OF Y(I)
1	12	22	13	22
2	23	18	34	16
3	12	23	13	23
4	34	13	34	14
5	45	8	34	15
6	45	7	56	7
7	34	11	35	13
8	43	10	56	8
9	23	19	45	11
10	24	17	24	19
11	31	14	41	12
12	15	21	23	21
13	31	15	32	18
14	61	5	68	3
15	67	2	65	5
16	58	6	54	9
17	34	12	64	6
18	25	16	72	2
19	45	9	52	10
20	79	1	89	1
21	65	3	67	4
22	65	4	23	20
23	23	20	34	17

```
A VALUE OF +1 INDICATES COMPLETE AGREEMENT IN ORDER OF RANK
A VALUE OF -1 INDICATES COMPLETE AGREEMENT IN OPPOSITE ORDER OF RANKS
CALCULATIONS COMPLETED

Ready
```

```
Ready

LIST
SRCC
100 DIM X(100),Y(100),R1(100),R2(100)
110 DIM X1(100),Y1(100)
120 PRINT"THIS PROGRAM CALCULATES SPEARMAN'S RANK CORRELATION COEFFICIENT FOR"
130 PRINT"N PAIRS OF OBSERVATIONS (X(I),Y(I))"
140 INPUT "ENTER NUMBER OF PAIRS OF OBSERVATIONS, N=";N
150 PRINT "ENTER NOW, SEPARATED BY COMMAS, ";N;"PAIRS OF OBSERVATIONS"
160 FOR I=1 TO N STEP 1
170 INPUT"ENTER ONE PAIR OF OBSERVATIONS";X(I),Y(I)
180 R1(I)=I
190 X1(I)=X(I)
200 Y1(I)=Y(I)
210 R2(I)=I
220 NEXT I
230 FOR I=1 TO N STEP 1
240 FOR J=I TO N STEP 1
250 IF(X(I)-X(J))<0 THEN 260 ELSE 320
260 J1=X(I)
270 X(I)=X(J)
280 X(J)=J1
290 J4=R1(J)
300 R1(J)=R1(I)
310 R1(I)=J4
320 NEXT J
330 NEXT I
340 FOR I=1 TO N STEP 1
350 FOR J=I TO N STEP 1
360 IF (Y(I)-Y(J))<0 THEN 370 ELSE 430
370 J1=Y(I)
380 Y(I) =Y(J)
390 Y(J) = J1
400 J4=R2(J)
410 R2(J)=R2(I)
420 R2(I)=J4
430 NEXT J
440 NEXT I
450 FOR I=1 TO N STEP 1
460 J=R1(I)
470 X(J)=I
480 L=R2(I)
490 Y(L)=I
500 NEXT I
510 FOR I=1 TO N STEP 1
520 R1(I)=X(I)
530 R2(I)=Y(I)
540 NEXT I
550 S5=0
560 FOR I=1 TO N STEP 1
570 S5=S5+(R1(I)-R2(I))**2
580 NEXT I
590 S6=1-(6*S5)/(N*(N*N-1))
600 PRINT"THE CALCULATED SPEARMAN'S CORRELATION COEFFICIENT IS=";S6
610 PRINT"THE RANKED RESULTS FOLLOW"
620 PRINT"I            X(I)         RANK OF X(I)   Y(I)         RANK OF Y(I)"
630 FOR I=1 TO N STEP 1
640 PRINT I,X1(I),X(I),Y1(I),Y(I)
650 NEXT I
660 PRINT"A VALUE OF +1 INDICATES COMPLETE AGREEMENT IN ORDER OF RANK"
670 PRINT"A VALUE OF -1 INDICATES COMPLETE AGREEMENT IN OPPOSITE ORDER OF RANKS"
680 PRINT"CALCULATIONS COMPLETED"
690 END

Ready
```

REGRESSION
AND CORRELATION

RUN#OIVR
ONE INDEPENDENT VARIABLE REGRESSION

This program calculates by the least squares method, the coefficients a, b for a set of N pairs of (x,y) values for the following alternative postulated functional relationships between the independent variable x and the dependent variable y.

	Postulated Equation	Linearized Equation
Linear	$y = a + bx$	$y = a + bx$
Exponential	$y = a\,e^{bx}$	$\ell ny = \ell na + bx$
Logarithmic	$y = a + b\,\ell nx$	$\ell ny = a + b\,\ell nx$
Power law	$y = ax^b$	$\ell ny = \ell na + b\,\ell nx$

PROGRAM RESTRICTIONS

Only 100 pairs of (x,y) values are permitted, that is, $N \leq 100$.

INPUT REQUIREMENTS

Integer N and N pairs of x_i, y_i values.

PROGRAM OUTPUT

For each of the four postulated models, the following parameters are evaluated:

A   = Regression coefficient a

B   = Regression coefficient b

STA   = Standard error of regression coefficient a

STB   = Standard error of regression coefficient b

STYONX   = Standard error of estimate of y on x

COEFFDET   = Coefficient of determination

The resulting four model equations are then evaluated and tabulated next to the original data.

REFERENCES

Hald, A., <u>Statistical Theory with Engineering Applications</u>, J. Wiley and Sons, New York, 1952.

Bartee, E. N., <u>Statistical Methods in Engineering Experiments</u>, Charles E. Merrill Books, Inc., Columbus, Ohio, 1966.

SAMPLE PROGRAM

Using the following data:

X	Y
1.1	2.1
2.1	3.1
3.1	3.9
4.1	5.1

plot the four approximating equations.

1. Which fits best?
2. Does your opinion agree with what the correlation coefficient tells you?
3. What sort of data do you expect to be best fit by each of the four equation forms given?

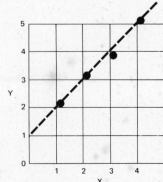

```
Ready

RUN
OIVR
THIS PROGRAM CALCULATES A TABLE OF ALTERNATIVE REGRESSION
COEFFICIENTS FOR LINEAR, EXPONENTIAL, LOGARITHMIC AND POWER
FUNCTION LEAST SQUARE REGRESSION LINES TO A GIVEN SET OF
N PAIRS OF (X(I),Y(I)) VALUES, X IS CONSIDERED THE INDEPENDENT
VARIABLE
NUMBER OF PAIRS OF (X(I),Y(I)) VALUES TO BE ENTERED, N=? 4
ENTER ONE PAIR OF (X(I),Y(I))? 1.1,2.1
ENTER ONE PAIR OF (X(I),Y(I))? 2.1,3.1
ENTER ONE PAIR OF (X(I),Y(I))? 3.1,3.9
ENTER ONE PAIR OF (X(I),Y(I))? 4.1,5.1

A           = REGRESSION COEFFICIENT
B           = REGRESSION COEFFICIENT
STA         = STANDARD ERROR OF REGRESSION COEFFICIENT A
STB         = STANDARD ERROR OF REGRESSION COEFFICIENT B
SEYONX      = STANDARD ERROR OF ESTIMATE OF Y ON X
COEFFDET    = COEFFICIENT OF DETERMINATION
COV         = COVARIANCE
CORRCOEFF   = CORRELATION COEFFICIENT

Y=A+B*X          A= 1.002 B= .98 STA= .149749 STB= .529113E-1
                 SEYONX= .118313 COEFFDET= .994203
                 COV= 1.63333 CORRCOEFF= .997097

Y=A*EXP(B*X)     A= 1.59059 B= .289148 STA= .672391E-1 STB= .237578E-1
                 SEYONX= .053124 COEFFDET= .986678
                 COV= .481914 CORRCOEFF= .993317

Y=A+B*LOG(X)     A= 1.72075 B= 2.16502 STA= .35715 STB= .364966
                 SEYONX= .360379 COEFFDET= .946222
                 COV= .70365 CORRCOEFF= .993317

Y=A*X**B         A= 1.93809 B= .655911 STA= .454356E-1 STB= .990078
                 SEYONX= .458465E-1 COEFFDET= .990078
                 COV= .213176 CORRCOEFF= .995027

X          Y=A+BX        Y=A*EXP(B*X)   Y=A+B*LOG(X)   Y=A*X**B

1.1        2.08          2.1862         1.9271         2.06312
2.1        3.06          2.91922        3.32706        3.15298
3.1        4.04          3.898          4.17026        4.07065
4.1        5.02          5.20496        4.77557        4.88997
EXPONENTIAL,LOGARITHMIC OR POWER REGRESSIONS WILL NOT BE CALCULATED
IF NEGATIVE OR ZERO VALUES APPEAR ON THE DATA. LINEAR REGRESSION WILL
OF COURSE ALWAYS BE PERFORMED REGARDLESS OF NEGATIVE VALUES
CALCULATIONS COMPLETED

Ready
```

```
Ready

LIST
OIVR
100 DIM C1(4),C2(4)
105 DIM X(200),Y(200),X1(200),Y1(200)
110 DIM A(4),B(4),S1(4),S2(4),S3(4),S4(4)
120 PRINT"THIS PROGRAM CALCULATES A TABLE OF ALTERNATIVE REGRESSION"
130 PRINT"COEFFICIENTS FOR LINEAR, EXPONENTIAL, LOGARITHMIC AND POWER"
140 PRINT"FUNCTION LEAST SQUARE REGRESSION LINES TO A GIVEN SET OF"
150 PRINT"N PAIRS OF (X(I),Y(I)) VALUES, X IS CONSIDERED THE INDEPENDENT"
160 PRINT"VARIABLE"
170 INPUT"NUMBER OF PAIRS OF (X(I),Y(I)) VALUES TO BE ENTERED, N="$N
180 FOR I=1 TO N STEP 1
190 INPUT"ENTER ONE PAIR OF (X(I),Y(I))"$X1(I),Y1(I)
200 NEXT I
210 REM - INPUT DATA IS NOW IN ARRAYS X1(I) AND Y1(I)
220 L2=1
230 L3=1
240 L4=1
250 FOR J=1 TO 4 STEP 1
260 ON J GO TO 270,320,410,500
270 FOR I=1 TO N STEP 1
280 X(I)=X1(I)
290 Y(I)=Y1(I)
300 NEXT I
310 GO TO 590
320 FOR I=1 TO N STEP 1
330 REM - X(I)=X1(I)
340 IF Y1(I)<0 OR Y1(I)=0 GO TO 380 ELSE 350
350 Y(I)=LOG(Y1(I))
360 NEXT I
370 GO TO 400
380 L2=2
390 GO TO 850
400 GO TO 590
410 FOR I=1 TO N STEP 1
420 IF X1(I)<0 OR X1(I)=0 GO TO 470 ELSE 430
430 X(I)=LOG(X1(I))
440 Y(I)=Y1(I)
450 NEXT I
460 GO TO 490
470 L3=2
480 GO TO 850
490 GO TO 590
500 FOR I=1 TO N STEP 1
510 IF X1(I)<0 OR X1(I)=0 OR Y1(I)<0 OR Y1(I)=0 GO TO 560 ELSE 530
520 REM - X(I)=LOG(X1(I))
530 Y(I)=LOG(Y1(I))
540 NEXT I
550 GO TO 580
560 L4=2
570 GO TO 850
580 GO TO 590
590 GO TO 600
600 Z5=0
610 Z2=0
620 Z6=0
630 Z7=0
640 Z9=0
650 FOR I=1 TO N STEP 1
660 Z5=Z5+X(I)*Y(I)
670 Z6=Z6+X(I)/N
680 Z7=Z7+Y(I)/N
690 Z9=Z9+(X(I)**2)
700 Z2=Z2+(Y(I)**2)
710 NEXT I
720 Z3=Z6*N
```

```
730 Z4=(Z3**2)/N
740 Z8=(Z6*N)*(Z7*N)
750 Z8=Z8/N
760 B(J)=((Z5-Z8)/(Z9-Z4))
770 A(J)=(Z7-B(J)*Z6)
780 S3(J)=B(J)/(Z2-(((Z7*N)**2)/N))*(Z5-Z8)
790 C1(J)=(1/(N-1))*(Z5-Z8)
800 C2(J)=C1(J)/((Z2-(((Z7*N)**2)/N))/(N-1))**0.5
810 C2(J)=C2(J)/((Z9-(((Z6*N)**2)/N))/(N-1))**0.5
820 S4(J)=((Z2-A(J)*Z7*N-B(J)*Z5)/(N-2))**0.5
830 S2(J)=S4(J)/((Z9-((Z6*N)**2)/N)**0.5)
840 S1(J)=((Z9/(N*(Z9-(((Z6*N)**2)/N))))**0.5)*S4(J)
850 GO TO 860
860 NEXT J
870 A(2)=EXP(A(2))
880 A(4)=EXP(A(4))
890 PRINT
900 PRINT"A          = REGRESSION COEFFICIENT"
910 PRINT"B          = REGRESSION COEFFICIENT"
920 PRINT"STA        = STANDARD ERROR OF REGRESSION COEFFICIENT A"
930 PRINT"STB        = STANDARD ERROR OF REGRESSION COEFFICIENT B"
940 PRINT"SEYONX     = STANDARD ERROR OF ESTIMATE OF Y ON X"
950 PRINT"COEFFDET   = COEFFICIENT OF DETERMINATION"
960 PRINT"COV        = COVARIANCE"
970 PRINT"CORRCOEFF  = CORRELATION COEFFICIENT"
980 PRINT
990PRINT"Y=A+B*X          A=";A(1);"B=";B(1);"STA=";S1(1);"STB=";S2(1)
1000PRINT"                 SEYONX=";S4(1);"COEFFDET=";S3(1)
1010PRINT"                 COV=";C1(1);"CORRCOEFF=";C2(1)
1020PRINT
1030 ON L2 GO TO 1040,1080
1040PRINT"Y=A*EXP(B*X)     A=";A(2);"B=";B(2);"STA=";S1(2);"STB=";S2(2)
1050PRINT"                 SEYONX=";S4(2);"COEFFDET=";S3(2)
1060PRINT"                 COV=";C1(2);"CORRCOEFF=";C2(2)
1070PRINT
1080 ON L3 GO TO 1090,1130
1090PRINT"Y=A+B*LOG(X)     A=";A(3);"B=";B(3);"STA=";S1(3);"STB=";S2(3)
1100PRINT"                 SEYONX=";S4(3);"COEFFDET=";S3(3)
1110PRINT"                 COV=";C1(3);"CORRCOEFF=";C2(2)
1120PRINT
1130 ON L4 GO TO 1140,1180
1140PRINT"Y=A*X**B         A=";A(4);"B=";B(4);"STA=";S1(4);"STB=";S3(4)
1150PRINT"                 SEYONX=";S4(4);"COEFFDET=";S3(4)
1160PRINT"                 COV=";C1(4);"CORRCOEFF=";C2(4)
1170PRINT
1180PRINT"X          Y=A+BX       Y=A*EXP(B*X)   Y=A+B*LOG(X)   Y=A*X**B"
1190PRINT
1200FOR I=1 TO N STEP 1
1210Y6=A(1)+B(1)*X1(I)
1220Y7=A(2)*EXP(B(2)*X1(I))
1230  IF L3=2 GO TO 1250 ELSE  Y8=A(3)+B(3)*LOG(X1(I))
1240  IF L4=2 GO TO 1250 ELSE Y9=EXP(LOG(A(4))+B(4)*LOG(X1(I)))
1250 PRINT X1(I),Y6,Y7,Y8,Y9
1260NEXT I
1270 PRINT"EXPONENTIAL,LOGARITHMIC OR POWER REGRESSIONS WILL NOT BE CALCULATED"
1280 PRINT"IF NEGATIVE OR ZERO VALUES APPEAR ON THE DATA, LINEAR REGRESSION WILL"
1290 PRINT"OF COURSE ALWAYS BE PERFORMED REGARDLESS OF NEGATIVE VALUES"
1300 REM - SHOULD ANY RUNNING DIFFICULTIES ARISE PLEASE REFER THEM
1310 REM - TO THE AUTHOR, JOSE ALONSO, SWINBURNE COLLEGE OF TECHNOLOGY
1320PRINT"CALCULATIONS COMPLETED"
1330 END
```

RUN#PR
POLYNOMIAL REGRESSION

This program calculates the polynomial regression coefficients B_j that fit the polynomial of power of p:

$$Y = B_0 + B_1 X + B_2 X^2 + B_3 X^3 + \ldots + B_j X^j + \ldots + B_p X^P$$

to set of N pairs of X, Y values where N > P. The design matrix is simply:

$$
\begin{array}{cc}
X_1 & Y_1 \\
X_2 & Y_2 \\
\cdot & \cdot \\
\cdot & \cdot \\
\cdot & \cdot \\
X_j & Y_j \\
\cdot & \cdot \\
\cdot & \cdot \\
\cdot & \cdot \\
X_p & Y_p \\
\cdot & \cdot \\
\cdot & \cdot \\
\cdot & \cdot \\
X_N & Y_N
\end{array}
$$

The program also prints an analysis of variance table due to regression and about regression.

PROGRAM RESTRICTIONS

Only 20 pairs of (X,Y) are permitted, that is, $N \geq 20$.
N must also be greater than (P + 1), that is, $N \geq (P + 1)$.
Preferably, N should be considerably greater than (P+1).

INPUT REQUIREMENTS

N pairs of real X, Y values.

PROGRAM OUTPUT

Value of B_0 and p values of B_j.

REFERENCES

Bartee, E. N., _Statistical Methods in Engineering Experiments_, Charles E. Merrill Books, Inc., Columbus, Ohio, 1966.
Hald, A., _Statistical Theory with Engineering Applications_, J. Wiley and Sons, New York 1952.

SAMPLE PROGRAM

The data for the problem is as follows:

1. Use program PE to calculate the values predicted by the equation

$$Y = (-0.690227) + (1.08718X) + (-0.022865)X^2 \text{ calculated by program PR}$$

2. Try also a cubic polynomial, a quartic, and a first order (the latter using program OIVR).

3. Compare your approximating functions by plotting them and by using program FD and the calculated mean squares ratio. Looking at the raw data, which of all your equations would you expect to fit better?

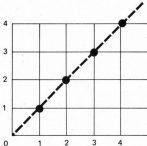

```
RUN
PR
THIS PROGRAM CALCULATES THE POLYNOMIAL REGRESSION COEFFICIENTS BJ
THAT FIT THE POLYNOMIAL OF POWER P
    Y=B0 + B1*X + B2*X**2 + ... + BP*X**P
TO A SET OF N PAIRS OF X,Y VALUES, WHERE N>P
POWER DESIRED FOR POLYNOMIAL REGRESSION EQUATION,P=? 2
ENTER NUMBER OF PAIRS OF X,Y, N=? 4
ENTER ONE PAIR OF X,Y SEPARATED BY COMMA? 1,1
ENTER ONE PAIR OF X,Y SEPARATED BY COMMA? 2,2
ENTER ONE PAIR OF X,Y SEPARATED BY COMMA? 3,3
ENTER ONE PAIR OF X,Y SEPARATED BY COMMA? 4.1,4
CORRELATION MATRICES FOLLOW, C X B = D, TO BE SOLVED FOR VECTOR B
WHERE C IS A PXP MATRIX AND B AND D ARE PX1 VECTORS
COEFFICIENT MATRIX C( 1 ,J) ELEMENTS
C( 1 , 1 )= 5.3075
C( 1 , 2 )= 27.1257
COEFFICIENT MATRIX C( 2 ,J) ELEMENTS
C( 2 , 1 )= 27.1257
C( 2 , 2 )= 143.262
CORRELATION MATRICES D(J) VECTOR ELEMENTS
D( 1 )= 5.15
D( 2 )= 26.215

CALCULATED POLYNOMIAL REGRESSION COEFFICIENTS

B 0 =-.690258E-1
P 1 = 1.08718
P 2 =-.228648E-1


                     SUM OF SQ        DEG OF FR      MEAN SQ
DUE TO REGRESSION      4.9996            2            2.4998
ABOUT REGRESSION       .398636E-3        1            .398636E-3
TOTAL                  5                 3            1.66667
COEFFICIENT OF POLYNOMIAL OR CURVILINEAR REGRESSION = .49996
CALCULATIONS COMPLETED

Ready
```

```
LIST
PR
100 DIM X(20),Y(20),X1(20),C(20,20),D(20),D1(20),X5(20)
110 PRINT"THIS PROGRAM CALCULATES THE POLYNOMIAL REGRESSION COEFFICIENTS BJ"
120 PRINT"THAT FIT THE POLYNOMIAL OF POWER P"
130 PRINT"     Y=B0 + B1*X + B2*X**2 + ... + BP*X**P"
140 PRINT"TO A SET OF N PAIRS OF X,Y VALUES, WHERE N>P"
150 INPUT"POWER DESIRED FOR POLYNOMIAL REGRESSION EQUATION,P=";P
160 INPUT"ENTER NUMBER OF PAIRS OF X,Y, N=";N
170 FOR I=1 TO N STEP 1
180 INPUT"ENTER ONE PAIR OF X,Y SEPARATED BY COMMA";X(I),Y(I)
190 NEXT I
200 MAT C=ZER(P,P)
210 MAT D=ZER(P)
220 MAT X5=ZER(P)
230 REM - COMPUTE MOMENTS
240 FOR I=1 TO P STEP 1
250 X1(I)=0
260 FOR I1=1 TO N STEP 1
270 X1(I)=X1(I)+X(I1)**I
280 NEXT I1
290 X1(I)=X1(I)/N
300 NEXT I
310 Y1=0
320 FOR I1=1 TO N STEP 1
330 Y1=Y1+Y(I1)
340 NEXT I1
350 Y1=Y1/N
360 REM - COMPUTE COEFFICIENTS
370 FOR J=1 TO P STEP 1
380 REM - CALCULATE D(J)
390 S1=0
400 FOR I=1 TO N STEP 1
410 S1=S1+(Y(I)-Y1)*(X(I)**J-X1(J))
420 NEXT I
430 D(J)=S1
440 S1=0
450 FOR K=J TO P STEP 1
460 IF J>K GO TO 540
470 REM - CALCULATE C(J,K)
480 S1=0
490 FOR I=1 TO N STEP 1
500 S1=S1+(X(I)**J-X1(J))*(X(I)**K-X1(K))
510 NEXT I
520 C(J,K)=S1
530 C(K,J)=C(J,K)
540 NEXT K
550 NEXT J
560 PRINT"CORRELATION MATRICES FOLLOW, C X B = D, TO BE SOLVED FOR VECTOR B"
570 PRINT"WHERE C IS A PXP MATRIX AND B AND D ARE PX1 VECTORS"
580 FOR I=1 TO P STEP 1
590 PRINT"COEFFICIENT MATRIX C(";I;",J) ELEMENTS"
600 FOR J=1 TO P STEP 1
610 PRINT"C(";I;",";J;")=";C(I,J)
620 NEXT J
630 NEXT I
640 PRINT"CORRELATION MATRICES D(J) VECTOR ELEMENTS"
650 FOR I=1 TO P STEP 1
660 PRINT"D(";I;")=";D(I)
670 NEXT I
680 FOR I=1 TO P STEP 1
690 D1(I)=D(I)
700 NEXT I
710 REM - SOLVE SYSTEM C X B = D FOR SOLUTION VECTOR B
720 REM-WHERE C IS THE COEFFICIENT MATRIX AND DI IS THE RIGHT HAND VECTOR
730 MAT C=INV(C)
740 MAT X5=C*D
750 M1=0
```

```
760 FOR I=1 TO P STEP 1
770 M1=M1+X5(I)*X1(I)
780 NEXT I
790 P0=Y1-M1
800 PRINT
810 PRINT"CALCULATED POLYNOMIAL REGRESSION COEFFICIENTS"
820 PRINT
830 PRINT"B 0 =";P0
840 FOR I=1 TO P STEP 1
850 PRINT "P";I;"=";X5(I)
860 NEXT I
870 PRINT
880 REM - WRITE ANOVA TABLE
890 PRINT
900 Y9=0
910 FOR I=1 TO N STEP 1
920 Y9=Y9+(Y(I)-Y1)**2
930 NEXT I
940 C9=Y9
950 C1=0
960 FOR I=1 TO P STEP 1
970 C1=C1+X5(I)*D1(I)
980 NEXT I
990 C2=C9-C1
1000 L=N-1
1010 K=L-P
1020 C8=C1/P
1030 C7=C2/K
1040 C6=C9/L
1050 PRINT"                          SUM OF SQ     DEG OF FR     MEAN SQ"
1060 PRINT"DUE TO REGRESSION",C1,P,C8
1070 PRINT"ABOUT REGRESSION ",C2,K,C7
1080 PRINT"TOTAL            ",C9,L,C6
1085 Z1=(1.0-(C2/C9))*0.5
1086 PRINT"COEFFICIENT OF POLYNOMIAL OR CURVILINEAR REGRESSION =";Z1
1090 PRINT"CALCULATIONS COMPLETED"
1100 END

Ready
```

RUN#PREE
POLYNOMIAL REGRESSION EQUATION EVALUATOR

This program evaluates a polynomial of order N at values of x from x_1 to x_2 in steps of x_3. ₁

$$y = a_0x^N + a_1x^{N-1} + a_2x^{N-2} + \ldots + a_{N-1}x + a_N$$

given values of a_0, a_1, a_2, $\ldots$, a_N.

The evaluation is done by Horner's method.

INPUT REQUIREMENTS

Real values of a_0, a_1, a_2, $\ldots$, a_N.

Integer values of N.

Real values of x_1, x_2, x_3.

PROGRAM OUTPUT

Values of y at values of x from x_1 to x_2 in steps of x_3.

REFERENCES

Any standard textbook on algebra.

SAMPLE PROGRAM

The polynomial $P(X) = 7.8X^4 + 5X^3 + 4.3X^2 + (-2.2)X + 1 = 0$

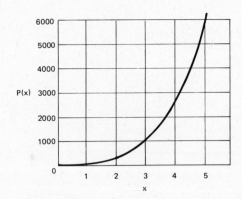

```
50   REM PROGRAM PREE
100  DIM A(30)
110  PRINT "THIS PROGRAM EVALUATES A POLYNOMIAL OF ORDER N"
120  PRINT "   Y=A0*X**N +A1*X**(N-1) +A2*X**(N-2) + ... + AN"
130  PRINT "AT VALUES OF X FROM X1 TO X2 IN STEPS OF X3"
140  PRINT "ENTER VALUE OF HIGHEST POWER N="
141  INPUT N
150  FOR I=1 TO N+1 STEP 1
160  PRINT "ENTER A(";I;")="
170  INPUT A(I)
180  NEXT I
190  PRINT "ENTER VALUE OF X1="
191  INPUT X1
200  PRINT "ENTER VALUE OF X2="
201  INPUT X2
210  PRINT "ENTER VALUE OF X3="
211  INPUT X3
```

```
220   FOR J=X1+1 TO X2+1 STEP X3
230   X=J-1
240   P=A(1)*X+A(2)
250   FOR I=3 TO N+1 STEP 1
260   P=X*P+A(I)
270   NEXT I
280   PRINT "VALUE OF P(";X;")=";P
290   NEXT J
300   PRINT "CALCULATIONS COMPLETED"
310   REM - SHOULD ANY EXECUTION TROUBLES BE ENCOUNTERED, PLEASE BRING THEM
320   REM - TO THE ATTENTION OF THE AUTHOR, JOSE ALONSO, SWINBURNE COLLEGE
330   REM - OF TECHNOLOGY LTD.
340   END
```

```
THIS PROGRAM EVALUATES A POLYNOMIAL OF ORDER N
    Y=A0*X**N +A1*X**(N-1) +A2*X**(N-2) + ... + AN
AT VALUES OF X FROM X1 TO X2 IN STEPS OF X3
ENTER VALUE OF HIGHEST POWER N=
?4
ENTER A( 1     )=
?7.8
ENTER A( 2     )=
?5
ENTER A( 3     )=
?4.3
ENTER A( 4     )=
?-2.2
ENTER A( 5     )=
?1
ENTER VALUE OF X1=
?1
ENTER VALUE OF X2=
?5
ENTER VALUE OF X3=
?.5
VALUE OF P( 1     )= 15.9
VALUE OF P( 1.5         )= 63.7375
VALUE OF P( 2     )= 178.6
VALUE OF P( 2.5         )= 405.187
VALUE OF P( 3     )= 799.9
VALUE OF P( 3.5         )= 1430.84
VALUE OF P( 4     )= 2377.8
VALUE OF P( 4.5         )= 3732.29
VALUE OF P( 5     )= 5597.5
CALCULATIONS COMPLETED

DONE
```

RUN#MLR
MULTIPLE LINEAR REGRESSION

This program calculates multiple linear regression coefficients B_j that fit the equation:

$$Y = B_0 + B_1 X_1 + B_2 X_2 + \ldots + B_j X_j + \ldots B_p X_p$$

to a set of N values of a dependent variable Y. Each of the N values correspond to p known values of the p independent variables x_j. The design matrix is:

$$
\begin{array}{ccccccc}
X_{11} & X_{12} & \ldots\ldots & X_{1j} & \ldots\ldots & X_{1p} & Y_1 \\
X_{21} & X_{22} & \ldots\ldots & X_{2j} & \ldots\ldots & X_{2p} & Y_2 \\
\cdot & \cdot & & \cdot & & \cdot & \cdot \\
\cdot & \cdot & & \cdot & & \cdot & \cdot \\
\cdot & \cdot & & \cdot & & \cdot & \cdot \\
X_{i1} & X_{i2} & & X_{ij} & & X_{ip} & Y_i \\
\cdot & \cdot & & \cdot & & \cdot & \cdot \\
\cdot & \cdot & & \cdot & & \cdot & \cdot \\
\cdot & \cdot & & \cdot & & \cdot & \cdot \\
X_{N1} & X_{N2} & & X_{Nj} & & X_{Np} & Y_N \\
\end{array}
$$

Independent   Dependent
Variables   (Observed)
                       Variable

1   2   j   p

This program also prints an analysis of variance table due to regression and about regression.

PROGRAM RESTRICTIONS

$(N \times p) \leq 225$.

$N \leq 30$.

$N \geq (p + 1)$.

INPUT REQUIREMENTS

$(N \times p)$ real values of X_{ij}.

N   real values of Y_i.

PROGRAM OUTPUT

Value of B_0 and p values of B_j.

REFERENCES

Bartee, E. N., _Statistical Methods in Engineering Experiments_, Charles E. Merrill Books, Inc., Columbus, Ohio, 1966.

Hald, A., _Statistical Theory with Engineering Applications_, J. Wiley and Sons, New York, 1952.

SAMPLE PROGRAM

The data for this problem is as follows:

Specified Variable X_1	Specified Variable X_2	Observed Variable Y	
3.1	15.7	0.7	Observation 1
4.1	17.8	0.72	Observation 2
2.5	13.9	0.58	Observation 3
5.7	18.6	0.81	Observation 4

The calculated equation is:

$$Y = (0.175812) + (0.267066)X_1 + (0.0256889)X_2$$

This program should be followed by program FD to test the correlation using the appropriate mean square ratio.

```
RUN
MLR
THISPROGRAM CALCULATES MULTIPLE REGRESSION COEFFICIENTS BJ
THAT FIT THE EQUATION
   Y=BO +B1*X1 +B2*X2+ ... +BJ*XJ+ ... +BP*XP
TO A SET OF N VALUES OF A DEPENDENT VARIABLE Y
EACH OF THE N VALUES CORRESPONDING TO P KNOWN VALUES OF THE
P INDEPENDENT VARIABLES XJ, WHERE 1<J<P
THEDESIGN MATRIX IS

X(1,1) X(1,2) ... X(1,J) ... X(1,P)        Y(1)
X(2,1) X(2,2) ... X(2,J) ... X(2,P)        Y(2)

X(I,1) X(I,2) ... X(I,J) ... X(I,P)        Y(I)

X(N,1) X(N,2) ... X(N,J) ... X(N,P)        Y(N)

MAXIMUM NUMBER OF Y VALUES PERMITTED IS 30
MAXIMUM NUMBER OF X VALUES PERMITED IS 225

ENTER NUMBER OF Y VALUES, N=? 4
ENTER NUMBER OF INDEPENDENT VARIABLES, P=? 2
ENTER X( 1 , 1 ) =
? 3.1
ENTER X( 1 , 2 ) =
? 15.7
ENTER NOW VALUE OF Y( 1 ) =
? .7
ENTER X( 2 , 1 ) =
? 4.1
ENTER X( 2 , 2 ) =
? 17.8
ENTER NOW VALUE OF Y( 2 ) =
? .72
ENTER X( 3 , 1 ) =
? 2.5
ENTER X( 3 , 2 ) =
? 13.9
ENTER NOW VALUE OF Y( 3 ) =
? .58
ENTER X( 4 , 1 ) =
? 5.7
```

```
ENTER X( 4 , 2 ) =
? 18.6
ENTER NOW VALUE OF Y( 4 ) =
? .81
CORRELATION MATRICES FOLLOW, C X B = D, TO BE SOLVED FOR VECTOR B
WHERE C IS A PXP MATRIX AND B AND D ARE PX1 VECTORS
COEFFICIENT MATRIX C( 1 ,J) ELEMENTS
C( 1 , 1 )= 5.87
C( 1 , 2 )= 8.32
COEFFICIENT MATRIX C( 2 ,J) ELEMENTS
C( 2 , 1 )= 8.32
C( 2 , 2 )= 13.5
COEFFICIENT MATRIX D(J) VECTOR ELEMENTS
D( 1 )= .3705
D( 2 )= .569


CALCULATED MULTIPLE LINEAR REGRESSION COEFFICIENTS

B 0 = .175812
B 1 = .267067E-1
B 2 = .256889E-1
```

	SUM OF SQ	DEG OF FR	MEAN SQ
DUE TO REGRESSION	.245118E-1	2	.122559E-1
ABOUT REGRESSION	.236317E-2	1	.236317E-2
TOTAL	.026875	3	.895834E-2

```
COEFFICIENT OF MULTIPLE CORRELATION = .955023
CALCULATIONS COMPLETED

Ready

LIST




MLR
100 REM - SHOULD ANY RUNNING DIFFICULTIES ARISE, PLEASE BRING THEM TO THE ATTENTION OF
    THE AUTHOR, JOSE ALONSO, SWINBURNE COLLEGE OF
    TECHNOLOGY
110 DIM X(15,15),Y(30),X1(15),C(15,15),D(15),D1(15),X5(15)
120 PRINT "THISPROGRAM CALCULATES MULTIPLE REGRESSION COEFFICIENTS BJ"
130 PRINT "THAT FIT THE EQUATION"
140 PRINT "   Y=BO +B1*X1 +B2*X2+ ... +BJ*XJ+ ... +BP*XP"
150 PRINT "TO A SET OF N VALUES OF A DEPENDENT VARIABLE Y"
160 PRINT "EACH OF THE N VALUES CORRESPONDING TO P KNOWN VALUES OF THE"
170 PRINT "P INDEPENDENT VARIABLES XJ, WHERE 1<J<P"
180 PRINT "THEDESIGN MATRIX IS"
190 PRINT
200 PRINT "X(1,1) X(1,2) ... X(1,J) ... X(1,P)        Y(1)"
210 PRINT "X(2,1) X(2,2) ... X(2,J) ... X(2,P)        Y(2)"
220 PRINT
230 PRINT "X(I,1) X(I,2) ... X(I,J) ... X(I,P)        Y(I)"
240 PRINT
250 PRINT "X(N,1) X(N,2) ... X(N,J) ... X(N,P)        Y(N)"
260 PRINT
270 PRINT"MAXIMUM NUMBER OF Y VALUES PERMITTED IS 30"
280 PRINT"MAXIMUM NUMBER OF X VALUES PERMITED IS 225"
290 PRINT
300 INPUT "ENTER NUMBER OF Y VALUES, N=";N
310 INPUT "ENTER NUMBER OF INDEPENDENT VARIABLES, P=";P
320 MAT C=ZER(P,P)
330 MAT D=ZER(P)
340 IF N*P>225 OR N>30 GO TO  1310 ELSE 350
350 MAT X=ZER(N,P)
360 FOR I=1 TO N STEP 1
370 FOR J=1 TO P STEP 1
```

```
380 PRINT "ENTER X(";I;",";J;") ="
390 INPUT X(I,J)
400 NEXT J
410 PRINT "ENTER NOW VALUE OF Y(";I;") ="
420 INPUT Y(I)
430 NEXT I
440 REM - COMPUTE MOMENTS
450 FOR I=1 TO P STEP 1
460 X1(I) =0
470 FOR I1=1 TO N STEP 1
480 X1(I)=X1(I)+X(I1,I)
490 NEXT I1
500 X1(I)=X1(I)/N
510 NEXT I
520 Y1=0
530 FOR I1=1 TO N STEP 1
540 Y1=Y1+Y(I1)
550 NEXT I1
560 Y1=Y1/N
570 REM - COMPUTE COEFFICIENTS
580 FOR J=1 TO P STEP 1
590 REM - CALCULATE D(J)
600 S1=0
610 FOR I=1 TO N STEP 1
620 S1=S1+(Y(I)-Y1)*(X(I,J)-X1(J))
630 NEXT I
640 D(J)=S1
650 S1=0
660 FOR K=J TO P STEP 1
670 IF J>K GO TO 750
680 REM - CALCULATE C(J,K)
690 S1=0
700 FOR I=1 TO N STEP 1
710 S1=S1+(X(I,J)-X1(J))*(X(I,K)-X1(K))
720 NEXT I
730 C(J,K)=S1
740 C(K,J)=C(J,K)
750 NEXT K
760 NEXT J
770 PRINT"CORRELATION MATRICES FOLLOW, C X B = D, TO BE SOLVED FOR VECTOR B"
780 PRINT"WHERE C IS A PXP MATRIX AND B AND D ARE PX1 VECTORS"
790 FOR I=1 TO P STEP 1
800 PRINT"COEFFICIENT MATRIX C(";I;",J) ELEMENTS"
810 FOR J=1 TO P STEP 1
820 PRINT "C(";I;",";J;")=";C(I,J)
830 NEXT J
840 NEXT I
850 PRINT"COEFFICIENT MATRIX D(J) VECTOR ELEMENTS"
860 FOR I=1 TO P STEP 1
870 PRINT"D(";I;")=";D(I)
880 NEXT I
890 FOR I=1 TO P STEP 1
900 D1(I)=D(I)
910 NEXT I
920 REM - SOLVE SYSTEM C X B = D FOR B
930 REM - WHERE C IS THE COEFFICIENT MATRIX AND D IS THE RIGHT HAND
VECTOR
940 MAT C=INV(C)
950 MAT X5=C*D
960 M1=0
970 FOR I=1 TO P STEP 1
980 M1=M1+X5(I)*X1(I)
990 NEXT I
1000 P0=Y1-M1
1010 PRINT
1020 PRINT "CALCULATED MULTIPLE LINEAR REGRESSION COEFFICIENTS"
1030 PRINT
1040 PRINT"B 0 =";P0
```

```
1050 FOR I=1 TO P STEP 1
1060 PRINT"B";I;"=";X5(I)
1070 NEXT I
1080 PRINT
1090 REM - WRITE ANOVA TABLE
1100 PRINT
1110 Y9=0
1120 FOR I=1 TO N STEP 1
1130 Y9=Y9+(Y(I)-Y1)**2
1140 NEXT I
1150 C9=Y9
1160 C1=0
1170 FOR I=1 TO P STEP 1
1180 C1=C1+X5(I)*D1(I)
1190 NEXT I
1200 C2=C9-C1
1210 L=N-1
1220 K=L-P
1230 C8=C1/P
1240 C7=C2/K
1250 C6=C9/L
1260 PRINT"                              SUM OF SQ    DEG OF FR     MEAN SQ"
1270 PRINT"DUE TO REGRESSION",C1,P,C8
1280 PRINT"ABOUT REGRESSION ",C2,K,C7
1290 PRINT"TOTAL           ",C9,L,C6
1295 Z1=(1.0-(C2/C9))**0.5
1296 PRINT"COEFFICIENT OF MULTIPLE CORRELATION =";Z1
1300 GO TO 1320
1310 PRINT"PROBLEM TOO LARGE FOR SYSTEM. PLEASE REREAD INSTRUCTIONS ABOVE"
1320 PRINT"CALCULATIONS COMPLETED"
1330 END
```

RUN#MLREE
MULTIPLE LINEAR REGRESSION EQUATION EVALUATOR

This program evaluates a multiple linear regression equation:

$$Y = k_0 + k_1x_1 + k_2x_2 + k_3x_3 + \ldots + k_ix_i + \ldots + k_nx_n$$

for values of x_1 from a_1 to b_1 in d_1 steps,

for values of x_2 from a_2 to b_2 in d_2 steps,

.
.
.

for values of x_i from a_i to b_i in d_i steps,

.
.
.

for values of x_n from a_n to b_n in d_n steps,

given the real values of k_0, k_1, k_2, ..., k_i, ..., k_n

and values of all a_i, b_i, and d_i.

PROGRAM RESTRICTIONS

$N \leq 20$.

INPUT REQUIREMENTS

Integer n, (n + 1) real values of k , k , ..., k_n, and n sets of (a_i, b_i, d_i), (real, real, integer), of course.

PROGRAM OUTPUT

Values of Y evaluated at specified combinations of values in tabular form.

REFERENCES

Bartee, E. N., Statistical Methods in Engineering Experiments, Charles E. Merrill Books, Inc., Columbus, Ohio, 1966.

SAMPLE PROGRAM

The multiple linear regression equation to be evaluated could have come from program MLR, from the literature, or from a hand calculation. It is:

$$Y = 2 + 3X_1 + 4X_2 + 5X_3 + 6X_4$$

for values of X_1 from $X_1 = 1$ to $X_1 = 5$ in 5 steps

X_2 from $X_2 = 1$ to $X_2 = 3$ in 1 step

X_3 from $X_3 = 1$ to $X_3 = 3$ in 1 step

X_4 from $X_4 = 1$ to $X_4 = 3$ in 1 step

The printout should be self-explanatory.

The program assumes that the equation given has 10 independent variables. If only 4 are given, (as in this case), it assumes the other 6 variables to be zero and prints them as zero.

```
RUN SIMPLE:MLREE
THIS PROGRAM EVALUATES A GIVEN MULTIPLE LINEAR REGRESSION EQUATION
Y=K0+K1*X1+K2*X2*.....+KI*XI+.....+KN*XN
GIVEN VALUE OF K0,K1,K2,..,KI,..KN
FOR VALUES OF X1 FROM A1 TO B1 IN N1 STEPS
FOR VALUES OF X2 FROM A2 TO B2 IN N2 STEPS
  "    "     "    "   "   "   "   "   "
FOR VALUES OF XN FROM AN TO BN IN NN STEPS
ENTER VALUE OF N=? 4
ENTER VALUE OF K0=? 2
ENTER NOW, SEPARATED BY COMMAS,  4 VALUES OF K1,K2,...,KN
? 3,4,5,6
ENTER NOW THE LIMITS AI,BI,AND THE NUMBER OF STEPS NI OF EACH VARIABLE
AS REQUESTED, FOR ONE VARIABLE AT A TIME, SEPARATED BY COMMAS
ENTER A 1 , B 1 , N 1
? 1,5,5
ENTER A 2 , B 2 , N 2
? 1,3,1
ENTER A 3 , B 3 , N 3
? 1,3,1
ENTER A 4 , B 4 , N 4
? 1,3,1
OUTPUT FORMAT
```

X1	X2	X3	X4	X5
X6	X7	X8	X9	Y
1.8	3	3	3	0
0	0	0	0	52.4
2.6	3	3	3	0
0	0	0	0	54.8
3.4	3	3	3	0
0	0	0	0	57.2
4.2	3	3	3	0
0	0	0	0	59.6
5	3	3	3	0
0	0	0	0	62

```
CALCULATIONS COMPLETED

Ready
```

```
1 DIM K(9),A(9),B(9),D(9),X(9)
10 PRINT"THIS PROGRAM EVALUATES A GIVEN MULTIPLE LINEAR REGRESSION EQUATION"
20 PRINT"Y=K0+K1*X1+K2*X2*.....+KI*XI+.....+KN*XN"
30 PRINT"GIVEN VALUE OF K0,K1,K2,..,KI,..KN"
40 PRINT"FOR VALUES OF X1 FROM A1 TO B1 IN N1 STEPS"
50 PRINT"FOR VALUES OF X2 FROM A2 TO B2 IN N2 STEPS"
60 PRINT'"    "     "   "   "    "   "   "   "   "   '
70 PRINT"FOR VALUES OF XN FROM AN TO BN IN NN STEPS"
80 INPUT"ENTER VALUE OF N=";N
90 INPUT"ENTER VALUE OF K0=";K0
100 PRINT"ENTER NOW, SEPARATED BY COMMAS, ";N;"VALUES OF K1,K2,...,KN"
110 MAT INPUT K(N)
120 PRINT"ENTER NOW THE LIMITS AI,BI,AND THE NUMBER OF STEPS NI OF EACH VARIABLE"
121 PRINT"AS REQUESTED, FOR ONE VARIABLE AT A TIME, SEPARATED BY COMMAS"
130 FOR I=1 TO N STEP 1
140 PRINT"ENTER A";I;", B";I;", N";I
150 INPUT A(I),B(I),D(I)
160 NEXT I
```

```
165 PRINT"OUTPUT FORMAT"
170 PRINT"X1                X2              X3              X4              X5"
171 PRINT"X6                X7              X8              X9              Y"
172 PRINT
180 ON N GO TO 380,370,360,350,340,330,320,310,300
300 FOR Q=1 TO D(9)
305 X9=A(9)+((B(9)-A(9))/D(9))*Q
310 FOR P=1 TO D(8)
315 X8=A(8)+((B(8)-A(8))/D(8))*P
320 FOR O=1 TO D(7)
325 X5=A(5)+((B(5)-A(5))/D(5))*N
330 FOR N=1 TO D(6)
335 X6=A(6)+((B(6)-A(6))/D(6))*N
340 FOR M=1 TO D(5)
345 X5=A(5)+((B(5)-A(5))/D(5))*M
350 FOR L=1 TO D(4)
355 X4=A(4)+((B(4)-A(4))/D(4))*L
360 FOR K=1 TO D(3)
365 X3=A(3)+((B(3)-A(3))/D(3))*K
370 FOR J=1 TO D(2)
375 X2=A(2)+((B(2)-A(2))/D(2))*J
380 FOR I=1 TO D(1)
385 X1=A(1)+((B(1)-A(1))/D(1))*I
390 Y=K0+K(1)*X1+K(2)*X2+K(3)*X3+K(4)*X4+K(5)*X5+K(6)*X6+K(7)*X7+K(8)*X8+K(9)*X9
392 PRINT X1,X2,X3,X4,X5
393 PRINT X6,X7,X8,X9,Y
394 PRINT
400 NEXT I
405 IF D(2)<=0 GO TO 490
410 NEXT J
415 IF D(3)<=0 GO TO 490
420 NEXT K
425 IF D(4)<=0 GO TO 490
430 NEXT L
435 IF D(5)<=0 GO TO 490
440 NEXT M
445 IF D(6)<=0 GO TO 490
450 NEXT N
455 IF D(7)<=0 GO TO 490
460 NEXT O
465 IF D(8)<=0 GO TO 490
470 NEXT P
475 IF D(9)<=0 GO TO 490
480 NEXT Q
490 PRINT"CALCULATIONS COMPLETED"
500 END
```

RUN#PCA
PRINCIPAL COMPONENT ANALYSIS

Principal components are the eigenvectors (often also called "characteristic" or "proper" vectors) of the covariance (or correlation) matrix. The variances of the principal components are the corresponding eigenvalues (characteristic values, proper values). This analysis produces linear combinations of variables with large variance.

Given M observations of N variables, this program calculates a covariance and then a correlation matrix from it. The correlation matrix is then used as input to a function which utilizes Jacobi's method for finding the eigenvalues and eigenvectors of a real symmetric matrix. The eigenvalues of a correlation matrix represent the amounts of variance attributable to each variable, and the eigenvectors are the respective principal components.

Program Restrictions

No checks are made on the validity of the data. Maximum observation matrix size is 100 rows by 10 columns, that is, up to 100 observations on up to 10 variables. These dimensions can naturally be varied according to machine capacity and virtual array-handling availability. The form of the program supplied may require some modification, as it uses DEC 11 virtual core and file handling syntax.

INPUT REQUIREMENTS

Up to 100 observations of up to 10 variables. Required input values are:

1. Number of variables N;

2. Number of sets of observations M, each set consisting of N values N x M observed values, entered by row, each row containing N values corresponding to one observation. M rows are entered successively.

PROGRAM OUTPUT

The program will print the observation matrix, means, standard deviations, covariance matrix, variance figures, and principal components. The observation matrix may be saved for subsequent use if desired.

REFERENCES

Bowdler, H., Martin, R. S., Reinsch, C., and Wilkinson, J. H., The QR and QL Algorithm for Symmetric Matrices, Springer Handbook Series on Linear Algebra, No.2, Vol.11, 1968.

SAMPLE PROGRAM

```
1!*****************************************************************
*****************************************************************
**                                                             **
**                                                             **
**              PRINCIPAL COMPONENT ANALYSIS                   **
**              -----------------------------                  **
**                                                             **
**                 AUTHOR:   BOB SCHORER                       **
**                                                             **
**         The program will input an observation matrix        **
**         from the user console one row at a time and         **
**         calculate a covariance and then a correlation       **
**         matrix from it.  The correlation matrix is          **
**         then used as input to a function which              **
**         utilizes Jacobi's method for finding the            **
**         eigenvalues and eigenvectors of a real              **
**         symmetric matrix.  ThJe eigenvalues of a            **
**         correlation matrix represent the amounts            **
**         of variance attributable to each variable           **
**         and the eigenvectors are the respective             **
**         principal components.                               **
**                                                             **
**         No checks are made on the validity of the           **
**         data.  Maximum observation matrix size is           **
**         100 rows by 10 columns (i.e. up to 100              **
**         observations on up to 10 variables) but             **
**         these dimensions could be easily increased          **
**         at a cost of greater disc space for the             **
**         virtual arrays.                                     **
**                                                             **
**         The program will print the observation              **
**         matrix, the means, the standard deviations,         **
**         the covariance matrix and the correlation           **
**         matrix if the user so desires, as well as           **
**         the variance figures and the principal              **
**         components.                                         **
**                                                             **
**         Note that the original observation matrix           **
**         may be saved on disc and used as input to           **
**         other statistical routines.                         **
**                                                             **
**                                                             **
*****************************************************************
*****************************************************************


100       EXTEND:
          OPEN "MATRIX.DAT" AS FILE 1%:
          OPEN "TEMP.FLE" AS FILE 2%:
          DIM #1%, BOUND%(2%), MATDATA(100%,10%):
          DIM #2%, MAT1(10%,100%):

          DIM CORRMAT(10%,10%),MEANS(10%),COMPS(10%,10%):

          INPUT "INPUT FROM KEYBOARD <KEY> OR DEFAULT <DISC>";A$:
          IF CVT$$(A$,2%) <> "KEY" GO TO 200
                  ELSE
                  INPUT "NO. VARIABLES ";BOUND%(2%):
                  INPUT "NO. OBSERVATIONS ";BOUND%(1%):
                  PRINT "TYPE IN OBSERVATION MATRIX ROW BY ROW":
                  PRINT "(SEPARATED BY COMMAS AND TERMINATED BY <LF>":
```

```
          FOR IZ = 1% TO BOUND%(1%):
          MAT INPUT MEANS(BOUND%(2%)):
          FOR JZ = 1% TO BOUND%(2%):
          MATDATA(IZ,JZ) = MEANS(JZ):
          NEXT JZ:
          NEXT IZ
```

```
!**************************************************************
*                                                            *
*                                                            *
*              Read data from the virtual array and store    *
*              it's transposed form in another virtual       *
*              array.  Calculate the means at the same       *
*              time.  Note that this duplication of data     *
*              is not really necessary but the processing     *
*              of virtual arrays is much faster if array     *
*              is accessed by column instead of by row.      *
*                                                            *
*              Print the observation matrix if user so       *
*              desires.                                       *
*                                                            *
```

```
200       M% = BOUND%(1%):
          N% = BOUND%(2%):
          FORMAT$ = "####.####  ":

          FOR IZ = 1% TO N%:
          MEANS(IZ) = 0.0:
            FOR JZ = 1% TO M%:
            MAT1(IZ,JZ) = MATDATA(JZ,IZ):
            MEANS(IZ) = MEANS(IZ)+MAT1(IZ,JZ):
            NEXT JZ:
          MEANS(IZ) = MEANS(IZ)/M%:
          NEXT IZ:
          PRINT:PRINT:
          INPUT "DO YOU WANT THE OBSERVATION MATRIX PRINTED ";A$:
          IF LEFT(CVT$$(A$,2%),1%) <> "Y" GO TO 300
                    ELSE
          PRINT:PRINT:
          PRINT "NUMBER OF VARIABLES = ";N%:
          PRINT "NUMBER OF OBSERVATIONS = ";M%:
          PRINT:
          PRINT "THE OBSERVATION MATRIX IS :-":
          PRINT:
          FOR IZ = 1% TO M%:
          PRINT USING FORMAT$, MATDATA(IZ,JZ); FOR JZ = 1% TO N%:
          PRINT:
          NEXT IZ:
          PRINT:PRINT
```

```
!**************************************************************
*                                                            *
*                                                            *
*              Now pre-multiply the observation matrix by     *
*              it's transpose.  Note that storage for the    *
*              transposed matrix is not neccessary and       *
*              that each element must be converted to a      *
*              displacement from the appropriate mean.       *
*                                                            *
*              Print the means, standard deviations and      *
*              the resultant covariance matrix if the        *
*              user requires them.                            *
*                                                            *
```

```
300      FOR IZ = 1% TO N%:
            FOR JZ = 1% TO N%:
                   CORRMAT(IZ,JZ) = 0.0:
                   FOR KZ = 1% TO M%:
                      CORRMAT(IZ,JZ) = CORRMAT(IZ,JZ)+(MAT1(IZ,KZ)-MEANS(IZ))*
                                                       (MAT1(JZ,KZ)-MEANS(JZ)):
                   NEXT KZ:
            CORRMAT(IZ,JZ) = CORRMAT(IZ,JZ)/(M%-1%):
            NEXT JZ:
         NEXT IZ:

         INPUT "DO YOU WANT MEANS AND S.D.'S PRINTED ";A$:
         IF LEFT(CVT$$(A$,2%),1%) <> "Y" GO TO 350
                 ELSE
         PRINT:PRINT:
         PRINT "THE MEANS ARE :- ":
         PRINT:
         PRINT USING FORMAT$, MEANS(IZ); FOR IZ = 1% TO N%:
         PRINT:PRINT:PRINT:
         PRINT"THE STANDARD DEVIATIONS ARE :-":
         PRINT:
         PRINT USING FORMAT$, SQR(CORRMAT(IZ,IZ)); FOR IZ = 1% TO N%:
         PRINT:PRINT:PRINT


350      INPUT "DO YOU WANT THE COVARIANCE MATRIX PRINTED ";A$:
         IF LEFT(CVT$$(A$,2%),1%) <> "Y" GO TO 400
                 ELSE
         PRINT:PRINT:
         PRINT "THE COVARIANCE MATRIX IS :-":
         PRINT:
         FOR IZ = 1% TO N%:
         PRINT USING FORMAT$,CORRMAT(IZ,JZ); FOR JZ = 1% TO N%:
         PRINT:
         NEXT IZ:
         PRINT:PRINT



!*****************************************************************************
*                                                                           *
*                                                                           *
*                  Convert the covariance matrix into a                     *
*                  correlation matrix by dividing each                      *
*                  element by the product of the square                     *
*                  roots of it's variances (the diagonal                    *
*                  elements) and, if required by the user,                  *
*                  print it out.                                            *
*                                                                           *
*                                                                           *


400      FOR IZ = 1% TO N%:
            FOR JZ = N% TO IZ STEP -1%:
                   CORRMAT(IZ,JZ) = CORRMAT(IZ,JZ)/SQR(CORRMAT(IZ,IZ)*
                                                       CORRMAT(JZ,JZ)):
            NEXT JZ:
         NEXT IZ:

         INPUT "DO YOU WANT THE CORRELATION MATRIX PRINTED ";A$:
         IF LEFT(CVT$$(A$,2%),1%) <> "Y" GO TO 500
                 ELSE
         PRINT:PRINT:
         PRINT "THE CORRELATION MATRIX IS :-":
         PRINT:
         FOR IZ = 1% TO N%:
         PRINT USING FORMAT$,CORRMAT(IZ,JZ); FOR JZ = 1% TO N%:
```

```
        PRINT:
        NEXT I%:
        PRINT:PRINT


!*******************************************************************
*                                                                 *
*                                                                 *
*               Call the Jacobi's method subroutine which         *
*               starts at line 2000 the print the variances       *
*               and principal components after sorting them       *
*               into ascending order for ease of reading.         *
*                                                                 *
*                                                                 *

500     EPS = 1E-5:
        GO SUB 2000:

        TEMP% = N%

550     TEMP% = TEMP%-1%:
        FLAG% = 0%:
        FOR I% = 1% TO TEMP%:
        IF CORRMAT(I%,I%) < CORRMAT(I%+1%,I%+1%) GO TO 600
                ELSE
                FLAG% = 1%:
                TEMP = CORRMAT(I%,I%):
                CORRMAT(I%,I%) = CORRMAT(I%+1%,I%+1%):
                CORRMAT(I%+1%,I%+1%) = TEMP:
                FOR J% = 1% TO N%:
                TEMP = COMPS(J%,I%):
                COMPS(J%,I%) = COMPS(J%,I%+1%):
                COMPS(J%,I%+1%) = TEMP:
                NEXT J%

600     NEXT I%:
        IF FLAG% = 1% GO TO 550
                ELSE
        PRINT "ACTUAL AMOUNTS OF VARIANCE CONTRIBUTED BY EACH VARIABLE":
        PRINT "(FOLLOWED BY PERCENTAGE OF TOTAL VARIANCE AND THEN BY":
        PRINT "THE CUMULATIVE PERCENTAGES) ARE :-":
        PRINT:
        SUM = 0.0:
        FOR I% = 1% TO N%:
        PRINT USING FORMAT$, CORRMAT(I%,I%);:
        SUM = SUM+CORRMAT(I%,I%):
        NEXT I%:
        PRINT:
        PRINT USING " (##.###%) ",(CORRMAT(I%,I%)/SUM*100.0); FOR I% = 1% TO N%:
        PRINT:
        TEMP = 0.0:
        FOR I% = 1% TO N%:
        TEMP = TEMP+CORRMAT(I%,I%)/SUM*100.0:
        PRINT USING "(###.###%) ", TEMP;:
        NEXT I%:
        PRINT:
        PRINT:
        PRINT:
        PRINT "PRINCIPAL COMPONENTS ARE :-":
        PRINT:
        FOR I% = 1% TO N%:
        PRINT USING FORMAT$, COMPS(I%,J%); FOR J% = 1% TO N%:
        PRINT:
        NEXT I%:

        PRINT:PRINT:
        CLOSE 1%,2%:
        KILL "TEMP.FLE":
```

```
      INPUT "DO YOU REQUIRE THE ORIGINAL OBSERVATION MATRIX TO BE SAVED";A$:
      IF LEFT(CVT$$(A$,2%),1%) = "Y" GO TO 32767
                ELSE
                KILL "MATRIX.DAT":
                GO TO 32767



  2000!**********************************************************************
      **********************************************************************
      **                                                                  **
      **                                                                  **
      **          The following function uses Jacobi's method             **
      **          to find the eigenvalues and eigenvectors of             **
      **          a real symmetric matrix.                                **
      **                                                                  **
      **          Because the 4-word math pack is being used              **
      **          on this system, all arithmetic is done in               **
      **          double precision.                                       **
      **                                                                  **
      **          Upon completion of this function, the array             **
      **          'CORRMAT' which held the original array as              **
      **          input, will contain, as it's diagonal                   **
      **          elements, the eigenvalues of the matrix, and            **
      **          the array 'COMPS' will contain the eigen-               **
      **          vectors.                                                **
      **                                                                  **
      **                                                                  **
      **********************************************************************
      **********************************************************************



      **********************************************************************
      *                                                                    *
      *          First set up an identity matrix in 'COMPS',               *
      *          this is used to calculate the eigenvectors                *
      *          for subsequent printing and serves no other              *
      *          useful purpose.  If eigenvalues only are                 *
      *          required then it could be deleted.                       *
      *                                                                    *
      *          Also calculate the sum of the squares of all             *
      *          matrix elements to serve as a test for                   *
      *          completion of the problem.                               *
      *          Also ensure matrix is symmetric.                         *
      *                                                                    *
      *                                                                    *



  2050    MAT COMPS = ZER:
          COMPS(I%,I%) = 1.0 FOR I% = 1% TO N%:

          SUMSQ = CORRMAT(N%,N%)**2:
          FOR I% = 1% TO N%-1%:
                SUMSQ = SUMSQ+CORRMAT(I%,I%)**2:
                FOR J% = I%+1% TO N%:
                SUMSQ = SUMSQ+CORRMAT(I%,J%)**2*2:
                CORRMAT(J%,I%) = CORRMAT(I%,J%):
                NEXT J%:
          NEXT I%:
          ITERNUM% = 0%


  !-------------------------------------------------------------------------!
  !                                                                         !
  !          Now enter loops which will progressively                      !
  !          zero each element in the matrix by pre-                       !
  !          and post-multiplying by a series of                           !
  !          orthogonal matrices which are calculated                      !
  !          on each pass to zero the 'i,j' element                        !
  !          for that pass.                                                !
```

```
!          The rotation angle for each pass is          !
!          calculated from -                            !
!          TAN(2A) = CORRMAT(i,j)/(CORRMAT(i,i)-CORRMAT(j,j))  !
!                                                        !
!          Note that since only the i and j rows and    !
!          columns are affected, it is not necessary    !
!          to multiply the whole of the matrix or       !
!          to store the orthogonal matrix.              !
!                                                        !
!          If, at the end of each pass through the      !
!          matrix, the diagonal elements have not       !
!          achieved the desired degree of dominance     !
!          then another pass through the matrix is      !
!          implemented, until sufficient accuracy       !
!          has been achieved.                           !


2150    ITERNUM% = ITERNUM%+1%:

        FOR I% = 1% TO N%-1%:
        FOR J% = I%+1% TO N%:

        IF ABS(CORRMAT(I%,J%)) < 1E-9 GO TO 2250
                ELSE
                COSALPH = SQR(0.5):
                SINALPH = COSALPH:
                IF ABS(CORRMAT(I%,I%)-CORRMAT(J%,J%)) > 1E-9 THEN
                        ALPH = ATN(CORRMAT(I%,J%)/(CORRMAT(I%,I%)-CORRMAT(J%,J%))):
                        COSALPH = COS(ALPH/2.0):
                        SINALPH = SIN(ALPH/2.0)

2200    FOR K% = 1% TO N%:
                TEMP = CORRMAT(I%,K%):
                CORRMAT(I%,K%) = TEMP*COSALPH+CORRMAT(J%,K%)*SINALPH:
                CORRMAT(J%,K%) = TEMP*SINALPH-CORRMAT(J%,K%)*COSALPH:
        NEXT K%:

        FOR K% = 1% TO N%:
                TEMP = CORRMAT(K%,I%):
                CORRMAT(K%,I%) = TEMP*COSALPH+CORRMAT(K%,J%)*SINALPH:
                CORRMAT(K%,J%) = TEMP*SINALPH-CORRMAT(K%,J%)*COSALPH:

                TEMP = COMPS(K%,I%):
                COMPS(K%,I%) = TEMP*COSALPH+COMPS(K%,J%)*SINALPH:
                COMPS(K%,J%) = TEMP*SINALPH-COMPS(K%,J%)*COSALPH:
        NEXT K%

2250    NEXT J%:
        NEXT I%:

        TEMP = 0.0:
        TEMP = TEMP+CORRMAT(I%,I%)**2 FOR I% = 1% TO N%:

        IF ABS(TEMP-SUMSQ) < EPS THEN RETURN
                ELSE
                IF ITERNUM% < 200% GO TO 2150
                        ELSE
                        PRINT "FUNCTION HAS NOT CONVERGED AFTER 200 ITERATIONS":
                        RETURN
!_____!
!                                                        !

32767   END
```

```
RUN SIMPLE:PCA
INPUT FROM KEYBOARD <KEY> OR DEFAULT <DISC>? KEY
NO. VARIABLES ? 6
NO. OBSERVATIONS ? 9
TYPE IN OBSERVATION MATRIX ROW BY ROW
(SEPARATED BY COMMAS AND TERMINATED BY <LF>
? 23,45,34,67,78,98
? 65,78,98,65,45,32
? 54,36,67,54,21,23
? 56,97,87,89,67,54
? 58,94,96,78,87,68
? 45,32,21,32,34,5\5\45
? 56,43,21,32,45,67
? 68,97,64,53,35,65,\,\
? 78,90,99,98,97,96


DO YOU WANT THE OBSERVATION MATRIX PRINTED ? Y


NUMBER OF VARIABLES =   6
NUMBER OF OBSERVATIONS =   9

THE OBSERVATION MATRIX IS :-

    23.0000     45.0000     34.0000     67.0000     78.0000     98.0000
    65.0000     78.0000     98.0000     65.0000     45.0000     32.0000
    54.0000     36.0000     67.0000     54.0000     21.0000     23.0000
    56.0000     97.0000     87.0000     89.0000     67.0000     54.0000
    58.0000     94.0000     96.0000     78.0000     87.0000     68.0000
    45.0000     32.0000     21.0000     32.0000     34.0000     45.0000
    56.0000     43.0000     21.0000     32.0000     45.0000     67.0000
    68.0000     97.0000     64.0000     53.0000     35.0000     65.0000
    78.0000     90.0000     99.0000     98.0000     97.0000     96.0000


DO YOU WANT MEANS AND S.D.'S PRINTED ? Y


THE MEANS ARE :-

    55.8889     68.0000     65.2222     63.1111     56.5556     60.8889


THE STANDARD DEVIATIONS ARE :-

    15.5197     28.3196     32.6488     23.0459     26.5429     25.7024


DO YOU WANT THE COVARIANCE MATRIX PRINTED ? Y


THE COVARIANCE MATRIX IS :-

   240.8610    274.1250    324.7780    115.6390     24.9445    -49.7639
     0.0000    802.0000    728.2500    466.3750    373.6250    170.7500
     0.0000      0.0000   1065.9400    611.0970    369.2360    -61.3472
     0.0000      0.0000      0.0000    531.1110    474.9310    231.2640
     0.0000      0.0000      0.0000      0.0000    704.5280    530.0700
     0.0000      0.0000      0.0000      0.0000      0.0000    660.6110


DO YOU WANT THE CORRELATION MATRIX PRINTED ? Y
```

```
THE CORRELATION MATRIX IS :-

    1.0000      0.6237      0.6410      0.3233      0.0606     -0.1248
    0.0000      1.0000      0.7876      0.7146      0.4971      0.2346
    0.0000      0.0000      1.0000      0.8122      0.4261     -0.0731
    0.0000      0.0000      0.0000      1.0000      0.7764      0.3904
    0.0000      0.0000      0.0000      0.0000      1.0000      0.7770
    0.0000      0.0000      0.0000      0.0000      0.0000      1.0000


FUNCTION HAS NOT CONVERGED AFTER 200 ITERATIONS
ACTUAL AMOUNTS OF VARIANCE CONTRIBUTED BY EACH VARIABLE
(FOLLOWED BY PERCENTAGE OF TOTAL VARIANCE AND THEN BY
THE CUMULATIVE PERCENTAGES) ARE :-

    0.0301      0.0741      0.2233      0.5302      1.6865      3.4559
 ( 0.502%)   ( 1.236%)   ( 3.722%)   ( 8.836%)   (28.107%)   (57.598%)
 ( 0.502%)   ( 1.737%)   ( 5.459%)   ( 14.295%)  ( 42.402%)  (100.000%)


PRINCIPAL COMPONENTS ARE :-

   -0.1735     -0.0298     -0.4555      0.6553     -0.4889      0.3053
   -0.1476      0.1155      0.8213      0.1892     -0.1695      0.4752
    0.7277      0.0951     -0.1349     -0.3537     -0.3244      0.4613
   -0.4304     -0.5967     -0.1655     -0.4189      0.0923      0.4973
   -0.2292      0.7000     -0.2685     -0.0647      0.4596      0.4123
    0.4251     -0.3616      0.0179      0.4796      0.6382      0.2257


DO YOU REQUIRE THE ORIGINAL OBSERVATION MATRIX TO BE SAVED? N

Ready
```

ANALYSIS OF VARIANCE

RUN#AV1
ANALYSIS OF VARIANCE—ONE INDEPENDENT VARIABLE

This program calculates an analysis of variance of a variable $Y(I,J)$ evaluated at K treatment levels indicated by subscript I, with unequal number of replications $N(I)$ at each level I. The experimental design matrix is as follows:

	1	2	J		N(I)	Different Number of Replications at Each Level
1	Y(1,1)	Y(1,2)	Y(1,J)		Y(1,N(1))	
2	Y(2,1)	Y(2,2)	Y(2,J)	Y(2,N(2))		
I	Y(I,1)	Y(I,2)	Y(I,J)			Y(I,N (I))
K	Y(K,1)	Y(K,2)	Y(K,J)	Y(K,N(K))		

Levels

INPUT REQUIREMENTS

One integer value of K.
K integer values of $N(I)$, the number of replications at each of the K levels.
$\Sigma N(I)$ real values of $Y(I,J)$, the observation matrix.

PROGRAM OUTPUT

Total SS			
Treat SS	Treat DF	Treat MS	F test ratio
Error SS	Error DF	Error MS	

REFERENCES

Bartee, E. M., _Engineering Experimental Design Fundamentals_, Prentice-Hall, N.J., 1968.

Hald, A., _Statistical Theory with Engineering Applications_, J. Wiley and Sons, New York, 1952.

SAMPLE PROGRAM

J →	1	2	3	4	5	N(K)
↓ K						
1	2	4	7	5		N(1) = 4
2	7	9	5			N(2) = 3
3	7	7	6	8	4	N(3) = 5

```
RUN
AV1
THIS PROGRAM CALCULATES AN ANALYSIS OF VARIANCE FOR A VARIABLE
Y(I,J) EVALUATED AT K TREATMENT LEVELS INDICATED BY
SUBSCRIPT I, WITH UNEQUAL NUMBER OF REPLICATIONS N(I) AT EACH
LEVEL I, INDICATED BY SUBSCRIPT J. THE EXPERIMENTAL DESIGN
MATRIX IS AS FOLLOWS:

      1        2      ...     J    ...              N(I) REPLICATIONS
1   Y(1,1)   Y(1,2)   ...              ...    Y(1,N(1))
2   Y(2,1)   Y(2,2)   ...   Y(1,N(2))
3   Y(3,1)   Y(3,2)   ...                      ...    Y(I,N(3))

I   Y(I,1)   Y(I,2)   ...   Y(I,J)   ...   ...   Y(I,N(I))
K   Y(K,1)   Y(K,2)   ...      Y(K,N(K))


ENTER VALUE OF K? 3
ENTER VALUE OF N( 1 ) =
? 4
ENTER VALUE OF N( 2 ) =
? 3
ENTER VALUE OF N( 3 ) =
? 5
ENTER VALUE OF Y( 1 , 1 ) =
? 2
ENTER VALUE OF Y( 1 , 2 ) =
? 4
ENTER VALUE OF Y( 1 , 3 ) =
? 7
ENTER VALUE OF Y( 1 , 4 ) =
? 5
ENTER VALUE OF Y( 2 , 1 ) =
? 7
ENTER VALUE OF Y( 2 , 2 ) =
? 9
ENTER VALUE OF Y( 2 , 3 ) =
? 5
ENTER VALUE OF Y( 3 , 1 ) =
? 7
ENTER VALUE OF Y( 3 , 2 ) =
? 7
ENTER VALUE OF Y( 3 , 3 ) =
? 6
ENTER VALUE OF Y( 3 , 4 ) =
? 8
ENTER VALUE OF Y( 3 , 5 ) =
? 4
TOTAL SS= 42.9167
TREAT SS= 12.7167
ERROR SS= 30.2
TREATMENT DEGREES OF FREEDOM= 2
ERROR DEGREES OF FREEDOM= 9
TREAT MS= 6.35834
ERROR MS= 3.35555
F-TEST RATIO= 1.89487 WITH 2 AND 9 DEGREES OF FREEDOM
CALCULATIONS COMPLETED

Ready
```

Program FD may now be entered with values of 2 and 9 for the degrees of freedom arguments and value of 1.89487 for the F-test ratio to calculate the F-test ratio percentile value.

```
Ready

LIST
AV1
100 DIM Y(20,20),N(20),S1(20)
110 PRINT"THIS PROGRAM CALCULATES AN ANALYSIS OF VARIANCE FOR A VARIABLE"
120 PRINT"Y(I,J) EVALUATED AT K TREATMENT LEVELS INDICATED BY "
130 PRINT"SUBSCRIPT I, WITH UNEQUAL NUMBER OF REPLICATIONS N(I) AT EACH"
140 PRINT"LEVEL I, INDICATED BY SUBSCRIPT J. THE EXPERIMENTAL DESIGN"
150 PRINT"MATRIX IS AS FOLLOWS:"
160 PRINT
170 PRINT"    1        2      ...    J   ...            N(I) REPLICATIONS
180 PRINT"1   Y(1,1)   Y(1,2)  ...          ...   Y(1,N(1))"
190PRINT"2   Y(2,1)   Y(2,2)   ...   Y(1,N(2))"
200PRINT"3   Y(3,1)   Y(3,2)   ...                ...   Y(I,N(3))"
210PRINT
220PRINT"I   Y(I,1)   Y(I,2)   ...   Y(I,J)  ...   ...   Y(I,N(I))"
230PRINT"K   Y(K,1)   Y(K,2)   ...       Y(K,N(K))"
240PRINT
250 REM - READ INPUT DATA
260 PRINT
270 PRINT
280 INPUT"ENTER VALUE OF K";K
290 N1=0
300 FOR I=1 TO K STEP 1
310 PRINT"ENTER VALUE OF N(";I;") ="
320 INPUT N(I)
330 N1=N1+N(I)
340 NEXT I
350 FOR I=1 TO K STEP 1
360 FOR J=1 TO N(I) STEP 1
370 PRINT"ENTER VALUE OF Y(";I;",";J;") ="
380 INPUT Y(I,J)
390 NEXT J
400 NEXT I
410 REM - CALCULATE SUM(I) TERMS S1(I)
420 FOR I=1 TO K STEP 1
430 S1(I)=0
440 FOR J=1 TO N(I) STEP 1
450 S1(I)=S1(I)+Y(I,J)
460 NEXT J
470 NEXT I
480 REM - CALCULATE TOTAL SS S2
490 T1=0
500 T2=0
510 FOR I=1 TO K STEP 1
520 FOR J=1 TO N(I) STEP 1
530 T1=T1+(Y(I,J)**2)
540 T2=T2+(Y(I,J))
550 NEXT J
560 NEXT I
570 S2=T1-(T2**2)/N1
580 REM - CALCULATE TREAT SS S3
590 T4=0
600 FOR I=1 TO K STEP 1
610 T3=0
620 FOR J=1 TO N(I) STEP 1
630 T3=T3+Y(I,J)
640 NEXT J
650 T4=T4+(T3**2)/N(I)
660 NEXT I
670 S3=T4-(T2**2)/N1
680 REM - CALCULATE ERROR SS S4
690 S4=S2-S3
700 REM - CALCULATE TREAT DEGREES OF FREEDOM D1
710 D1=K-1
720 REM - CALCULATE ERROR DEGREES OF FREEDOM D2
730 D2=0
```

```
740 FOR I=1 TO K STEP 1
750 D2=D2+(N(I))
760 NEXT I
770 D2=D2-K
780 REM - CALCULATE TREAT MS M1
790 M1=S3/D1
800 REM - CALCULATE ERROR MS M2
810 M2=S4/D2
820 REM - CALCULATE F TEST RATIO F
830 F=M1/M2
840 REM - PRINT OUTPUT DATA
850 FOR I=1TO M STEP 1
860 PRINT"TOTAL SS=";S1(I)
870 NEXT I
880 PRINT"TOTAL SS=";S2
890 PRINT"TREAT SS=";S3
900 PRINT"ERROR SS=";S4
910 PRINT"TREATMENT DEGREES OF FREEDOM=";D1
920 PRINT"ERROR DEGREES OF FREEDOM="D2
930 PRINT"TREAT MS=";M1
940 PRINT"ERROR MS=";M2
950 M3=K-1
960 M4=N1-K
970 PRINT"F-TEST RATIO=";F;"WITH";M3;"AND";M4;"DEGREES OF FREEDOM"
980 PRINT"CALCULATIONS COMPLETED"
990 REM - SHOULD ANY EXECUTION TROUBLES DEVELOP, PLEASE REFER THEM TO
1000 REM - THE AUTHOR, JOSE ALONSO, SWINBURNE COLLEGE OF TECHNOLOGY LTD
1010 END

Ready
```

RUN#AV2
ANALYSIS OF VARIANCE—TWO INDEPENDENT VARIABLES

This program evaluates the analysis of variance for two independent variables, a and b, evaluated at k treatment levels indicated by subscript k.

For k = 1, IE· without replications, only classification is calculated.
For k > 1, interaction is also calculated.

The experimental design matrix is as follows:

	Var. 2.				
	Level 1	Level 2	Level 3		Level J
Var. 1					
Level 1	(1,1,1)	(1,2,1)	(1,3,1)	. . . . .	(1,J,1)
	(1,1,2)	(1,2,2)	(1,3,2)	. . . . .	(1,J,2)
	(1,1,3)	(1,2,3)	(1,3,3)	. . . . .	(1,J,3)
	·	·	·		·
	·	·	·		·
	(1,1,K)	(1,2,K)	(1,3,K)	. . . .	(1,J,K)
Level 2	(2,1,1)	(2,2,1)	(2,3,1)	. . . . .	(2,J,1)
	(2,1,2)	(2,2,2)	(2,3,2)	. . . . .	(2,J,2)
	(2,1,3)	(2,2,3)	(2,3,3)	. . . . .	(2,J,3)
	·	·	·		·
	(2,1,K)	(2,2,K)	(2,3,K)	. . . .	(2,J,K)
	·	·	·	. . . . .	·
	·	·	·	. . . . .	·
	·	·	·	. . . . .	·
Level 1	(I,1,1)	(I,2,1)	(I,3,1)	. . . . .	(I,J,1)
	(I,1,2)	(I,2,2)	(I,3,2)	. . . . .	(I,J,1)
	(I,1,3)	(I,2,3)	(I,3,3)	. . . . .	(I,J,3)
	·	·	·		·
	(I,1,K)	(I,2,K)	(I,3,K)	. . . . .	(I,J,K)

PROGRAM RESTRICTIONS

I, J, K may all be different integers, none greater than 10.

INPUT REQUIREMENTS

Integers I, J, and K.

Real values of Y(I,J,K).

PROGRAM OUTPUT

For factors A and B, as well as for the interaction term, the following is calculated: the sum of squares, degrees of freedom, mean sum of squares, F-test ratio and the F-test ratio percentiles.

The error term and its associated sum of squares, degrees of freedom and mean sum of squares are also tabulated, along with the total of the sum of squares and degrees of freedom.

REFERENCES

Walpole, R. E., and Myers, R. H., <u>Probability and Statistics for Engineers and Scientists</u>, Macmillan, New York, 1972.

Mendenhall, W., <u>Introduction to Probability and Statistics</u>, Duxbury Press, New Jersey, 1968.

Bartee, E. M., <u>Engineering Experimental Design Fundamentals</u>, Prentice-Hall, New Jersey, 1968.

Hald, A., <u>Statistical Theory with Engineering Applications</u>, J. Wiley and Sons, New York, 1952.

SAMPLE PROGRAM

In an experiment conducted to determine which of three missile systems is preferable, as well as to determine which of four propellant types is preferable, the observed variable is the distance traveled. Two replications were made of each experimental cell. The experimental design matrix is as follows:

Propellant Type (Four Levels)

Missile System (3 levels)	B1	B2	B3	B4
A1	34.0	30.1	29.8	29.0
	32.7	32.8	26.7	28.9
A2	32.0	30.2	28.7	27.7
	33.2	29.8	28.1	27.8
A3	28.4	27.3	29.7	28.8
	29.3	28.9	27.3	29.1

Or for those readers who prefer a true hierarchical form:

Variable 1, A Missile System	|	i=1				i=2				i=3			
Variable 2, B Propellant Type	j=1	j=2	j=2	j=4	j=1	j=2	j=3	j=4	j=1	j=2	j=3	j=4
Y (k=1)	34	30.1	29.8	29	32	30.2	28.7	27.6	28.4	27.3	29.7	28.8
Y (k=2)	32.7	32.8	26.7	28.9	33.2	29.8	28.1	27.8	29.3	28.9	27.3	29.1

Actual program run begins on page 151.

```
LIST
AV2
1 PRINT"PROGRAM AV2, ANALYSIS OF VARIANCE, TWO INDEPENDENT VARIABLES"
2 PRINT"SHOULD THE MESSAGE 'PROTECTION VIOLATION AT LINE 20' APPEAR"
3 PRINT"YOU SHOULD WAIT FOR A FEW MINUTES AND THEN TRY TO RUN AGAIN"
4 PRINT"THIS PROGRAM USES LARGE VIRTUAL FILES THAT ALLOW ONLY ONE USER"
5 PRINT"TO ACCESS THE VIRTUAL FILES AT ANY ONE TIME FROM ONE ACCOUNT"
10 DIM T(100)
20 OPEN "AV2VIR"AS FILE 1
30 DIM #1,Y(10,100),X(10,10)
40 OPEN "AV2VIS"AS FILE 2
50 DIM #2,S(5),D(5),M(4),F(3),A$(1),B$(1),Z(1)
60 PRINT "THIS PROGRAM CALCULATES A TWO WAY ANALYSIS OF VARIANCE."
70 PRINT "WITH ONE OBSERVATION PER CELL,ONLY CLASSIFICATION IS "
80 PRINT "CALCULATED.IF THE NUMBER OF UNITS PER CELL IS MORE THAN"
90 PRINT "ONE,INTERACTION IS ALSO CALCULATED."
100 PRINT
110 PRINT "FACTOR 1 IS DESIGNATED BY 'VAR.1',AND"
120 PRINT "FACTOR 2 IS DESIGNATED BY 'VAR.2."
130 PRINT
```

```
140 PRINT "A CELL IS DEFINED AS AN INDIVIDUAL (I,J) BLOCK,"
150 PRINT "WITH K REPLICATIONS IN EACH BLOCK."
160 PRINT
170 PRINT "THE EXPERIMENTAL DESIGN MATRIX IS AS FOLLOWS:"
180 PRINT "                    VAR.2."
190 PRINT "        LEVEL     LEVEL     LEVEL          LEVEL"
200 PRINT "VAR.1.    1         2         3    ......    J"
210 PRINT " LEVEL"
220 PRINT "   1.   (1,1,1)   (1,2,1)   (1,3,1) ...... (1,J,1)"
230 PRINT "        (1,1,2)   (1,2,2)   (1,3,2) ...... (1,J,2)"
240 PRINT "        (1,1,3)   (1,2,3)   (1,3,3) ...... (1,J,3)"
250 PRINT "           .         .         .            . "
260 PRINT "           .         .         .            . "
270 PRINT "           .         .         .            . "
280 PRINT "        (1,1,K)   (1,2,K)   (1,3,K) ...... (1,J,K)"
290 PRINT
300 PRINT " LEVEL"
310 PRINT "   2.   (2,1,1)   (2,2,1)   (2,3,1) ...... (2,J,1)"
320 PRINT "        (2,1,2)   (2,2,2)   (2,3,2) ...... (2,J,2)"
330 PRINT "        (2,1,3)   (2,2,3)   (2,3,3) ...... (2,J,3)"
340 PRINT "           .         .         .            . "
350 PRINT "           .         .         .            . "
360 PRINT "           .         .         .            . "
370 PRINT "        (2,1,K)   (2,2,K)   (2,3,K) ...... (2,J,K)"
380 PRINT
390 PRINT "   .       .         .         .     ......   . "
400 PRINT "   .       .         .         .     ......   . "
410 PRINT "   .       .         .         .     ......   . "
420 PRINT "   .       .         .         .     ......   . "
430 PRINT
440 PRINT
450 PRINT " LEVEL"
460 PRINT "   I.   (I,1,1)   (I,2,1)   (I,3,1) ...... (I,J,1)"
470 PRINT "        (I,1,2)   (I,2,2)   (I,3,2) ...... (I,J,2)"
480 PRINT "        (I,1,3)   (I,2,3)   (I,3,3) ...... (I,J,3)"
490 PRINT "           .         .         .            . "
500 PRINT "           .         .         .            . "
510 PRINT "           .         .         .            . "
520 PRINT "        (I,1,K)   (I,2,K)   (I,3,K) ...... (I,J,K)"
530 PRINT
540 PRINT
550 PRINT
560 PRINT "MAX NO OF OBSERVATIONS IS "
570 PRINT "I=10,J=10,K=10"
580 REM - INPUT NAMES OF PARAMETERS
590 PRINT "INPUT ,NAME OF FACTOR 1"
600 INPUT A$(1)
610 PRINT "INPUT ,NAME OF FACTOR 2"
620 INPUT B$(1)
630 REM - READ INPUT DATA PARAMETERS
640 PRINT
650 INPUT "NO OF LEVELS FOR 1,I=",X
660 INPUT "NO OF LEVELS FOR 2,J=",Y
670 INPUT "NO OF REPLICATIONS,K=",Z
680 PRINT
690 REM - CHECK INPUT DATA
700 IF X<2 GO TO 740
710 IF Y<2 GO TO 740
720 IF Z<1 GO TO 740
730 GO TO 760
740 PRINT "INPUT DATA INCORRECT PLEASE RE-ENTER"
750 GO TO 650
760 PRINT
770 REM-ARRAY SET-UP
780 FOR J=1 TO Y STEP 1
790 FOR K=1 TO Z STEP 1
800 X(J,K)=10*J+K
810 NEXT K
```

```
820 NEXT J
830 REM - ENTER DATA
840 PRINT
850 FOR I=1 TO X STEP 1
860   IF Z=1 GO TO 1050
870 F=0
880 FOR J=1 TO Y
890 FOR K=1 TO Z
900 F=F+1
920 PRINT "ENTER VALUE OF Y(";I;",";J;",";K;") ="
930 INPUT T(F)
940 NEXT K
950 NEXT J
960 GOSUB 1140
970 F=0
980 FOR J=1 TO Y
990 FOR K=1 TO Z
1000 F=F+1
1010 Y(I,X(J,K))=T(F)
1020 NEXT K
1030 NEXT J
1040 GO TO 1210
1050 FOR J=1 TO Y
1060 PRINT"ENTER VALUE OF Y(";I;",";J;")="
1070 INPUT T(J)
1080 NEXT J
1090 GOSUB 1140
1100 FOR J=1 TO Y
1110 Y(I,X(J,K))=T(J)
1120 NEXT J
1130 GO TO 1210
1140 REM-CHECK ID DATA IS CORRECT
1150 PRINT "IF DATA IS CORRECT IN LAST BLOCK"
1160 INPUT "PRESS'RETURN',IF INCORRECT PRINT'NO'",C$
1170 PRINT
1180 IF C$ <>"NO"GO TO 1200
1190 I=I-1
1200 RETURN
1210 NEXT I
1220 REM-CALCULATE SUM OF SQUARES
1230 REM- SUM OF ROWS SQUARED   T(1)
1240 T(1)=0
1250 FOR I=1 TO X STEP 1
1260 S1=0
1270 FOR J=1 TO Y STEP 1
1280 FOR K=1 TO Z STEP 1
1290 S1=S1+Y(I,X(J,K))
1300 NEXT K
1310 NEXT J
1320 T(1)=T(1)+(S1**2)
1330 NEXT I
1340 T(1)=T(1)/(Y*Z)
1350 REM- SUM OF COLUMNS SQUARED T(2)
1360 T(2)=0
1370 FOR  J=1 TO Y STEP1
1380 S1=0
1390 FOR I =1 TO X STEP 1
1400   FOR  K=1 TO Z STEP 1
1410 S1=S1 +Y(I,X(J,K))
1420 NEXT K
1430 NEXT I
1440 T(2)=T(2)+(S1**2)
1450 NEXT J
1460 T(2)=T(2)/(X*Z)
1470 REM -TOTAL SUM OF SQUARES   T(3)
1480 REM- TOTAL SUM SQUARED   T(4)
1490   T(3)=0
1500 T(4)=0
```

```
1510 FOR I=1 TO X STEP 1
1520 FOR J=1 TO Y STEP 1
1530 FOR K=1 TO Z STEP 1
1540 T(3)=T(3)+(Y(I,X(J,K))**2)
1550 T(4)=T(4)+Y(I,X(J,K))
1560 NEXT K
1570 NEXT J
1580 NEXT I
1590 T(4)=(T(4)**2)/(X*Y*Z)
1600 IF Z=1 GO TO 1730
1610 REM - SUM OF THE SUM OF EACH CELL SQUARED   T(5)
1620 T(5)=0
1630 FOR  I=1 TO X STEP 1
1640 FOR J=1 TO Y STEP 1
1650 S1=0
1660 FOR K=1 TO Z STEP 1
1670 S1= S1+Y(I,X(J,K))
1680 NEXT K
1690 T(5) =T(5)+(S1**2)
1700 NEXT J
1710 NEXT I
1720 T(5)=T(5)/Z
1730 REM -SUM OF SQUARES      S
1740 REM - DEGREES OF FREEDOM    D
1750 REM - MEAN SUM OF SQUARES    M
1760 REM - ROWS,COLUMNS,TOTAL
1770 S(1)=T(1)-T(4)
1780 D(1)=X-1
1790 M(1)=S(1)/D(1)
1800 S(2)=T(2)-T(4)
1810 D(2)=Y-1
1820 M(2)=S(2)/D(2)
1830 S(5)=T(3)-T(4)
1840 D(5)=(X*Y*Z)-1
1850 REM - RESIDUAL FOR CLASSIFICATION
1860 IF Z>1 GO TO 1920
1870 S(4)=S(5)-S(1)-S(2)
1880 D(4) =(X-1)*(Y-1)
1890 M(4)=S(4)/D(4)
1900 GO TO 2020
1910  REM -RESIDUAL FOR INTERACTION
1920 S(4)=T(3)-T(5)
1930 D(4)=(X*Y*(Z-1))
1940 M(4)=S(4)/D(4)
1950 REM-INTERACTION
1960 S(3)=T(5) -T(4)-(S(1)+S(2))
1970 D(3)=(X-1)*(Y-1)
1980 M(3)=S(3)/D(3)
1990 REM -F TESTS CALCULATED
2000 IF M(4)=0 GO TO 2040
2010 F(3)=M(3)/M(4)
2020 F(1)=M(1)/M(4)
2030 F(2)=M(2)/M(4)
2040 REM - CALCULATIONS COMPLETED
2050 KILL "AV2VIR"
2060 Z(1)=Z
2070 CLOSE #2
2080 CHAIN"(2,4)AV22.BAS"10
2090 PRINT "CALCULATIONS COMPLETED"
2100 END
```

Ready

```
Ready

LIST
AV22
10 OPEN "AV2VIS"AS FILE 2
20 DIM #2,S(5),D(5),M(4),F(3),A$(1),B$(1),Z(1)
30 REM -PRINT RESULTS
40N$(1)="  FACTOR 1"
50 N$(2)="  FACTOR 2"
60 N$(3)="  INTERACTION"
70N$(4)="  ERROR"
80 N$(5)="  TOTAL"
90 L$=" "
100 M$="     "
105 Z=Z(1)
110 PRINT
120 PRINT
130 PRINT
140 PRINT "   SOURCE OF","   SUM  OF"," DEGREES  OF",
150 PRINT "  MEAN  SUM","   F  TEST"
160 PRINT "   VARIATION","   SQUARES","   FREEDOM",
170 PRINT " OF  SQUARES","    RATIO"
180 PRINT " _____"," _____"," _____",
190 PRINT " _____"," _____"
200 PRINT
210 FOR I=1 TO3 STEP 1
220 IF I<3 GO TO 240
230 IF Z=1 GO TO 260
240 PRINT N$(I),L$;S(I),M$;D(I),L$;M(I),L$;F(I)
250 PRINT
260 NEXT I
270 PRINT N$(4),L$;S(4),M$;D(4),L$;M(4)
280 PRINT
290 PRINT N$(5),L$;S(5),M$;D(5)
300 PRINT
310 PRINT
320 PRINT
330 PRINT"FACTOR 1 IS ";A$(1)
340 PRINT "FACTOR 2 IS ";B$(1)
350 PRINT
370 IF M(4)<>0 GO TO 420
380 PRINT"SINCE THE ERROR MEAN SUM OF SQUARES,IS ZERO"
390 PRINT "THEN THE PERCENTILES FOR THE F TEST RATIO'S"
400 PRINT"WILL BE 100%,i.e.PERFECT CORRELATION."
410 GO TO 1480
420 FOR V=1 TO 3 STEP 1
430 IF V<3 GO TO 450
440 IF Z=1 GO TO 900
450 M1=D(V)
460 M2=D(4)
470 X=F(V)
480 C1=INT(M1/2)
490 C2=INT(M2/2)
500 IF (C1-M1/2)==0 GO TO 530
510 IF (C2-M2/2)==0 GO TO 560
520 GO TO 590
530 L=1
540 K=(M1-2)/2
550 GO TO 620
560 L=2
570 K=(M2-2)/2
580 GO TO 620
590 L=3
600 T3=ATN(((M1/M2)*X)**(1/2))
610 GO TO 920
620 T=M2/(M2+M1*X)
630 P=1
640 FOR I=1 TO K STEP 1
```

```
650 ON L GO TO 660,720,780
660 N1=1
670 FOR J=1 TO I STEP 1
680 N1=N1*(M2+2*J-2)/(2*J)
690 NEXT J
700 P=P+N1*(1-T)**I
710 GO TO 800
720 N1=1
730 FOR J=1 TO I STEP 1
740 N1=N1*(M1+2*J-2)/(2*J)
750 NEXT J
760 P=P+N1*T**I
770 GO TO 800
780 N1=1
790 GO TO 800
800  REM NEXT SUM TERM
810 NEXT I
820 ON L GO TO 830,850,860
830 F=P*(T**(M2/2))
840 GO TO 860
850 F=1-((1-T)**(M1/2))*P
860 F=(1-F)*100
870 PRINT "THE F TEST RATIO FOR";N$(V)
880 PRINT "ON THE ";F;"PERCENTILE"
890 PRINT
900 NEXT V
910 GO TO 1480
920 REM M1 AND M2 ARE BOTH ODD
930 REM F=1-A+B3=1-C4+B3
940 REM CALCULATE A
950 IF M2=1 THEN 1110
960 C4=COS (T3)
970 FOR I2=M2-2 TO 3 STEP -2
980 G3=1
990 G6=1
1000 FOR I3=I2-1 TO 2 STEP -2
1010 G3=G3*I3
1020 G6=G6*(I3+1)
1030 NEXT I3
1040 C3=(G3/G6)*(COS(T3)**I2)
1050 C4=C4+C3
1060 NEXT I2
1070 C4=C4*SIN(T3)
1080 C4=C4+T3
1090 C4=(C4*2)/(3.14159)
1100 GO TO 1120
1110 C4=(2*T3)/(3.14159)
1120 REM CALCULATE B3
1130 IF M1=1 THEN 1440
1140 A5=1
1150 FOR I2=2 TO M1-3 STEP 2
1160 A4=1
1170 A2=1
1180 FOR I3=3 TO I2+1 STEP 2
1190 A4=A4*I3
1200 NEXT I3
1210 FOR I3=M2+1 TO M2+(I2-1) STEP 2
1220 A2=A2*I3
1230 NEXT I3
1240 A5=A5+(A2/A4)*(SIN(T3)**I2)
1250 NEXT I2
1260 A5=A5*SIN(T3)*(COS(T3)**M2)
1270 A5=A5*2/(3.14159**.5)
1280 REM CALCULATE TOP FACTORIAL A8
1290 A8=1
1300 FOR A7=1 TO (M2-1)/2 STEP 1
1310 A8=A8*A7
1320 NEXT A7
```

```
1330 REM CALCULATE BOTTOM FACTORIAL B2
1340 Z=((M2-2)/2)+6
1350 G5=((2*3.14159/Z)**.5)*(Z**Z)
1360 E5=-(Z-(1/(12*Z))+(1/(360*Z*Z*Z)))
1370 E5 = EXP(E5)
1380 G5=G5*E5
1390 Z=Z-5
1400 B2=G5/((Z+4)*(Z+3)*(Z+2)*(Z+1)*(Z))
1410 A5=A5*A8/B2
1420 B3=A5
1430 GO TO 1450
1440 B3=0
1450 REM CALCULATE F
1460 F=1-C4+B3
1470 GO TO 860
1480 PRINT "WAIT FOR 'CALCULATIONS COMPLETED'  !!!!!"
1490 KILL "AV2VIS"
1500 CHAIN"(2,4)AV2.BAS"2090
1510 END

Ready
```

```
RUN
AV2
PROGRAM AV2, ANALYSIS OF VARIANCE, TWO INDEPENDENT VARIABLES
SHOULD THE MESSAGE 'PROTECTION VIOLATION AT LINE 20' APPEAR
YOU SHOULD WAIT FOR A FEW MINUTES AND THEN TRY TO RUN AGAIN
THIS PROGRAM USES LARGE VIRTUAL FILES THAT ALLOW ONLY ONE USER
TO ACCESS THE VIRTUAL FILES AT ANY ONE TIME FROM ONE ACCOUNT
THIS PROGRAM CALCULATES A TWO WAY ANALYSIS OF VARIANCE.
WITH ONE OBSERVATION PER CELL,ONLY CLASSIFICATION IS
CALCULATED.IF THE NUMBER OF UNITS PER CELL IS MORE THAN
ONE,INTERACTION IS ALSO CALCULATED.

FACTOR 1 IS DESIGNATED BY 'VAR.1',AND
FACTOR 2 IS DESIGNATED BY 'VAR.2.

A CELL IS DEFINED AS AN INDIVIDUAL (I,J) BLOCK,
WITH K REPLICATIONS IN EACH BLOCK.

THE EXPERIMENTAL DESIGN MATRIX IS AS FOLLOWS:
                      VAR.2.
        LEVEL     LEVEL     LEVEL          LEVEL
VAR.1.    1         2         3    ......     J
  LEVEL
    1.   (1,1,1)   (1,2,1)   (1,3,1) ......  (1,J,1)
         (1,1,2)   (1,2,2)   (1,3,2) ......  (1,J,2)
         (1,1,3)   (1,2,3)   (1,3,3) ......  (1,J,3)
            .         .         .               .
            .         .         .               .
            .         .         .               .
         (1,1,K)   (1,2,K)   (1,3,K) ......  (1,J,K)


  LEVEL
    2.   (2,1,1)   (2,2,1)   (2,3,1) ......  (2,J,1)
         (2,1,2)   (2,2,2)   (2,3,2) ......  (2,J,2)
         (2,1,3)   (2,2,3)   (2,3,3) ......  (2,J,3)
            .         .         .               .
            .         .         .               .
            .         .         .               .
         (2,1,K)   (2,2,K)   (2,3,K) ......  (2,J,K)


      .         .         .         .      ......     .
      .         .         .         .      ......     .
      .         .         .         .      ......     .
      .         .         .         .      ......     .
```

```
LEVEL
  I.   (I,1,1)   (I,2,1)   (I,3,1) ......  (I,J,1)
       (I,1,2)   (I,2,2)   (I,3,2) ......  (I,J,2)
       (I,1,3)   (I,2,3)   (I,3,3) ......  (I,J,3)
          .         .         .              .
          .         .         .              .
          .         .         .              .
       (I,1,K)   (I,2,K)   (I,3,K) ......  (I,J,K)
```

```
MAX NO OF OBSERVATIONS IS
I=10,J=10,K=10
INPUT ,NAME OF FACTOR 1
? MISSILE SYSTEM
INPUT ,NAME OF FACTOR 2
? PROPELLANT TYPE

NO OF LEVELS FOR 1,I=        ? 3
NO OF LEVELS FOR 2,J=        ? 4
NO OF REPLICATIONS,K=        ? 2


ENTER VALUE OF Y( 1 , 1 , 1 ) =
? 34
ENTER VALUE OF Y( 1 , 1 , 2 ) =
? 32.7
ENTER VALUE OF Y( 1 , 2 , 1 ) =
? 30.1
ENTER VALUE OF Y( 1 , 2 , 2 ) =
? 32.8
ENTER VALUE OF Y( 1 , 3 , 1 ) =
? 29.8
ENTER VALUE OF Y( 1 , 3 , 2 ) =
? 26.7
ENTER VALUE OF Y( 1 , 4 , 1 ) =
? 29.0
ENTER VALUE OF Y( 1 , 4 , 2 ) =
? 28.9
IF DATA IS CORRECT IN LAST BLOCK
PRESS'RETURN',IF INCORRECT PRINT'NO'        ?

ENTER VALUE OF Y( 2 , 1 , 1 ) =
? 32
ENTER VALUE OF Y( 2 , 1 , 2 ) =
? 33.2
ENTER VALUE OF Y( 2 , 2 , 1 ) =
? 30.2
ENTER VALUE OF Y( 2 , 2 , 2 ) =
? 29.8
ENTER VALUE OF Y( 2 , 3 , 1 ) =
? 28.7
ENTER VALUE OF Y( 2 , 3 , 2 ) =
? 28.1
ENTER VALUE OF Y( 2 , 4 , 1 ) =
? 27.6
ENTER VALUE OF Y( 2 , 4 , 2 ) =
? 27.8
IF DATA IS CORRECT IN LAST BLOCK
PRESS'RETURN',IF INCORRECT PRINT'NO'        ?

ENTER VALUE OF Y( 3 , 1 , 1 ) =
? 28.4
ENTER VALUE OF Y( 3 , 1 , 2 ) =
? 29.3
ENTER VALUE OF Y( 3 , 2 , 1 ) =
? 27.3
```

```
ENTER VALUE OF Y( 3 , 2 , 2 ) =
? 28.9
ENTER VALUE OF Y( 3 , 3 , 1 ) =
? 29.7
ENTER VALUE OF Y( 3 , 3 , 2 ) =
? 27.3
ENTER VALUE OF Y( 3 , 4 , 1 ) =
? 28.8
ENTER VALUE OF Y( 3 , 4 , 2 ) =
? 29.1
IF DATA IS CORRECT IN LAST BLOCK
PRESS'RETURN',IF INCORRECT PRINT'NO'        ?
```

SOURCE OF VARIATION	SUM OF SQUARES	DEGREES OF FREEDOM	MEAN SUM OF SQUARES	F TEST RATIO
FACTOR 1	14.5254	2	7.2627	5.8444
FACTOR 2	40.084	3	13.3613	10.7521
INTERACTION	22.1602	6	3.69336	2.9721
ERROR	14.9121	12	1.24268	
TOTAL	91.6816	23		

```
FACTOR 1 IS MISSILE SYSTEM
FACTOR 2 IS PROPELLANT TYPE

THE F TEST RATIO FOR  FACTOR 1
ON THE  98.3102 PERCENTILE

THE F TEST RATIO FOR  FACTOR 2
ON THE  99.8979 PERCENTILE

THE F TEST RATIO FOR  INTERACTION
ON THE  94.8788 PERCENTILE

WAIT FOR 'CALCULATIONS COMPLETED'  !!!!!
CALCULATIONS COMPLETED

Ready
```

RUN#AV3
ANALYSIS OF VARIANCE—THREE INDEPENDENT VARIABLES

This program evaluates the analysis of variance for three independent variables, A, B, and C, evaluated at L treatment levels, indicated by the subscript L.

For L = 1, that is, without replications, only classification is calculated.
For L > 1, interaction as well as classification is calculated.

The experimental design matrix is as follows:

```
                        Variable B = 1

                        Variable C

           Level       Level                    Level
  Var. A   1           2                         J
  Level
   1      (1,1,1,1)    (1,1,2,1)   . . . . .     (1,1,K,1)
          (1,1,1,2)    (1,1,2,2)   . . . . .     (1,1,K,2)
             .            .                         .
             .            .                         .
             .            .                         .
          (1,1,1,L)    (1,1,2,L)   . . . . .     (1,1,K,L)

  Level
   2      (2,1,1,1)    (2,1,2,1)   . . . . .     (2,1,K,1)
          (2,1,1,2)    (2,1,2,2)   . . . . .     (2,1,K,2)
             .            .                         .
             .            .                         .
          (2,1,1,L)    (2,1,2,L)   . . . . .     (2,1,K,L)

     .        .            .       . . . . .        .
     .        .            .       . . . . .        .
     .        .            .       . . . . .        .

  Level
   I      (I,1,1,1)    (I,1,2,1)   . . . . .     (I,1,K,1)
          (I,1,1,2)    (I,1,2,2)   . . . . .     (I,1,K,2)
             .            .                         .
             .            .                         .
          (I,1,1,L)    (I,1,2,L)   . . . . .     (I,1,K,L)
```

The above then repeats itself, except that B = 2, and then B = 3, and so on until B = J. The last line for B = 2 would then become:

```
             .            .                         .
          (I,1,2,L)    (I,2,2,L)   . . . . .     (I,2,K,L)
```

And then B = 3 and so on until B = J, thus making the last line:

```
             .            .                         .
          (I,1,K,L)    (I,2,K,L)   . . . . .     (I,J,K,L)
```

PROGRAM RESTRICTIONS

I, J, K, and L may all be different integers, none greater than 9.

INPUT REQUIREMENTS

Integers I, J, K, and L.
Real values of Y(I,J,K,L).

PROGRAM OUTPUT

For one-factor classification, two-factor interaction, and three-factor interaction, the following is calculated: the sum of squares, degrees of freedom, mean sum of squares, F-test ratio, and the F-test ratio percentiles.

The error term and its associated sum of squares, degrees of freedom, and mean sum of squares are also tabulated, along with the total of the sum of squares and degrees of freedom.

REFERENCES

Walpole, R. E., and Myers, R. H., <u>Probability and Statistics for Engineers and Scientists</u>, Macmillan, New York, 1972.

Mendenhall, W., <u>Introduction to Probability and Statistics</u>, Duxbury Press, Massachusetts, 1975.

Bartee, E. M., <u>Engineering Experimental Design Fundamentals</u>, Prentice-Hall, New Jersey, 1968.

Hald, A., <u>Statistical Theory with Engineering Applications</u>, J. Wiley and Sons, New York, 1952.

SAMPLE PROGRAM

In the production of a particular material, three variables are of interest:

A. the operator used,

B. the catalyst type, and

C. the washing time, minutes per batch.

The observed variable Y is the weight of product produced in one batch. Three replications were made of each experimental cell. The experimental design matrix is as follows:

	Catalyst Type					
	B1		B2		B3	
	Washing Time					
Operator	C1	C2	C1	C2	C1	C2
A1	10.7	10.9	10.3	10.5	11.2	12.2
	10.8	12.1	10.2	11.1	11.6	11.7
	11.3	11.5	10.5	10.3	12.0	11.0
A2	11.4	9.8	10.2	12.6	10.7	10.8
	11.8	11.3	10.9	7.5	10.5	10.2
	11.5	10.9	10.5	9.9	10.2	11.5
A3	13.6	10.7	12.0	10.2	11.1	11.9
	14.1	11.7	11.6	11.5	11.0	11.6
	14.5	12.7	11.5	10.9	11.5	12.2

Or, for those readers who prefer a true hierarchical form:

Variable 1, A Operator	i=1						i=2						i=3					
Variable 2, B Catalyst Type	j=1		j=2		j=3		j=1		j=2		j=3		j=1		j=2		j=3	
Variable 3, C Washing Time	k=1	k=2	k=1	k=2	k=1	k=2	k=1	k=2	k=1	k=2	k=1	k=2	k=1	k=2	k=1	k=2	k=1	k=2
$Y (\ell = 1)$	10.7	10.9	10.3	10.5	11.2	12.2	11.4	9.8	10.2	12.6	10.7	10.8	13.6	10.7	12.0	10.2	11.1	11.9
$Y (\ell = 2)$	10.8	12.1	10.2	11.1	11.6	11.7	11.8	11.3	10.9	7.5	10.5	10.2	14.1	11.7	11.2	11.5	11.0	11.6
$Y (\ell = 3)$	11.3	11.5	10.5	10.3	12.0	11.0	11.5	10.9	10.5	9.9	10.2	11.5	14.5	12.7	11.3	10.9	11.5	12.2

```
RUN  ZAV3
THIS PROGRAM CALCULATES A THREE WAY ANALYSIS OF VARIANCE.
WITH ONE OBSERVATION PER CELL,ONLY CLASSIFICATION IS
CALCULATED.IF THE NUMBER PER CELL IS GREATER THAN ONE,
INTERACTION IS ALSO CALCULATED FOR THE DEPENDENT
VARIABLE WITH EACH OF THE INDEPENDENT VARIABLES,AND
IT IS ALSO CALCULATED FOR THE INDEPENDENT VARIABLES
IN RELATION TO EACH OTHER.

CONSIDER THE FOLLOWING COMPLETE FACTORIAL DESIGN WITH
THREE INDEPENDENT VARIABLES A,B AND C AND ONE DEPENDENT
VARIABLE Y.

VARIABLE A IS EVALUATED AT I LEVELS,i=1,2,....,I
VARIABLE B IS EVALUATED AT J LEVELS,j=1,2,....,J
VARIABLE C IS EVALUATED AT K LEVELS,k=1,2,....,K
EVERY VALUE OF Y(A,B,C) IS REPLICATED L TIMES,l=1,2,....,L

THE EXPERIMENTAL DESIGN MATRIX IS AS FOLLOWS:


             VARIABLE B=1

                 VARIABLE C
         LEVEL    LEVEL              LEVEL
VAR.A     1        2                  K
  LEVEL
   1.   (1,1,1,1) (1,1,2,1) ...... (1,1,K,1)
        (1,1,1,2) (1,1,2,2) ...... (1,1,K,2)
           .         .               .
           .         .               .
           .         .               .
        (1,1,1,L) (1,1,2,L) ...... (1,1,K,L)


  LEVEL
   2.   (2,1,1,1) (2,1,2,1) ...... (2,1,K,1)
        (2,1,1,2) (2,1,2,2) ...... (2,1,K,2)
           .         .               .
           .         .               .
           .         .               .
        (2,1,1,L) (2,1,2,L) ...... (2,1,K,L)


     .        .         .    ......    .
     .        .         .    ......    .
     .        .         .    ......    .

  LEVEL
   I.   (I,1,1,1) (I,1,2,1) ...... (I,1,K,1)
        (I,1,1,2) (I,1,2,2) ...... (I,1,K,2)
           .         .               .
           .         .               .
           .         .               .
        (I,1,1,L) (I,1,2,L) ...... (I,1,K,L)

THE ABOVE THEN REPEATS ITSELF,EXCEPT THAT B=2,
AND THEN B=3 AND SO ON UNTIL B=J.

THE LAST LINE FOR B=2 WOULD THEN BECOME:
           .         .               .
           .         .               .
        (I,1,2,L) (I,2,2,L) ...... (I,2,K,L)'

AND THEN B=3 AND SO ON UNTIL B=J,THUS MAKING THE LAST LINE:
           .         .               .
           .         .               .
        (I,1,K,L) (I,2,K,L) ...... (I,J,K,L)

INPUT,NAME OF FACTOR 1
? OPERATORS
```

```
INPUT,NAME OF FACTOR 2
? CATALYSTS

INPUT,NAME OF FACTOR 3
? WASHING TIME

MAXIMUM No. OF LEVELS FOR ; I=9 , J=9 , K-9 , L=9
NO OF LEVELS FOR 1,I=         ? 3
NO OF LEVELS FOR 2,J=         ? 3
NO OF LEVELS FOR 3,K=         ? 2
NO OF REPLICATIONS,L=         ? 3


ENTER VALUE OF Y( 1 , 1 , 1 , 1 ) =
? 10.7
ENTER VALUE OF Y( 1 , 1 , 1 , 2 ) =
? 10.8
ENTER VALUE OF Y( 1 , 1 , 1 , 3 ) =
? 11.3
ENTER VALUE OF Y( 1 , 1 , 2 , 1 ) =
? 10.9
ENTER VALUE OF Y( 1 , 1 , 2 , 2 ) =
? 12.1
ENTER VALUE OF Y( 1 , 1 , 2 , 3 ) =
? 11.5

IF DATA IS CORRECT , IN LAST BLOCK
PRESS 'RETURN' , IF INCORRECT PRINT 'NO'  ?

ENTER VALUE OF Y( 1 , 2 , 1 , 1 ) =
?
ENTER VALUE OF Y( 1 , 2 , 1 , 2 ) =
? 10.2
ENTER VALUE OF Y( 1 , 2 , 1 , 3 ) =
? 10.5
ENTER VALUE OF Y( 1 , 2 , 2 , 1 ) =
? 10.5
ENTER VALUE OF Y( 1 , 2 , 2 , 2 ) =
? 11.1
ENTER VALUE OF Y( 1 , 2 , 2 , 3 ) =
? 10.3

IF DATA IS CORRECT , IN LAST BLOCK
PRESS 'RETURN' , IF INCORRECT PRINT 'NO'  ? NO

ENTER VALUE OF Y( 1 , 2 , 1 , 1 ) =
? 10.3
ENTER VALUE OF Y( 1 , 2 , 1 , 2 ) =
? 10.2
ENTER VALUE OF Y( 1 , 2 , 1 , 3 ) =
? 10.5
ENTER VALUE OF Y( 1 , 2 , 2 , 1 ) =
? 10.5
ENTER VALUE OF Y( 1 , 2 , 2 , 2 ) =
? 11.1
ENTER VALUE OF Y( 1 , 2 , 2 , 3 ) =
? 10.3

IF DATA IS CORRECT , IN LAST BLOCK
PRESS 'RETURN' , IF INCORRECT PRINT 'NO'  ?

ENTER VALUE OF Y( 1 , 3 , 1 , 1 ) =
? 11.2
ENTER VALUE OF Y( 1 , 3 , 1 , 2 ) =
? 11.6
ENTER VALUE OF Y( 1 , 3 , 1 , 3 ) =
? 12.0
```

```
ENTER VALUE OF Y( 1 , 3 , 2 , 1 ) =
? 12.2
ENTER VALUE OF Y( 1 , 3 , 2 , 2 ) =
? 11.7
ENTER VALUE OF Y( 1 , 3 , 2 , 3 ) =
? 11.0


IF DATA IS CORRECT , IN LAST BLOCK
PRESS 'RETURN' , IF INCORRECT PRINT 'NO'  ?

ENTER VALUE OF Y( 2 , 1 , 1 , 1 ) =
? 11.4
ENTER VALUE OF Y( 2 , 1 , 1 , 2 ) =
? 11.8
ENTER VALUE OF Y( 2 , 1 , 1 , 3 ) =
? 11.5
ENTER VALUE OF Y( 2 , 1 , 2 , 1 ) =
? 9.8
ENTER VALUE OF Y( 2 , 1 , 2 , 2 ) =
? 11.3
ENTER VALUE OF Y( 2 , 1 , 2 , 3 ) =
? 10.9


IF DATA IS CORRECT , IN LAST BLOCK
PRESS 'RETURN' , IF INCORRECT PRINT 'NO'  ?

ENTER VALUE OF Y( 2 , 2 , 1 , 1 ) =
? 10.2
ENTER VALUE OF Y( 2 , 2 , 1 , 2 ) =
? 10.9
ENTER VALUE OF Y( 2 , 2 , 1 , 3 ) =
? 10.5
ENTER VALUE OF Y( 2 , 2 , 2 , 1 ) =
? 12.6
ENTER VALUE OF Y( 2 , 2 , 2 , 2 ) =
? 7.5
ENTER VALUE OF Y( 2 , 2 , 2 , 3 ) =
? 9.9


IF DATA IS CORRECT , IN LAST BLOCK
PRESS 'RETURN' , IF INCORRECT PRINT 'NO'  ?

ENTER VALUE OF Y( 2 , 3 , 1 , 1 ) =
? 10.7
ENTER VALUE OF Y( 2 , 3 , 1 , 2 ) =
? 10.5
ENTER VALUE OF Y( 2 , 3 , 1 , 3 ) =
? 10.2
ENTER VALUE OF Y( 2 , 3 , 2 , 1 ) =
? 10.8
ENTER VALUE OF Y( 2 , 3 , 2 , 2 ) =
? 10.2
ENTER VALUE OF Y( 2 , 3 , 2 , 3 ) =
? 11.5


IF DATA IS CORRECT , IN LAST BLOCK
PRESS 'RETURN' , IF INCORRECT PRINT 'NO'  ?

ENTER VALUE OF Y( 3 , 1 , 1 , 1 ) =
? 13.6
ENTER VALUE OF Y( 3 , 1 , 1 , 2 ) =
? 14.1
ENTER VALUE OF Y( 3 , 1 , 1 , 3 ) =
? 14.5
ENTER VALUE OF Y( 3 , 1 , 2 , 1 ) =
? 10.7
ENTER VALUE OF Y( 3 , 1 , 2 , 2 ) =
? 11.7
ENTER VALUE OF Y( 3 , 1 , 2 , 3 ) =
? 12.7
```

```
IF DATA IS CORRECT , IN LAST BLOCK
PRESS 'RETURN' , IF INCORRECT PRINT 'NO'  ?

ENTER VALUE OF Y( 3 , 2 , 1 , 1 ) =
? 12.0
ENTER VALUE OF Y( 3 , 2 , 1 , 2 ) =
? 11.6
ENTER VALUE OF Y( 3 , 2 , 1 , 3 ) =
? 11.5
ENTER VALUE OF Y( 3 , 2 , 2 , 1 ) =
? 10.2
ENTER VALUE OF Y( 3 , 2 , 2 , 2 ) =
? 11.5
ENTER VALUE OF Y( 3 , 2 , 2 , 3 ) =
? 10.9

IF DATA IS CORRECT , IN LAST BLOCK
PRESS 'RETURN' , IF INCORRECT PRINT 'NO'  ?

ENTER VALUE OF Y( 3 , 3 , 1 , 1 ) =
? 11.1
ENTER VALUE OF Y( 3 , 3 , 1 , 2 ) =
? 11.0
ENTER VALUE OF Y( 3 , 3 , 1 , 3 ) =
? 11.5
ENTER VALUE OF Y( 3 , 3 , 2 , 1 ) =
? 11.9
ENTER VALUE OF Y( 3 , 3 , 2 , 2 ) =
? 11.6
ENTER VALUE OF Y( 3 , 3 , 2 , 3 ) =
? 12.2

IF DATA IS CORRECT , IN LAST BLOCK
PRESS 'RETURN' , IF INCORRECT PRINT 'NO'  ?
```

SOURCE OF VARIATION	SUM OF SQUARES	DEGREES OF FREEDOM	MEAN SUM OF SQUARES	F TEST RATIO
1 FACTOR CLASSIFICATION				
1	13.98	2	6.98999	11.6428
2	10.1802	2	5.09009	8.47827
3	1.18408	1	1.18408	1.97226
2 FACTOR INTERACTION				
1*2	4.77783	4	1.19446	1.98954
2*3	3.63574	2	1.81787	3.02792
1*3	2.91504	2	1.45752	2.42771
3 FACTOR INTERACTION				
1*2*3	4.90479	4	1.2262	2.0424
ERROR	21.6133	36	.600369	
TOTAL	63.1909	53		

FACTOR   1   IS OPERATORS

FACTOR   2   IS CATALYSTS

FACTOR   3   IS WASHING TIME

1 FACTOR   CLASSIFICATION

THE F TEST RATIO FOR 1 LIES
     ON THE   99.9874 PERCENTILE

THE F TEST RATIO FOR 2 LIES
     ON THE   99.9039 PERCENTILE

THE F TEST RATIO FOR 3 LIES
     ON THE   83.1222 PERCENTILE

2 FACTOR   INTERACTION

THE F TEST RATIO FOR 1*2 LIES
     ON THE   88.3047 PERCENTILE

THE F TEST RATIO FOR 2*3 LIES
     ON THE   93.9107 PERCENTILE

THE F TEST RATIO FOR 1*3 LIES
     ON THE   89.7446 PERCENTILE

3 FACTOR   INTERACTION

THE F TEST RATIO FOR 1*2*3 LIES
     ON THE   89.0948 PERCENTILE

WAIT FOR 'CALCULATIONS COMPLETED' !!!!
CALCULATIONS COMPLETED

Ready

```
Ready

LIST
AV3
10 DIM C(81)
20 OPEN "AV3VIR" AS FILE 1
30 DIM #1,Z(9,729),Y(9,81),X(9,9)
40 OPEN "AV3VIS" AS FILE 2
50 DIM #2,S(9),D(9),M(9),F(9),A$(3),N(1)
60 REM - ANALYSIS OF VARIANCE 3 WAY
70 PRINT "THIS PROGRAM CALCULATES A THREE WAY ANALYSIS OF VARIANCE."
80 PRINT "WITH ONE OBSERVATION PER CELL,ONLY CLASSIFICATION IS"
90 PRINT "CALCULATED.IF THE NUMBER PER CELL IS GREATER THAN ONE,"
100 PRINT "INTERACTION IS ALSO CALCULATED FOR THE DEPENDENT"
110 PRINT "VARIABLE WITH EACH OF THE INDEPENDENT VARIABLES,AND"
120 PRINT "IT IS ALSO CALCULATED FOR THE INDEPENDENT VARIABLES"
130 PRINT "IN RELATION TO EACH OTHER."
140 PRINT
150 PRINT "CONSIDER THE FOLLOWING COMPLETE FACTORIAL DESIGN WITH"
160 PRINT "THREE INDEPENDENT VARIABLES A,B AND C AND ONE DEPENDENT"
170 PRINT "VARIABLE Y."
180 PRINT
190 PRINT "VARIABLE A IS EVALUATED AT I LEVELS,i=1,2,.....,I"
200 PRINT "VARIABLE B IS EVALUATED AT J LEVELS,j=1,2,.....,J"
210 PRINT "VARIABLE C IS EVALUATED AT K LEVELS,k=1,2,.....,K"
220 PRINT "EVERY VALUE OF Y(A,B,C) IS REPLICATED L TIMES,l=1,2,.....,L"
230 PRINT
240 PRINT "THE EXPERIMENTAL DESIGN MATRIX IS AS FOLLOWS:"
250 PRINT
260 PRINT "                    VARIABLE B=1"
270 PRINT
280 PRINT "                    VARIABLE C"
290 PRINT "          LEVEL        LEVEL              LEVEL"
300 PRINT "VAR.A       1            2                  K"
310 PRINT " LEVEL"
320 PRINT "    1.  (1,1,1,1)  (1,1,2,1) ...... (1,1,K,1)"
330 PRINT "        (1,1,1,2)  (1,1,2,2) ...... (1,1,K,2)"
340 PRINT "            .          .               ."
350 PRINT "            .          .               ."
360 PRINT "            .          .               ."
370 PRINT "        (1,1,1,L)  (1,1,2,L) ...... (1,1,K,L)"
380 PRINT
390 PRINT " LEVEL"
400 PRINT "    2.  (2,1,1,1)  (2,1,2,1) ...... (2,1,K,1)"
410 PRINT "        (2,1,1,2)  (2,1,2,2) ...... (2,1,K,2)"
420 PRINT "            .          .               ."
430 PRINT "            .          .               ."
440 PRINT "            .          .               ."
450 PRINT "        (2,1,1,L)  (2,1,2,L) ...... (2,1,K,L)"
460 PRINT
470 PRINT "     .        .          .      ......    ."
480 PRINT "     .        .          .      ......    ."
490 PRINT "     .        .          .      ......    ."
500 PRINT
510 PRINT " LEVEL"
520 PRINT "    I.  (I,1,1,1)  (I,1,2,1) ...... (I,1,K,1)"
530 PRINT "        (I,1,1,2)  (I,1,2,2) ...... (I,1,K,2)"
540 PRINT "            .          .               ."
550 PRINT "            .          .               ."
560 PRINT "            .          .               ."
570 PRINT "        (I,1,1,L)  (I,1,2,L) ...... (I,1,K,L)"
580 PRINT
590 PRINT "THE ABOVE THEN REPEATS ITSELF,EXCEPT THAT B=2,"
600 PRINT "AND THEN B=3 AND SO ON UNTIL B=J."
610 PRINT
620 PRINT "THE LAST LINE FOR B=2 WOULD THEN BECOME:"
630 PRINT "        .          .          .      ."
640 PRINT "        .          .          .      ."
```

```
650 PRINT "          (I,1,2,L)  (I,2,2,L) ....... (I,2,K,L)'
660 PRINT
670 PRINT "AND THEN B=3 AND SO ON UNTIL B=J,THUS MAKING THE LAST LINE:"
680 PRINT "            .              .                  ."
690 PRINT "            .              .                  ."
700 PRINT "          (I,1,K,L)  (I,2,K,L) ....... (I,J,K,L)"
710 PRINT
720 REM-INPUT NAMES OF PARAMETERS
730 FOR I=1 TO 3 STEP 1
740 PRINT "INPUT,NAME OF FACTOR";I
750 INPUT A$(I)
760 PRINT
770 NEXT I
780 REM-READ INPUT DATA PARAMETERS
790 PRINT "MAXIMUM No. OF LEVELS FOR ; I=9 , J=9 , K-9 , L=9"
800 INPUT "NO OF LEVELS FOR 1,I=",X
810 INPUT "NO OF LEVELS FOR 2,J=",Y
820 INPUT "NO OF LEVELS FOR 3,K=",Z
830 INPUT "NO OF REPLICATIONS,L=",N
840 PRINT
850 REM-CHECK INPUT DATA
860 IF X<2 GO TO 910
870 IF Y<2 GO TO 910
880 IF Z<2 GO TO 910
890 IF N<1 GO TO 910
900 GO TO 930
910 PRINT "INPUT DATA INCORRECT PLEASE RE-ENTER"
920 GO TO 800
930 PRINT
940 REM-ARRAY SET-UP
950 FOR J=1 TO Y STEP 1
960 FOR K=1 TO Z STEP 1
970 FOR L=1 TO N STEP 1
980 X(K,L) = 9*K+L-9
990 Y(J,X(K,L)) = 81*J+X(K,L)-81
1000 NEXT L
1010 NEXT K
1020 NEXT J
1030 REM-ENTER DATA
1040 FOR I=1 TO X STEP 1
1050 FOR J=1 TO Y STEP 1
1060 F=0
1070 IF N=1 GO TO 1240
1080 FOR K=1 TO Z STEP 1
1090 FOR L=1 TO N STEP 1
1100 F=F+1
1110 PRINT "ENTER VALUE OF Y(";I;",";J;",";K;",";L;") ="
1120 INPUT C(F)
1130 NEXT L
1140 NEXT K
1150 F=0
1160 FOR K=1 TO Z STEP 1
1170 FOR L=1 TO N STEP 1
1180 F = F + 1
1190 Z(I,Y(J,X(K,L)))=C(F)
1200 NEXT L
1210 NEXT K
1220 GOSUB 1330
1230 GO TO 1410
1240 FOR K=1 TO Z STEP 1
1250 PRINT "ENTER VALUE OF Y(";I;",";J;",";K;") ="
1260 INPUT C(K)
1270 NEXT K
1280 FOR K=1 TO Z STEP 1
1290 Z(I,Y(J,X(K,L)))=C(K)
1300 NEXT K
1310 GOSUB 1330
1320 GO TO 1410
```

```
1330 PRINT
1340 REM-CHECK IF DATA CORRECT
1350 PRINT "IF DATA IS CORRECT , IN LAST BLOCK"
1360 INPUT "PRESS 'RETURN' , IF INCORRECT PRINT 'NO'",B$
1370 PRINT
1380 IF B$<>"NO"GO TO 1400
1390 J = J - 1
1400 RETURN
1410 NEXT J
1420 NEXT I
1430 REM-CALCULATE TOTAL SUMS THEN SQUARE
1440 FOR F= 1 TO 9 STEP 1
1450 ON F GO TO 1460,1500,1540,1460,1500,1540,1460,1460,1460
1460 B=X
1470 C=Y
1480 D=Z
1490 GO TO 1570
1500 B=Y
1510 C=Z
1520 D=X
1530 GO TO 1570
1540 B=Z
1550 C=X
1560 D=Y
1570 S(F)=0
1580 T(F) = 0
1590 FOR I=1 TO B STEP 1
1600 IF F>3 GO TO 1620
1610 S(F)=0
1620 FOR J=1 TO C STEP 1
1630 IF F>6 GO TO 1660
1640 IF F <4 GO TO 1660
1650 S(F)=0
1660 FOR K=1 TO D STEP 1
1670 IF F<>7 GO TO 1690
1680 S(F)=0
1690 FOR L=1 TO N STEP 1
1700 ON F GO TO 1710,1730,1750,1710,1730,1750,1710,1710,1770
1710 S(F)=S(F)+Z(I,Y(J,X(K,L)))
1720 GO TO 1780
1730 S(F)=S(F)+Z(K,Y(I,X(J,L)))
1740 GO TO 1780
1750 S(F)=S(F)+Z(J,Y(K,X(I,L)))
1760 GO TO 1780
1770 S(F)=S(F)+(Z(I,Y(J,X(K,L))))**2)
1780 NEXT L
1790 IF F<>7 GO TO 1810
1800 T(F)=T(F)+(S(F)**2)
1810 NEXT K
1820 IF F >6 GO TO 1850
1830 IF F <4 GO TO 1850
1840 T(F)=T(F)+(S(F)**2)
1850 NEXT J
1860 IF F>3 GO TO 1880
1870 T(F)=T(F)+(S(F)**2)
1880 NEXT I
1890 ON F GO TO 1900,1900,1900,1920,1920,1920,1940,1960,1980
1900 T(F)=T(F)/(C*D*N)
1910 GO TO 1990
1920 T(F)=T(F)/(D*N)
1930 GO TO 1990
1940 T(F)=T(F)/N
1950 GO TO 1990
1960 T(F)=(S(F)**2)/(B*C*D*N)
1970 GO TO 1990
1980 T(F)=S(F)
1990 NEXT F
2000 REM-CALCULATE SUM OF SQUARES,DEGREES OF FREEDOM.
```

```
2010 S(1)=T(1)-T(8)
2020 D(1)=X-1
2030 S(2)=T(2)-T(8)
2040 D(2)=Y-1
2050 S(3)=T(3)-T(8)
2060 D(3)=Z-1
2070 S(4)=T(4)-T(1)-T(2)+T(8)
2080 D(4)=D(1)*D(2)
2090 S(5)=T(5)-T(2)-T(3)+T(8)
2100 D(5)=D(2)*D(3)
2110 S(6)=T(6)-T(1)-T(3)+T(8)
2120 D(6)=D(1)*D(3)
2130 IF N=1 GO TO 2190
2140 S(7)=T(7)-S(4)-T(5)-T(6)+T(3)
2150 D(7) =D(4)*D(3)
2160 S(8)=T(9)-T(7)
2170 D(8)=X*Y*Z*(N-1)
2180 GO TO 2210
2190 S(8)=T(9)+T(3)-S(4)-T(5)-T(6)
2200 D(8)=(X*Y*Z)-(X*Y)-(Y*Z)-(X*Z)+X+Y+Z-1
2210 S(9)=T(9)-T(8)
2220 D(9)=(X*Y*Z*N)-1
2230 REM -CALCULATE MEAN SQUARES
2240 FOR F=1 TO 8 STEP 1
2250 IF F<>7 GO TO 2270
2260 IF N=1 GO TO 2280
2270 M(F)=S(F)/D(F)
2280 NEXT F
2290 REM -CALCULATE F TEST RATIO
2300 IF M(8) <> 0 GO TO 2320
2310 GO TO 2370
2320 FOR G=1 TO 7 STEP 1
2330 IF G<>7 GO TO 2350
2340 IF N=1 GO TO 2360
2350 F(G)=M(G)/M(8)
2360 NEXT G
2370 KILL "AV3VIR"
2380 N(1) = N
2390 CLOSE # 2
2400 CHAIN "(2,4)AV33.BAS<40>"10
2410 PRINT "CALCULATIONS COMPLETED"
2420 END
```

Ready

```
Ready

LIST
AV33
10 OPEN "AV3VIS" AS FILE 2
20 DIM #2,S(9),D(9),M(9),F(9),A$(3),N(1)
30 N=N(1)
40 N$(1)="1"
50 N$(2)="2"
60 N$(3)="3"
70 N$(4)="1*2"
80 N$(5)="2*3"
90 N$(6)="1*3"
100 N$(7)="1*2*3"
110 N$(8)="ERROR"
120 N$(9)="TOTAL"
130 L$=" "
140 M$="       "
150 PRINT
160 PRINT
170 PRINT
180 PRINT " SOURCE OF","  SUM  OF"," DEGREES  OF",
190 PRINT "  MEAN  SUM","  F  TEST"
200 PRINT " VARIATION","  SQUARES","   FREEDOM",
210 PRINT " OF  SQUARES","  RATIO"
220 PRINT " _____","  _____"," _____",
230 PRINT " _____","  _____"
240 PRINT
250 G$(1)="CLASSIFICATION"
260 G$(2)="INTERACTION"
270 G$(3)=G$(2)
280 F$=" FACTOR "
290 I=0
300 FOR F=1 TO 3 STEP 1
310 IF F<3 GO TO 330
320 IF N=1 GO TO 450
330 PRINT F;F$
340 PRINT G$(F)
350 PRINT
360 FOR G=1 TO 3 STEP 1
370 IF F<3 GO TO 390
380 IF G>1 GO TO 430
390 I=I+1
400 IF M(8) = 0 THEN F(I) = 0
410 PRINT M$;N$(I),L$;S(I),M$;D(I),L$;M(I),L$;F(I)
420 PRINT
430 NEXT G
440 PRINT
450 NEXT F
460 PRINT M$;N$(8),L$;S(8),M$;D(8),L$;M(8)
470 PRINT
480 PRINT M$;N$(9),L$;S(9),M$;D(9)
490 PRINT
500 PRINT
510 PRINT
520 PRINT
530 FOR I=1 TO 3 STEP 1
540 PRINT F$;I;" IS ";A$(I)
550 PRINT
560 NEXT I
570 IF M(8) <> 0 GO TO 620
580 PRINT "SINCE THE ERROR MEAN SUM OF SQUARES,IS ZERO"
590 PRINT "THEN THE PERCENTILES FOR THE F TEST RATIO'S"
600 PRINT "WILL BE  100 % ie PERFECT CORRELATION"
610 GO TO 1820
620 REM - CALCULATE F TEST PERCENTILES
630 FOR V=1 TO 7 STEP 1
640 IF V<7 GO TO 660
```

```
650 IF N = 1 GO TO 1080
660 M1 = D(V)
670 M2 = D(8)
680 X=ABS(F(V))
690 C1=INT(M1/2)
700 C2=INT(M2/2)
710 IF (C1-M1/2)==0 GO TO 740
720 IF (C2-M2/2)==0 GO TO 770
730 GO TO 800
740 L=1
750 K=(M1-2)/2
760 GO TO 830
770 L=2
780 K=(M2-2)/2
790 GO TO 830
800 L=3
810 T3=ATN(((M1/M2)*X)**(1/2))
820 GO TO 1260
830 T=M2/(M2+M1*X)
840 P=1
850 FOR I=1 TO K STEP 1
860 ON L GO TO 870,930,990
870 N1=1
880 FOR J=1 TO I STEP 1
890 N1=N1*(M2+2*J-2)/(2*J)
900 NEXT J
910 P=P+N1*(1-T)**I
920 GO TO 1010
930 N1=1
940 FOR J=1 TO I STEP 1
950 N1=N1*(M1+2*J-2)/(2*J)
960 NEXT J
970 P=P+N1*T**I
980 GO TO 1010
990 N1=1
1000 GO TO 1010
1010   REM NEXT SUM TERM
1020 NEXT I
1030 ON L GO TO 1040,1060,1070
1040 F=P*(T**(M2/2))
1050 GO TO 1070
1060 F=1-((1-T)**(M1/2))*P
1070 U(V) = (1-F)*100
1080 NEXT V
1090 I = 0
1100 FOR G = 1 TO 3 STEP 1
1110 IF G < 3 GO TO 1130
1120 IF N = 1 GO TO 1240
1130 PRINT G;F$;" ";G$(G)
1140 PRINT
1150 FOR H = 1 TO 3 STEP 1
1160 IF G < 3 GO TO 1180
1170 IF H > 1 GO TO 1220
1180 I = I + 1
1190 PRINT L$;"THE F TEST RATIO FOR ";N$(I);" LIES"
1200 PRINT M$;"ON THE ";U(I);" PERCENTILE"
1210 PRINT
1220 NEXT H
1230 PRINT
1240 NEXT G
1250 GO TO 1820
1260 REM M1 AND M2 ARE BOTH ODD
1270 REM F=1-A+B3=1-C4+B3
1280 REM CALCULATE A
1290 IF M2=1 THEN 1450
1300 C4=COS(T3)
1310 FOR I2 =M2-2 TO 3 STEP -2
1320 G3=1
```

```
1330 G6=1
1340 FOR I3=I2-1 TO 2 STEP -2
1350 G3=G3*I3
1360 G6=G6*(I3+1)
1370 NEXT I3
1380 C3=(G3/G6)*(COS(T3)**I2)
1390 C4=C4+C3
1400 NEXT I2
1410 C4=C4*SIN(T3)
1420 C4=C4+T3
1430 C4=(C4*2)/(3.14159)
1440 GO TO 1460
1450 C4=(2*T3)/(3.14159)
1460 REM CALCULATE B3
1470 IF M1=1 THEN 1780
1480 A5=1
1490 FOR I2=2 TO M1-3 STEP 2
1500 A4=1
1510 A2=1
1520 FOR I3=3 TO I2+1 STEP 2
1530 A4=A4*I3
1540 NEXT I3
1550 FOR I3=M2+1 TO M2+(I2-1) STEP 2
1560 A2=A2*I3
1570 NEXT I3
1580 A5=A5+(A2/A4)*(SIN(T3)**I2)
1590 NEXT I2
1600 A5=A5*SIN(T3)*(COS(T3)**M2)
1610 A5=A5*2/(3.14159**.5)
1620 REM CALCULATE TOP FACTORIAL A8
1630 A8=1
1640 FOR A7=1 TO (M2-1)/2 STEP 1
1650 A8=A8*A7
1660 NEXT A7
1670 REM CALCULATE BOTTOM FACTORIAL B2
1680 Z=((M2-2)/2)+6
1690 G5=((2*3.14159/Z)**.5)*(Z**Z)
1700 E5=-(Z-(1/(12*Z))+(1/(360*Z*Z*Z)))
1710 E5 = EXP(E5)
1720 G5=G5*E5
1730 Z=Z-5
1740 B2=G5/((Z+4)*(Z+3)*(Z+2)*(Z+1)*(Z))
1750 A5=A5*A8/B2
1760 B3=A5
1770 GO TO 1790
1780 B3=0
1790 REM CALCULATE F
1800 F=1-C4+B3
1810 GO TO 1070
1820 PRINT "WAIT FOR 'CALCULATIONS COMPLETED'  !!!!"
1830 KILL "AV3VIS"
1840 CHAIN"(2,4)AV3.BAS<40>"2410
1850 END

Ready
```

FACTORIAL
INFORMATION MATRICES

170

RUN#PCA
PRINCIPAL COMPONENT ANALYSIS

Principal components are the eigenvectors (often also called "characteristic" or "proper" vectors) of the covariance (or correlation) matrix. The variances of the principal components are the corresponding eigenvalues (characteristic values, proper values). This analysis produces linear combinations of variables with large variance.

Given M observations of N variables, this program calculates a covariance and then a correlation matrix from it. The correlation matrix is then used as input to a function which utilizes Jacobi's method for finding the eigenvalues and eigenvectors of a real symmetric matrix. The eigenvalues of a correlation matrix represent the amounts of variance attributable to each variable, and the eigenvectors are the respective principal components.

PROGRAM RESTRICTIONS

No checks are made on the validity of the data. Maximum observation matrix size is 100 rows by 10 columns, that is, up to 100 observations on up to variables. These dimensions can naturally be varied according to machine capacity and virtual array-handling availability. The form of the program supplied may require some modification, as it uses DEC 11 virtual core and file-handling syntax.

INPUT REQUIREMENTS

Up to 100 observations of up to 10 variables. Required input values are:

1. Number of variables N;

2. Number of sets of observations M, each set consisting of N values N x M observed values, entered by row, each row containing N values corresponding to one observation. M rows are entered successively.

PROGRAM OUTPUT

The program will print the observation matrix, means, standard deviations, covariance matrix, variance figures, and principal components. The observation matrix may be saved for subsequent use if desired.

REFERENCES

Bowdler, H., Martin, R. S., Reinsch, C., and Wilkinson, J. H., The QR and QL Algorithm for Symmetric Matrices, Springer Handbook Series on Linear Algebra, No. 2, Vol. 11, 1968.

SAMPLE PROGRAM

```
LIST
PCA
1 !**********************************************************************
**********************************************************************
**                                                                  **
**                                                                  **
**                  PRINCIPAL COMPONENT ANALYSIS                    **
**              ------------------------------------                **
**                                                                  **
**                     AUTHOR:  BOB SCHORER                         **
**                                                                  **
**          The program will input an observation matrix           **
**          from the user console one row at a time and            **
**          calculate a covariance and then a correlation          **
**          matrix from it.  The correlation matrix is             **
**          then used as input to a function which                 **
**          utilizes Jacobi's method for finding the               **
**          eigenvalues and eigenvectors of a real                 **
**          symmetric matrix.  ThJe eigenvalues of a               **
**          correlation matrix represent the amounts               **
**          of variance attributable to each variable              **
**          and the eigenvectors are the respective                **
**          principal components.                                  **
**                                                                  **
**          No checks are made on the validity of the              **
**          data.  Maximum observation matrix size is              **
**          100 rows by 10 columns (i.e. up to 100                 **
**          observations on up to 10 variables) but                **
**          these dimensions could be easily increased             **
**          at a cost of greater disc space for the                **
**          virtual arrays.                                        **
**                                                                  **
**          The program will print the observation                 **
**          matrix, the means, the standard deviations,            **
**          the covariance matrix and the correlation              **
**          matrix if the user so desires, as well as              **
**          the variance figures and the principal                 **
**          components.                                            **
**                                                                  **
**          Note that the original observation matrix              **
**          may be saved on disc and used as input to              **
**          other statistical routines.                            **
**                                                                  **
**                                                                  **
**********************************************************************
**********************************************************************


100     EXTEND:
        OPEN "MATRIX.DAT" AS FILE 1%:
        OPEN "TEMP.FLE" AS FILE 2%:
        DIM #1%, BOUND%(2%), MATDATA(100%,10%):
        DIM #2%, MAT1(10%,100%):

        DIM CORRMAT(10%,10%),MEANS(10%),COMPS(10%,10%):

        INPUT "INPUT FROM KEYBOARD <KEY> OR DEFAULT <DISC>";A$:
        IF CVT$$(A$,2%) <> "KEY" GO TO 200
                ELSE
                INPUT "NO. VARIABLES ";BOUND%(2%):
                INPUT "NO. OBSERVATIONS ";BOUND%(1%):
                PRINT "TYPE IN OBSERVATION MATRIX ROW BY ROW":
                PRINT "(SEPARATED BY COMMAS AND TERMINATED BY <LF>":
                FOR I% = 1% TO BOUND%(1%):
                MAT INPUT MEANS(BOUND%(2%)):
                FOR J% = 1% TO BOUND%(2%):
                MATDATA(I%,J%) = MEANS(J%):
                NEXT J%:
                NEXT I%
```

```
!*******************************************************************
*                                                                 *
*                                                                 *
*                  Read data from the virtual array and store     *
*                  it's transposed form in another virtual        *
*                  array.  Calculate the means at the same        *
*                  time.  Note that this duplication of data      *
*                  is not really necessary but the processing     *
*                  of virtual arrays is much faster if array      *
*                  is accessed by column instead of by row.       *
*                                                                 *
*                  Print the observation matrix if user so        *
*                  desires.                                        *
*                                                                 *

200     M% = BOUND%(1%):
        N% = BOUND%(2%):
        FORMAT$ = "####.####   ":

        FOR I% = 1% TO N%:
        MEANS(I%) = 0.0:
          FOR J% = 1% TO M%:
          MAT1(I%,J%) = MATDATA(J%,I%):
          MEANS(I%) = MEANS(I%)+MAT1(I%,J%):
          NEXT J%:
        MEANS(I%) = MEANS(I%)/M%:
        NEXT I%:


        PRINT:PRINT:
        INPUT "DO YOU WANT THE OBSERVATION MATRIX PRINTED ";A$:
        IF LEFT(CVT$$(A$,2%),1%) <> "Y" GO TO 300
                ELSE
        PRINT:PRINT:
        PRINT "NUMBER OF VARIABLES = ";N%:
        PRINT "NUMBER OF OBSERVATIONS = ";M%:
        PRINT:
        PRINT "THE OBSERVATION MATRIX IS :-":
        PRINT:
        FOR I% = 1% TO M%:
        PRINT USING FORMAT$, MATDATA(I%,J%); FOR J% = 1% TO N%:
        PRINT:
        NEXT I%:
        PRINT:PRINT



!*******************************************************************
*                                                                 *
*                                                                 *
*                  Now pre-multiply the observation matrix by     *
*                  it's transpose.  Note that storage for the     *
*                  transposed matrix is not neccessary and        *
*                  that each element must be converted to a       *
*                  displacement from the appropriate mean.        *
*                                                                 *
*                  Print the means, standard deviations and       *
*                  the resultant covariance matrix if the         *
*                  user requires them.                            *
*                                                                 *

300     FOR I% = 1% TO N%:
          FOR J% = I% TO N%:
                CORRMAT(I%,J%) = 0.0:
                FOR K% = 1% TO M%:
                  CORRMAT(I%,J%) = CORRMAT(I%,J%)+(MAT1(I%,K%)-MEANS(I%))*
                                          (MAT1(J%,K%)-MEANS(J%)):
```

```
              NEXT K%:
        CORRMAT(I%,J%) = CORRMAT(I%,J%)/(M%-1%):
          NEXT J%:
      NEXT I%:

      INPUT "DO YOU WANT MEANS AND S.D.'S PRINTED ";A$:
      IF LEFT(CVT$$(A$,2%),1%) <> "Y" GO TO 350
              ELSE
      PRINT:PRINT:
      PRINT "THE MEANS ARE :- ":
      PRINT:
      PRINT USING FORMAT$, MEANS(I%); FOR I% = 1% TO N%:
      PRINT:PRINT:PRINT:
      PRINT"THE STANDARD DEVIATIONS ARE :-":
      PRINT:
      PRINT USING FORMAT$, SQR(CORRMAT(I%,I%)); FOR I% = 1% TO N%:
      PRINT:PRINT:PRINT


350   INPUT "DO YOU WANT THE COVARIANCE MATRIX PRINTED ";A$:
      IF LEFT(CVT$$(A$,2%),1%) <> "Y" GO TO 400
              ELSE
      PRINT:PRINT:
      PRINT "THE COVARIANCE MATRIX IS :-":
      PRINT:
      FOR I% = 1% TO N%:
      PRINT USING FORMAT$,CORRMAT(I%,J%); FOR J% = 1% TO N%:
      PRINT:
      NEXT I%:
      PRINT:PRINT




! ******************************************************************
*                                                                *
*                                                                *
*              Convert the covariance matrix into a              *
*              correlation matrix by dividing each               *
*              element by the product of the square              *
*              roots of it's variances (the diagonal             *
*              elements) and, if required by the user,           *
*              print it out.                                     *
*                                                                *
*                                                                *


400   FOR I% = 1% TO N%:
        FOR J% = N% TO I% STEP -1%:
            CORRMAT(I%,J%) = CORRMAT(I%,J%)/SQR(CORRMAT(I%,I%)*
                                               CORRMAT(J%,J%)):
          NEXT J%:
      NEXT I%:

      INPUT "DO YOU WANT THE CORRELATION MATRIX PRINTED ";A$:
      IF LEFT(CVT$$(A$,2%),1%) <> "Y" GO TO 500
              ELSE
      PRINT:PRINT:
      PRINT "THE CORRELATION MATRIX IS :-":
      PRINT:
      FOR I% = 1% TO N%:
      PRINT USING FORMAT$,CORRMAT(I%,J%); FOR J% = 1% TO N%:
      PRINT:
      NEXT I%:
      PRINT:PRINT
```

```
!*********************************************************************
*                                                                   *
*                                                                   *
*              Call the Jacobi's method subroutine which            *
*              starts at line 2000 the print the variances          *
*              and principal components after sorting them          *
*              into ascending order for ease of reading.            *
*                                                                   *
*                                                                   *

500      EPS = 1E-5:
         GO SUB 2000:

         TEMP% = N%

550      TEMP% = TEMP%-1%:
         FLAG% = 0%:
         FOR I% = 1% TO TEMP%:
         IF CORRMAT(I%,I%) < CORRMAT(I%+1%,I%+1%) GO TO 600
                 ELSE
                 FLAG% = 1%:
                 TEMP = CORRMAT(I%,I%):
                 CORRMAT(I%,I%) = CORRMAT(I%+1%,I%+1%):
                 CORRMAT(I%+1%,I%+1%) = TEMP:
                 FOR J% = 1% TO N%:
                 TEMP = COMPS(J%,I%):
                 COMPS(J%,I%) = COMPS(J%,I%+1%):
                 COMPS(J%,I%+1%) = TEMP:
                 NEXT J%

600      NEXT I%:
         IF FLAG% = 1% GO TO 550
                 ELSE
         PRINT "ACTUAL AMOUNTS OF VARIANCE CONTRIBUTED BY EACH VARIABLE":
         PRINT "(FOLLOWED BY PERCENTAGE OF TOTAL VARIANCE AND THEN BY":
         PRINT "THE CUMULATIVE PERCENTAGES) ARE :-":
         PRINT:
         SUM = 0.0:
         FOR I% = 1% TO N%:
         PRINT USING FORMAT$, CORRMAT(I%,I%);:
         SUM = SUM+CORRMAT(I%,I%):
         NEXT I%:
         PRINT:
         PRINT USING " (##.###%) ",(CORRMAT(I%,I%)/SUM*100.0); FOR I% = 1% TO N%:
         PRINT:
         TEMP = 0.0:
         FOR I% = 1% TO N%:
         TEMP = TEMP+CORRMAT(I%,I%)/SUM*100.0:
         PRINT USING "(###.###%) ", TEMP;:
         NEXT I%:
         PRINT:
         PRINT:
         PRINT:
         PRINT "PRINCIPAL COMPONENTS ARE :-":
         PRINT:
         FOR I% = 1% TO N%:
         PRINT USING FORMAT$, COMPS(I%,J%); FOR J% = 1% TO N%:
         PRINT:
         NEXT I%:

         PRINT:PRINT:
         CLOSE 1%,2%:
         KILL "TEMP.FLE":
         INPUT "DO YOU REQUIRE THE ORIGINAL OBSERVATION MATRIX TO BE SAVED";A$:
         IF LEFT(CVT$$(A$,2%),1%) = "Y" GO TO 32767
                 ELSE
                 KILL "MATRIX.DAT":
                 GO TO 32767
```

```
2000 !**************************************************************
     ****************************************************************
     **                                                          **
     **                                                          **
     **        The following function uses Jacobi's method       **
     **        to find the eigenvalues and eigenvectors of       **
     **        a real symmetric matrix.                          **
     **                                                          **
     **        Because the 4-word math pack is being used        **
     **        on this system, all arithmetic is done in         **
     **        double precision.                                 **
     **                                                          **
     **        Upon completion of this function, the array       **
     **        'CORRMAT' which held the original array as        **
     **        input, will contain, as it's diagonal             **
     **        elements, the eigenvalues of the matrix, and      **
     **        the array 'COMPS' will contain the eigen-         **
     **        vectors.                                          **
     **                                                          **
     **                                                          **
     ****************************************************************
     ****************************************************************


     ****************************************************************
     *                                                            *
     *          First set up an identity matrix in 'COMPS',       *
     *          this is used to calculate the eigenvectors        *
     *          for subsequent printing and serves no other       *
     *          useful purpose.  If eigenvalues only are          *
     *          required then it could be deleted.                *
     *                                                            *
     *          Also calculate the sum of the squares of all      *
     *          matrix elements to serve as a test for            *
     *          completion of the problem.                        *
     *          Also ensure matrix is symmetric.                  *
     *                                                            *
     *                                                            *
```

```
2050     MAT COMPS = ZER:
         COMPS(IZ,IZ) = 1.0 FOR IZ = 1% TO N%:

         SUMSQ = CORRMAT(N%,N%)**2:
         FOR IZ = 1% TO N%-1%:
                 SUMSQ = SUMSQ+CORRMAT(I%,I%)**2:
                 FOR J% = I%+1% TO N%:
                 SUMSQ = SUMSQ+CORRMAT(I%,J%)**2*2:
                 CORRMAT(J%,I%) = CORRMAT(I%,J%):
                 NEXT J%:
         NEXT I%:
         ITERNUM% = 0%
```

```
!---------------------------------------------------------------!
!                                                               !
!              Now enter loops which will progressively         !
!              zero each element in the matrix by pre-          !
!              and post-multiplying by a series of              !
!              orthogonal matrices which are calculated         !
!              on each pass to zero the 'i,j' element           !
!              for that pass.                                    !
!                                                               !
!              The rotation angle for each pass is              !
!              calculated from -                                !
!              TAN(2A) = CORRMAT(i,j)/(CORRMAT(i,i)-CORRMAT(j,j))!
!                                                               !
!              Note that since only the i and j rows and        !
!              columns are affected, it is not necessary        !
!              to multiply the whole of the matrix or           !
!              to store the orthogonal matrix.                  !
```

```
!                                                                        !
!                  If, at the end of each pass through the               !
!                  matrix, the diagonal elements have not                !
!                  achieved the desired degree of dominance              !
!                  then another pass through the matrix is               !
!                  implemented, until sufficient accuracy                !
!                  has been achieved.                                    !
!                                                                        !


2150      ITERNUM% = ITERNUM%+1%:

          FOR I% = 1% TO N%-1%:
          FOR J% = I%+1% TO N%:

          IF ABS(CORRMAT(I%,J%)) < 1E-9 GO TO 2250
                  ELSE
                  COSALPH = SQR(0.5):
                  SINALPH = COSALPH:
                  IF ABS(CORRMAT(I%,I%)-CORRMAT(J%,J%)) > 1E-9 THEN
                          ALPH = ATN(CORRMAT(I%,J%)/(CORRMAT(I%,I%)-CORRMAT(J%,J%))):
                          COSALPH = COS(ALPH/2.0):
                          SINALPH = SIN(ALPH/2.0)

2200      FOR K% = 1% TO N%:
                  TEMP = CORRMAT(I%,K%):
                  CORRMAT(I%,K%) = TEMP*COSALPH+CORRMAT(J%,K%)*SINALPH:
                  CORRMAT(J%,K%) = TEMP*SINALPH-CORRMAT(J%,K%)*COSALPH:
          NEXT K%:

          FOR K% = 1% TO N%:
                  TEMP = CORRMAT(K%,I%):
                  CORRMAT(K%,I%) = TEMP*COSALPH+CORRMAT(K%,J%)*SINALPH:
                  CORRMAT(K%,J%) = TEMP*SINALPH-CORRMAT(K%,J%)*COSALPH:

                  TEMP = COMPS(K%,I%):
                  COMPS(K%,I%) = TEMP*COSALPH+COMPS(K%,J%)*SINALPH:
                  COMPS(K%,J%) = TEMP*SINALPH-COMPS(K%,J%)*COSALPH:
          NEXT K%

2250      NEXT J%:
          NEXT I%:

          TEMP = 0.0:
          TEMP = TEMP+CORRMAT(I%,I%)**2 FOR I% = 1% TO N%:

          IF ABS(TEMP-SUMSQ) < EPS THEN RETURN
                  ELSE
                  IF ITERNUM% < 200% GO TO 2150
                          ELSE
                          PRINT "FUNCTION HAS NOT CONVERGED AFTER 200 ITERATIONS":
                          RETURN
!                                                                        !
!                                                                        !
----------------------------------------------------------------------------

32767     END

Ready
```

```
RUN
PCA
INPUT FROM KEYBOARD <KEY> OR DEFAULT <DISC>? KEY
NO. VARIABLES ? 6
NO. OBSERVATIONS ? 9
TYPE IN OBSERVATION MATRIX ROW BY ROW
(SEPARATED BY COMMAS AND TERMINATED BY <LF>
? 23,45,34,67,78,98
? 65,78,98,65,45,32
? 54,36,67,54,21,23
? 56,97,87,89,67,54
? 58,94,96,78,87,68
? 45,32,21,32,34,45,\,\
? 56,43,21,32,45,67
? 68,97,64,53,35,65
? 78,90,99,98,97,96


DO YOU WANT THE OBSERVATION MATRIX PRINTED ? Y


NUMBER OF VARIABLES =  6
NUMBER OF OBSERVATIONS =  9

THE OBSERVATION MATRIX IS :-

    23.0000     45.0000     34.0000     67.0000     78.0000     98.0000
    65.0000     78.0000     98.0000     65.0000     45.0000     32.0000
    54.0000     36.0000     67.0000     54.0000     21.0000     23.0000
    56.0000     97.0000     87.0000     89.0000     67.0000     54.0000
    58.0000     94.0000     96.0000     78.0000     87.0000     68.0000
    45.0000     32.0000     21.0000     32.0000     34.0000     45.0000
    56.0000     43.0000     21.0000     32.0000     45.0000     67.0000
    68.0000     97.0000     64.0000     53.0000     35.0000     65.0000
    78.0000     90.0000     99.0000     98.0000     97.0000     96.0000


DO YOU WANT MEANS AND S.D.'S PRINTED ? Y


THE MEANS ARE :-

    55.8889     68.0000     65.2222     63.1111     56.5556     60.8889


THE STANDARD DEVIATIONS ARE :-

    15.5197     28.3196     32.6488     23.0459     26.5429     25.7024


DO YOU WANT THE COVARIANCE MATRIX PRINTED ? Y


THE COVARIANCE MATRIX IS :-

   240.8610    274.1250    324.7780    115.6390     24.9445    -49.7639
     0.0000    802.0000    728.2500    466.3750    373.6250    170.7500
     0.0000      0.0000   1065.9400    611.0970    369.2360    -61.3472
     0.0000      0.0000      0.0000    531.1110    474.9310    231.2640
     0.0000      0.0000      0.0000      0.0000    704.5280    530.0700
     0.0000      0.0000      0.0000      0.0000      0.0000    660.6110


DO YOU WANT THE CORRELATION MATRIX PRINTED ? Y
```

```
THE CORRELATION MATRIX IS :-

     1.0000      0.6237      0.6410      0.3233      0.0606     -0.1248
     0.0000      1.0000      0.7876      0.7146      0.4971      0.2346
     0.0000      0.0000      1.0000      0.8122      0.4261     -0.0731
     0.0000      0.0000      0.0000      1.0000      0.7764      0.3904
     0.0000      0.0000      0.0000      0.0000      1.0000      0.7770
     0.0000      0.0000      0.0000      0.0000      0.0000      1.0000


FUNCTION HAS NOT CONVERGED AFTER 200 ITERATIONS
ACTUAL AMOUNTS OF VARIANCE CONTRIBUTED BY EACH VARIABLE
(FOLLOWED BY PERCENTAGE OF TOTAL VARIANCE AND THEN BY
THE CUMULATIVE PERCENTAGES) ARE :-

     0.0301      0.0741      0.2233      0.5302      1.6865      3.4559
   ( 0.502%)  ( 1.236%)  ( 3.722%)  ( 8.836%)  (28.107%)  (57.598%)
   ( 0.502%)  ( 1.737%)  ( 5.459%)  (14.295%)  (42.402%) (100.000%)


PRINCIPAL COMPONENTS ARE :-

    -0.1735     -0.0298     -0.4555      0.6553     -0.4889      0.3053
    -0.1476      0.1155      0.8213      0.1892     -0.1695      0.4752
     0.7277      0.0951     -0.1349     -0.3537     -0.3244      0.4613
    -0.4304     -0.5967     -0.1655     -0.4189      0.0923      0.4973
    -0.2292      0.7000     -0.2685     -0.0647      0.4596      0.4123
     0.4251     -0.3616      0.0179      0.4796      0.6382      0.2257


DO YOU REQUIRE THE ORIGINAL OBSERVATION MATRIX TO BE SAVED? Y

Ready
```

ANALYSIS OF TIME SERIES

RUN#FCAST
FORECASTING: MONTHLY DATA: DECOMPOSITION

This program calculates:

1. seasonal indices,

2. deseasonalized data,

3. trends, and

4. irregular and cyclical variations as a percentage deviation from the trend line.

The only input data required is a set of equal interval time dependent data values. The table below shows the input data and the calculated result:

	Original Data	Seasonally ADJ Data	% Deviation From Trend	Trend Values
1951				
January	318	265	$-0.399213E-1$	264.698
February	281	263	-1.17269	266.344
March	278	268	$-0.857362E-1$	276.99
April	250	270	0.058131	269.635
-	-	-	-	-
-	-	-	-	-
-	-	-	-	-
1952				
January	342	285	$0.399213E-1$	284.448
February	309	289	1.17269	286.094
March	299	288	$0.857362E-1$	287.74
-	-	-	-	-
-	-	-	-	-
-	-	-	-	-
December	364	300	-0.983821	302.552

The algorithm used assumes a multiplicative relationship where the time series variable F is a product of the variables T, C, S, I.

$$F = T\,C\,I\,S$$

where:

T = trend values (secular),

C = cyclical variations,

I = irregular variations,

S = seasonal variations.

PROGRAM RESTRICTIONS

Number of years N to be analyzed must be less than or equal to 20.

INPUT REQUIREMENTS

Number of years to be analyzed.

First year in which data is to be studied.

Six monthly groups of data beginning with January of the first year.

PROGRAM OUTPUT

1. seasonal indices,

2. original data,

3. seasonally adjusted data,

4. irregular and cyclical variations as a percentage,

5. deviation from trend, and

6. trend values.

REFERENCES

Spiegel, Murray R., Theory and Problems of Statistics, "Schaum's Outline Series," McGraw-Hill Book Company, New York, 1968.

SAMPLE PROGRAM

```
RUN
FCAST

GIVEN A SET OF MONTHLY DATA COVERING SEVERAL YEARS,
THIS PROGRAM WILL GENERATE SEASONAL INDICES AND
DESEASONALIZE THE DATA, CALCULATE THE TREND AND
ISOLATE IRREGULAR AND CYCLICAL VARIATIONS AS A
PERCENTAGE DEVIATION FROM THE TREND LINE.



AT PRESENT THE PROGRAM CONTAINS A SET OF SAMPLE DATA
WHICH RESULTS IN THE OUT DISPLAYED BELOW
NEW DATA MUST BE INPUT IN THE FORM OF DATA STATEMENTS
BETWEEN LINE NUMBER 1350 AND 3000

THE FIRST LINE OF DATA CONTAINS THE NUMBER OF YEARS
TO BE ANALYSED
THE SECOND LINE OF DATA CONTAINS THE FIRST YEAR
IN WHICH DATA IS TO BE STUDIED
THE REMAINING LINES CONTAIN THE MONTHLY DATA
FOR THE PERIOD SPECIFIED
THE DATA SHOULD BE INPUT IN SIX MONTHLY GROUPS,
BEGINNING WITH JANUARY OF THE FIRST YEAR.

TO SEE THE FORMAT OF THE DATA STATEMENTS
LIST LINES 1350 TO 3000 AFTER CALCULATIONS
COMPLETED IS PRINTED


SEASONAL INDICES
----------------

JANUARY        119.948
FEBRUARY       107.027
MARCH          103.714
APRIL          93.2996
MAY            86.7587
```

```
JUNE            81.2208
JULY            83.1867
AUGUST          89.6555
SEPTEMBER       96.5562
OCTOBER         106.354
NOVEMBER        112.894
DECEMBER        119.605
```

	ORIGINAL DATA	SEASONALLY ADJ DATA	% DEVIATION FROM TREND	TREND VALUES
1951				
JANUARY	318	265	4.68106	253.259
FEBRUARY	281	263	2.77725	255.457
MARCH	278	268	4.03297	257.655
APRIL	250	268	3.11768	259.853
MAY	231	266	1.60479	262.05
JUNE	216	266	.640808	264.248
JULY	223	268	.610146	266.446
AUGUST	245	273	1.72138	268.644
SEPTEMBER	269	279	2.86232	270.842
OCTOBER	302	284	3.99888	273.04
NOVEMBER	325	288	4.59364	275.237
DECEMBER	347	290	4.5726	277.435
1952				
JANUARY	342	285	1.96323	279.633
FEBRUARY	309	289	2.44203	281.831
MARCH	299	288	1.50168	284.029
APRIL	268	287	.356384	286.227
MAY	249	287	-.492821	288.424
JUNE	236	291	$-.194321E-1$	290.622
JULY	242	291	-.651619	292.82
AUGUST	262	292	-.945076	295.018
SEPTEMBER	288	298	.355293	297.216
OCTOBER	321	302	.804726	299.414
NOVEMBER	342	303	.440216	301.611
DECEMBER	364	304	.172951	303.809
1953				
JANUARY	367	306	$-.136795E-1$	306.007
FEBRUARY	328	306	-.564247	308.205
MARCH	320	309	-.599449	310.403
APRIL	287	308	-1.59612	312.601
MAY	269	310	-1.50667	314.798
JUNE	251	309	-2.51179	316.996
JULY	259	311	-2.45811	319.194
AUGUST	284	317	-1.43867	321.392
SEPTEMBER	309	320	-1.10294	323.59
OCTOBER	345	324	-.429222	325.788
NOVEMBER	367	325	-.884659	327.985
DECEMBER	394	329	-.23201	330.183
1954				
JANUARY	392	327	-1.67685	332.381
FEBRUARY	349	326	-2.53803	334.579
MARCH	342	330	-2.08521	336.777
APRIL	311	333	-1.6638	338.975

MAY	290	334	-2.02592	341.172
JUNE	273	336	-2.11133	343.37
JULY	282	339	-1.90164	345.568
AUGUST	305	340	-2.17812	347.766
SEPTEMBER	328	340	-2.93326	349.964
OCTOBER	364	342	-2.81332	352.162
NOVEMBER	389	345	-2.76224	354.359
DECEMBER	417	349	-2.21846	356.557

1955

JANUARY	420	350	-2.39833	358.755
FEBRUARY	378	353	-2.15253	360.953
MARCH	370	357	-1.76209	363.151
APRIL	334	358	-2.01509	365.349
MAY	314	362	-1.52986	367.546
JUNE	296	364	-1.435	369.744
JULY	305	367	-1.4241	371.942
AUGUST	330	368	-1.62085	374.14
SEPTEMBER	356	369	-2.03028	376.338
OCTOBER	396	372	-1.63608	378.536
NOVEMBER	422	374	-1.8205	380.734
DECEMBER	452	378	-1.31124	382.931

1956

JANUARY	453	378	-1.93864	385.129
FEBRUARY	412	385	-.613388	387.327
MARCH	398	384	-1.48274	389.525
APRIL	362	388	-.950996	391.723
MAY	341	393	-.22242	393.921
JUNE	322	396	.837326E-1	396.118
JULY	335	403	1.10281	398.316
AUGUST	359	400	-.230331E-1	400.514
SEPTEMBER	392	406	.811813	402.712
OCTOBER	427	401	-.844414	404.91
NOVEMBER	454	402	-1.21838	407.108
DECEMBER	483	404	-1.338	409.305

1957

JANUARY	487	406	-1.33528	411.503
FEBRUARY	440	411	-.625595	413.701
MARCH	429	414	-.543312	415.899
APRIL	393	421	.74791	418.097
MAY	370	426	1.46942	420.295
JUNE	347	427	1.12144	422.492
JULY	357	429	1.0514	424.69
AUGUST	398	433	1.37737	426.888
SEPTEMBER	415	430	.166763	429.086
OCTOBER	457	430	-.367592	431.284
NOVEMBER	491	435	.332207	433.482
DECEMBER	516	431	-.97773	435.679

1958

JANUARY	529	441	.718552	437.877
FEBRUARY	477	446	1.27449	440.075
MARCH	463	446	.938103	442.273
APRIL	423	453	2.00407	444.471
MAY	398	459	2.70342	446.669
JUNE	380	468	4.23154	448.866
JULY	389	468	3.67107	451.064
AUGUST	419	467	3.10694	453.262

SEPTEMBER	448	464	1.87032	455.46
OCTOBER	493	464	1.28697	457.658
NOVEMBER	526	466	1.31966	459.856
DECEMBER	560	468	1.33187	462.053

CALCULATION COMPLETED

Ready

Ready

```
LIST
FCAST
10 OPEN "FCAST 1" AS FILE 1
20 DIM #1,X(20,12),Y9(20,12)
30 DIM M$(20),T(20),Y6(12)
40 DIM S(20),X2(20),Y4(20),L(20),L1(20),G(20),Y8(20,12)
50 PRINT
60 PRINT "GIVEN A SET OF MONTHLY DATA COVERING SEVERAL YEARS,"
70 PRINT "THIS PROGRAM WILL GENERATE SEASONAL INDICES AND"
80 PRINT "DESEASONALIZE THE DATA, CALCULATE THE TREND AND"
90 PRINT "ISOLATE IRREGULAR AND CYCLICAL VARIATIONS AS A"
100 PRINT "PERCENTAGE DEVIATION FROM THE TREND LINE."
110PRINT
120 PRINT
130 PRINT
140 M$(1) ="JANUARY"
150 M$(2) ="FEBRUARY"
160 M$(3) ="MARCH"
170 M$(4) ="APRIL"
180 M$(5) ="MAY"
190 M$(6) ="JUNE"
200 M$(7) ="JULY"
210 M$(8) ="AUGUST"
220 M$(9) ="SEPTEMBER"
230 M$(10) = "OCTOBER"
240 M$(11) ="NOVEMBER"
250 M$(12) ="DECEMBER"
260 REM ... INPUT DATA INTO ARRAY X(I,J)
270 READ N
280 READ F
290 FOR I = 1 TO N
300 FOR J = 1 TO 12 STEP 1
310 READ X(I,J)
320 NEXT J
330 NEXT I
340 IF X(1,1) = 318 GO TO 350 ELSE 520
350 PRINT "AT PRESENT THE PROGRAM CONTAINS A SET OF SAMPLE DATA"
360 PRINT "WHICH RESULTS IN THE OUT DISPLAYED BELOW"
370 PRINT "NEW DATA MUST BE INPUT IN THE FORM OF DATA STATEMENTS"
380 PRINT "BETWEEN LINE NUMBER 1350 AND 3000
390 PRINT
400 PRINT "THE FIRST LINE OF DATA CONTAINS THE NUMBER OF YEARS"
410 PRINT "TO BE ANALYSED"
420 PRINT "THE SECOND LINE OF DATA CONTAINS THE FIRST YEAR"
430 PRINT "IN WHICH DATA IS TO BE STUDIED"
440 PRINT "THE REMAINING LINES CONTAIN THE MONTHLY DATA"
450 PRINT "FOR THE PERIOD SPECIFIED"
460 PRINT "THE DATA SHOULD BE INPUT IN SIX MONTHLY GROUPS,"
470 PRINT "BEGINNING WITH JANUARY OF THE FIRST YEAR."
480 PRINT
490 PRINT "TO SEE THE FORMAT OF THE DATA STATEMENTS"
500 PRINT "LIST LINES 1350 TO 3000 AFTER CALCULATIONS"
501 PRINT "COMPLETED IS PRINTED"
502 PRINT
504 PRINT
```

```
510 REM _ CALCULATE MONTHLY AVERAGES
520 FOR I = 1 TO N
530 T(I) = 0
540 FOR J = 1 TO 12 STEP 1
550 T(I) = X(I,J) + T(I)
560 NEXT J
570 S(I) = T(I)/12
580 NEXT I
590 REM _ CALCULATE EQUATION OF TREND LINE
600 S1 = 0
610 FOR I = 1 TO N
620 S1 = S1 + I-1
630 G(I) = I-1
640 NEXT I
650 M1 = S1/N
660 REM G(I) CONTAINS THE GIVEN VALUES
670 Y =0
680 FOR I = 1TON STEP 1
690 Y = Y+S(I)
700 NEXT I
710 Y1 = Y/N
720 L(I) = 0
730 A=0
740 B=0
750 FOR I = 1 TO N STEP 1
760 L(I) = G(I) - M1
770 L1(I) = S(I) - Y1
780 X2(I) = L(I)**2
790 Y4(I) = L1(I)*L(I)
800 A = A+X2(I)
810 B = B + Y4(I)
820 NEXT I
830 Y5 = B/A
840 L = Y1-(Y5*(M1+0.5))
850 REM - GENERATE MONTHLY VALUES TO FIT TREND LINE
860 Y5 = Y5/12
870 Z = L-(Y5*0.5)
880 K=0
890 FOR I = 1 TO N
900 FOR J = 1 TO 12
910 K = K+1
920 Y8(I,J) = Z + (K*Y5)
930 REM CALCULATE SEASONAL INDICES
940 Y9(I,J) = 100 * X(I,J)/Y8(I,J)
950 NEXT J
960 NEXT I
970 Y4 = 0
980 FOR J = 1 TO 12
990 Y6 = 0
1000 FOR I = 1 TO N
1010 Y6 = Y6 + Y9(I,J)
1020 NEXT I
1030 Y6(J) = Y6/N
1040 Y4 = Y4 + Y6(J)
1050 NEXT J
1060 Y4 = 1200/Y4
1070 PRINT "SEASONAL INDICES"
1080 PRINT "_____"
1090 PRINT
1100 FOR J = 1 TO 12
1110 PRINT M$(J),Y6(J)
1120 NEXT J
1130 PRINT
1140 PRINT
1150 REM - PRINT HEADINGS
1160 PRINT,"ORIGINAL","SEASONALLY","% DEVIATION","TREND"
1170 PRINT, " DATA  ","ADJ DATA  ","FROM TREND ","VALUES"
1180 PRINT ,"_____"
```

```
1190 PRINT
1200 REM - CALCULATE DESEASONALISED AND DETRENDED DATA AND PRINT
1210 FOR I = 1 TO N
1220 PRINT F
1230 F = F+1
1240 PRINT " _____"
1250 PRINT
1260 FOR J = 1 TO 12
1270 Y9(I,J) = X(I,J)/Y6(J)
1280 PRINT M$(J),X(I,J),INT((Y9(I,J)*100)+0.5),Y9(I,J)*10000/Y8(I,J)-100,Y8(I,J)
1290 NEXT J
1300 PRINT
1310 NEXT I
1320 KILL "FCAST1"
1330 PRINT "CALCULATION COMPLETED"
1340 REM
1350 DATA 8
1360 DATA 1951
1370 DATA 318,281,278,250,231,216
1380 DATA 223,245,269,302,325,347
1390 DATA 342,309,299,268,249,236
1400 DATA 242,262,288,321,342,364
1410 DATA 367,328,320,287,269,251
1420 DATA 259,284,309,345,367,394
1430 DATA 392,349,342,311,290,273
1440 DATA 282,305,328,364,389,417
1450 DATA 420,378,370,334,314,296
1460 DATA 305,330,356,396,422,452
1470 DATA 453,412,398,362,341,322
1480 DATA 335,359,392,427,454,483
1490 DATA 487,440,429,393,370,347
1500 DATA 357,388,415,457,491,516
1510 DATA 529,477,463,423,398,380
1520 DATA 389,419,448,493,526,560
3000 END
```

Ready

MISCELLANEOUS
BUSINESS CALCULATIONS

RUN#LRIR
LOAN REPAYMENT: INTEREST RATE

This program calculates the interest rate on a loan of value V, lent over N time periods. Payments P are made at the end of each period. This program solves the equation f(I) by an iteration for I using Newton's method:

$$I_{k+1} = I_k - \frac{f(I)}{f'(I)}$$

given:

$$f(I) = \frac{1 - (1 + I)^{-N}}{I} - \frac{V}{P}$$

f'(I) = the first derivative of f(I).

I = interest rate per time period.

N = number of payment periods.

V = present value or principal.

P = payment at the end of each period.

k = iteration index.

INPUT REQUIREMENTS

Values of V, P, N.

PROGRAM OUTPUT

Value of I expressed as a percentage per period.

REFERENCES

Any standard business or accounting textbook.

SAMPLE PROGRAM

Calculations for a rate of interest of 7.5% per annum:

Year	Amount Owed, Amount Borrowed or Principal	Yearly Payment	Fraction of Yearly Payment to Pay Interest	Fraction of Yearly Payment to Pay Principal	Unpaid Balance	Accumulated Interest
0	15,000					
1		1,700	1,125	575	14,425	1,125
2		1,700	1,082	618	13,806	2,206
3		1,700	1,035	664	13,142	3,242
.		.	.	.	.	.
.		.	.	.	.	.
.		.	.	.	.	.
14		1,700	227	1,472	1,564	10,364
15		1,700	117	1,582	-18	10,482

Given:

Calculate:

```
RUN
LRIR
                DIRECT REDUCTION LOAN INTEREST RATE
THIS PROGRAM CALCULATES THE INTEREST RATE ON A MORTGAGE WHERE PAYMENTS
ARE MADE AT THE END OF THE PERIOD.
THE DATA REQUIRED IS :
V=PRESENT VALUE OR PRINCIPAL.
P=PAYMENT.
N=NUMBER OF PAYMENTS.

ENTER VALUE OF V=
? 15000
ENTER VALUE OF P=
? 1700
ENTER VALUE OF N=
? 15

THE INTEREST RATE = 7.50656 %
CAREFUL!!!INTEREST RATE ABOVE IS PER PAYMENT PERIOD
YOU MAY HAVE TO CONVERT IT TO A TRUE PER ANNUM RATE
CALCULATIONS COMPLETED

Ready

Ready

LIST
LRIR
00100 PRINT"                DIRECT REDUCTION LOAN INTEREST RATE"
00110 PRINT"THIS PROGRAM CALCULATES THE INTEREST RATE ON A MORTGAGE WHERE PAYMENTS"
00120 PRINT"ARE MADE AT THE END OF THE PERIOD."
00130 PRINT"THE DATA REQUIRED IS :"
00140 PRINT"V=PRESENT VALUE OR PRINCIPAL."
00150 PRINT"P=PAYMENT."
00160 PRINT "N=NUMBER OF PAYMENTS."
00170 PRINT
00180 PRINT"ENTER VALUE OF V="
00181 INPUT V
00190 PRINT"ENTER VALUE OF P="
00191 INPUT P
00200 PRINT"ENTER VALUE OF N="
00201 INPUT N
00210 PRINT
00220 M = V/P
00230 I1=.004
00240 F1=(1-EXP(LOG(1)-N*LOG(1+I1)))/I1-M
00250 I1=.003
00260 F2=(1-EXP(LOG(1)-N*LOG(1+I1)))/I1-M
00270 F3=(F2-F1)/(.003-.004)
00280 I2=.003
00290 I1=I2-(F2/F3)
00300 F1=F2
00310 FOR J=1 TO 100 STEP 1
00320 F2 =(1-EXP(LOG(1)-N*LOG(1+I1)))/I1-M
00330 F3 = (F2-F1)/(I1-I2)
00340 I2=I1
00350 I1 = I1-(F2/F3)
00360 F1 = F2
00370 IF F2<.0000001 THEN 400
00371 GO TO 380
00380 NEXT J
00390 PRINT
00400 I1 = I1*100
00410 PRINT"THE INTEREST RATE =";I1;"%"
00420 PRINT"CAREFUL!!!INTEREST RATE ABOVE IS PER PAYMENT PERIOD"
00430 PRINT"YOU MAY HAVE TO CONVERT IT TO A TRUE PER ANNUM RATE"
00440 PRINT"CALCULATIONS COMPLETED"
00450 END

Ready
```

RUN#LRP
LOAN REPAYMENT: PAYMENTS

This program calculates the required payment amount for a direct reduction loan.

$$A = P\left(\frac{I}{1 - (1 + I)^{-N}}\right)$$

given

A = payment at the end of each period.

P = present value or principal.

I = interest rate per time period.

N = number of payment periods.

Note: You may have to divide yearly I by 12 to find the monthly interest rate, if you are dealing with monthly repayments.

INPUT REQUIREMENTS

Values of N, P, I.

PROGRAM OUTPUT

Value of A.

REFERENCES

Any standard business or accounting textbooks.

SAMPLE PROGRAM

Calculations for a rate of interest of 7.5% per annum:

Year	Amount Owed, Amount Borrowed or Principal	Yearly Payment	Fraction of Yearly Payment to Pay Interest	Fraction of Yearly Payment to Pay Principal	Unpaid Balance	Accumulated Interest
0	15,000					
1		1,700	1,125	575	14,425	1,125
2		1,700	1,082	618	13,806	2,206
3		1,700	1,035	664	13,142	3,242
.		.	.	.	.	.
.		.	.	.	.	.
.		.	.	.	.	.
14		1,700	227	1,472	1,564	10,364
15		1,700	117	1,582	-18	10,482

Given:

Calculate:

```
RUN
LRP
THIS PROGRAM CALCULATES THE PAYMENT AMOUNT OF A MORTGAGE
GIVEN :
N=NUMBER OF PAYMENT PERIODS
P=PRESENT VALUE OR PRINCIPAL
I=INTEREST RATE,PERCENT,FOR THE LENGTH OF THE PERIOD ABOVE
ENTER VALUE OF N=? 15
ENTER VALUE OF P=? 15000
ENTER VALUE OF I IN PERCENT BUT PLEASE DO NOT USE THE '%' SYMBOL I=? 7.5
THE PAYMENT AMOUNT = 1699.31
CALCULATIONS COMPLETED

Ready



Ready

LIST
LRP
100 PRINT"THIS PROGRAM CALCULATES THE PAYMENT AMOUNT OF A MORTGAGE"
110 PRINT"GIVEN :"
120 PRINT"N=NUMBER OF PAYMENT PERIODS"
130 PRINT"P=PRESENT VALUE OR PRINCIPAL"
140 PRINT"I=INTEREST RATE,PERCENT,FOR THE LENGTH OF THE PERIOD ABOVE"
150INPUT"ENTER VALUE OF N=";N
160INPUT"ENTER VALUE OF P=";P
170INPUT"ENTER VALUE OF I IN PERCENT BUT PLEASE DO NOT USE THE '%' SYMBOL I=";I
180 I=I/100
190 A = P*(I/(1-(1+I)**-N))
200 PRINT"THE PAYMENT AMOUNT =";A
210 PRINT"CALCULATIONS COMPLETED"
220 END

Ready
```

RUN#LRPW
LOAN REPAYMENT: PRESENT WORTH

This program calculates the present value or principal for a direct reduction loan:

$$P = A\left[\frac{1 - (1 + I)^{-N}}{I}\right]$$

given P = present value or principal.

A = payment at the end of each period.

I = interest rate per time period.

N = number of payment periods.

Note: You may have to divide I by 12 to find the monthly interest rate.

INPUT REQUIREMENTS

Values of A, I, N.

PROGRAM OUTPUT

Value of P.

REFERENCES

Any standard business or accounting textbook.

SAMPLE PROGRAM

Calculations for a rate of interest of 7.5% per annum:

Year	Amount Owed, Amount Borrowed or Principal	Yearly Payment	Fraction of Yearly Payment to Pay Interest	Fraction of Yearly Payment to Pay Principal	Unpaid Balance	Accumulated Interest
0	15,000					
1		1,700	1,125	575	14,425	1,125
2		1,700	1,082	618	13,806	2,206
3		1,700	1,035	664	13,142	3,242
.		.	.	.	.	.
.		.	.	.	.	.
.		.	.	.	.	.
14		1,700	227	1,472	1,564	10,364
15		1,700	117	1,582	-18	10,482

Given:

Calculate:

```
RUN
LRPW
THIS PROGRAM CALCULATES THE PRESENT VALUE OF A MORTGAGE
GIVEN :
N=NUMBER OF PAYMENT PERIODS
A=PAYMENT AMOUNT
I=INTEREST RATE,PERCENT,FOR THE LENGTH OF THE PERIOD ABOVE
ENTER VALUE OF N=? 15
ENTER VALUE OF A=? 1700
ENTER VALUE OF I IN PERCENT BUT PLEASE DO NOT USE THE '%' SYMBOL I=? 7.5
THE PRESENT VALUE = 15006.1
CALCULATIONS COMPLETED

Ready


Ready

LIST
LRPW
100 PRINT"THIS PROGRAM CALCULATES THE PRESENT VALUE OF A MORTGAGE"
110 PRINT"GIVEN :"
120 PRINT"N=NUMBER OF PAYMENT PERIODS"
130 PRINT"A=PAYMENT AMOUNT"
140 PRINT"I=INTEREST RATE,PERCENT,FOR THE LENGTH OF THE PERIOD ABOVE"
150INPUT"ENTER VALUE OF N=";N
160 INPUT"ENTER VALUE OF A=";A
170INPUT"ENTER VALUE OF I IN PERCENT BUT PLEASE DO NOT USE THE '%' SYMBOL I=";I
180 I=I/100
190 P = A*((1-(1+I)**-N)/I)
200 PRINT"THE PRESENT VALUE =";P
210 PRINT"CALCULATIONS COMPLETED"
220 END

Ready
```

RUN#LRNTP
LOAN REPAYMENT: NUMBER OF TIME PERIODS

This program calculates the number of payment periods required for the loan:

$$N = \frac{-\ell n(1 - I\frac{P}{A})}{\ell n(1 + I)}$$

given N = number of payment periods.

   I = interest rate per time periods.

   A = payment at the end of each period.

   P = present value or principal.

INPUT REQUIREMENTS

Values of I, P, A.

PROGRAM OUTPUT

Value of N.

REFERENCES

Any standard business or accounting textbook.

SAMPLE PROGRAM

Calculations for a rate of interest of 7.5% per annum:

Year	Amount Owed, Amount Borrowed or Principal	Yearly Payment	Fraction of Yearly Payment to Pay Interest	Fraction of Yearly Payment to Pay Principal	Unpaid Balance	Accumulated Interest
0	15,000					
1		1,700	1,125	575	14,425	1,125
2		1,700	1,082	618	13,806	2,206
3		1,700	1,035	664	13,142	3,242
.		.	.	.	.	.
.		.	.	.	.	.
14		1,700	227	1,472	1,564	10,364
15		1,700	117	1,582	-18	10,482

Given:

Calculate:

```
RUN
LRNTP
THIS PROGRAM CALCULATES THE NUMBER OF PAYMENT PERIODS OF A MORTGAGE
GIVEN :
P=PRESENT VALUE OR PRINCIPAL
A=PAYMENT AMOUNT
I=INTEREST RATE,PERCENT,FOR THE LENGTH OF THE PERIOD ABOVE
ENTER VALUE OF P =? 15000
ENTER VALUE OF A=? 1700
ENTER VALUE OF I IN PERCENT BUT PLEASE DO NOT USE THE '%' SYMBOL I=? 7.5
THE NUMBER OF PAYMENT PERIODS = 14.989
CALCULATIONS COMPLETED

Ready


Ready

LIST
LRNTP
100 PRINT"THIS PROGRAM CALCULATES THE NUMBER OF PAYMENT PERIODS OF A MORTGAGE"
110 PRINT"GIVEN :"
120 PRINT"P=PRESENT VALUE OR PRINCIPAL"
130 PRINT"A=PAYMENT AMOUNT"
140 PRINT"I=INTEREST RATE,PERCENT,FOR THE LENGTH OF THE PERIOD ABOVE"
150 INPUT"ENTER VALUE OF P =";P
160 INPUT"ENTER VALUE OF A=";A
170INPUT"ENTER VALUE OF I IN PERCENT BUT PLEASE DO NOT USE THE '%' SYMBOL I=";I
180 I=I/100
190 N = -(LOG(1-I*P/A)/LOG(1+I))
200 PRINT"THE NUMBER OF PAYMENT PERIODS =";N
210 PRINT"CALCULATIONS COMPLETED"
220 END

Ready
```

RUN#LRAI
LOAN REPAYMENT: ACCUMULATED INTEREST

Consider a loan to be repaid in N periodic payments of A dollars each. The monies were lent at an interest rate of I percent per payment period. This program calculates the interest accumulated between payments number C and K, both included. This calculation is useful in deciding whether to pay off a loan or to keep on carrying it for the full lending period.

PROGRAM RESTRICTIONS

None.

INPUT REQUIREMENTS

Integer values of N, C, K, where, naturally, $C < K \leq N$.
Real values of I and A.

PROGRAM OUTPUT

Accumulated interest between payment C and K.

REFERENCES

Any standard business or accounting textbook.

SAMPLE PROGRAM

Calculations for a rate of interest of 7.5% per annum:

Year	Amount Owed, Amount Borrowed or Principal	Yearly Payment	Fraction of Yearly Payment to Pay Interest	Fraction of Yearly Payment to Pay Principal	Unpaid Balance	Accumulated Interest	
0	15,000						ai = yearly interest
1		1,700	1,125	575	14,425	1,125	
2		1,700	1,082	618	13,806	2,206	Year 9
3		1,700	1,035	664	13,142	3,242	$\sum$ai
.		.	.	.	.	.	Year 1
9		.	.	.	.	.	
.		.	.	.	.	.	
14		1,700	227	1,472	1,564	10,364	
15		1,700	117	1,582	-18	10,482	

Given:

Calculate:

```
RUN
LRAI
THIS PROGRAM FINDS THE ACCUMULATED INTEREST OF A MORTGAGE, BETWEEN
THE PAYMENTS OF C THROUGH TO K
GIVEN :
A=PAYMENT AMOUNT
N=NUMBER OF PAYMENT PERIODS
I=INTEREST RATE,PERCENT,FOR THE LENGTH OF THE PERIOD ABOVE
C=INITIAL PAYMENT TO BE CONSIDERED
K=FINAL PAYMENT TO BE CONSIDERED

ENTER VALUE OF A=? 1700
ENTER VALUE OF I IN PERCENT BUT PLEASE DO NOT USE THE '%' SYMBOL I=? 7.5
ENTER VALUE OF N=? 15
ENTER PAYMENT NUMBER, C=? 1
ENTER PAYMENT NUMBER, K=? 9

THE ACCUMULATED INTEREST PAID BY PAYMENTS 1 THROUGH TO 9 = 8273.43
CALCULATIONS COMPLETED

Ready


Ready

LIST
LRAI
100 PRINT"THIS PROGRAM FINDS THE ACCUMULATED INTEREST OF A MORTGAGE, BETWEEN"
110PRINT"THE PAYMENTS OF C THROUGH TO K"
120 PRINT"GIVEN :"
130 PRINT"A=PAYMENT AMOUNT"
140 PRINT "N=NUMBER OF PAYMENT PERIODS"
150 PRINT"I=INTEREST RATE,PERCENT,FOR THE LENGTH OF THE PERIOD ABOVE"
160 PRINT"C=INITIAL PAYMENT TO BE CONSIDERED"
170 PRINT"K=FINAL PAYMENT TO BE CONSIDERED"
180PRINT
190 INPUT"ENTER VALUE OF A=";A
200INPUT"ENTER VALUE OF I IN PERCENT BUT PLEASE DO NOT USE THE '%' SYMBOL I=";I
210 I=I/100
220 INPUT"ENTER VALUE OF N=";N
230 INPUT"ENTER PAYMENT NUMBER, C=";C
240 INPUT"ENTER PAYMENT NUMBER, K=";K
250 D=A*(K-(C-1)-((1+I)**(K-N)/I)*(1-(1+I)**((C-1)-K)))
260PRINT
270PRINT"THE ACCUMULATED INTEREST PAID BY PAYMENTS";C;"THROUGH TO";K;"=";D
280 PRINT"CALCULATIONS COMPLETED"
290 END

Ready
```

RUN#LRRB
LOAN REPAYMENT: REMAINING BALANCE

Consider a loan to be repaid in N periodic payments of A dollars each. The monies were lent at an interest rate of I percent per payment period. This program calculates the amount still left to be paid after payment K has been made.

This calculation is useful in deciding whether to pay off a loan or to keep carrying it for the full lending period.

PROGRAM RESTRICTIONS

None.

INPUT REQUIREMENTS

Integer values of N and K, where K < N; and real values of I and A.

PROGRAM OUTPUT

Amount remaining to be paid after payment number K.

REFERENCES

Any standard business or accounting textbook.

SAMPLE PROGRAM

Calculations for a rate of interest of 7.5% per annum:

Year	Amount Owed, Amount Borrowed or Principal	Yearly Payment	Fraction of Yearly Payment to Pay Interest	Fraction of Yearly Payment to Pay Principal	Unpaid Balance	Accumulated Interest
0	15,000					
1=K		1,700	1,125	575	14,425	1,125
2		1,700	1,082	618	13,806	2,206
3		1,700	1,035	664	13,142	3,242
.		.	.	.	.	.
.		.	.	.	.	.
14		1,700	227	1,472	1,564	10,364
15		1,700	117	1,582	-18	10,482

Given:

Calculated

```
RUN
LRRB
THIS PROGRAM FINDS THE REMAINING BALANCE OF A MORTGAGE AFTER PAYMENT K
GIVEN :
A=PAYMENT AMOUNT
N=NUMBER OF PAYMENT PERIODS
I=INTEREST RATE,PERCENT,FOR THE LENGTH OF THE PERIOD ABOVE
K=PAYMENT NUMBER FROM WHICH BALANCE IS TO BE CALCULATED


ENTER VALUE OF A=
? 1700
ENTER VALUE OF I IN PERCENT BUT PLEASE DO NOT USE % SYMBOL, I=
? 7.5
ENTER VALUE OF N=
? 15
ENTER PAYMENT NUMBER, K=
? 1


THE REMAINING BALANCE AFTER PAYMENT  1 = 14431.6
CALCULATIONS COMPLETED

Ready




Ready

LIST
LRRB
00100 PRINT"THIS PROGRAM FINDS THE REMAINING BALANCE OF A MORTGAGE AFTER PAYMENT K"
00110 PRINT"GIVEN :"
00120 PRINT"A=PAYMENT AMOUNT"
00130 PRINT "N=NUMBER OF PAYMENT PERIODS"
00140 PRINT"I=INTEREST RATE,PERCENT,FOR THE LENGTH OF THE PERIOD ABOVE"
00150 PRINT"K=PAYMENT NUMBER FROM WHICH BALANCE IS TO BE CALCULATED"
00160PRINT
00170PRINT
00180 PRINT"ENTER VALUE OF A="
00181 INPUT A
00190 PRINT"ENTER VALUE OF I IN PERCENT BUT PLEASE DO NOT USE % SYMBOL, I="
00191 INPUT I
00200 I=I/100
00210 PRINT"ENTER VALUE OF N="
00211 INPUT N
00220 PRINT"ENTER PAYMENT NUMBER, K="
00221 INPUT K
00230 B=A*(1-(1+I)**(K-N))/I
00240PRINT
00250PRINT
00260PRINT"THE REMAINING BALANCE AFTER PAYMENT ";K;"=";B
00270 PRINT"CALCULATIONS COMPLETED"
00280 END

Ready
```

RUN#LRAS
LOAN REPAYMENT: AMORTIZATION SCHEDULE

Consider a loan of LØ dollars, lent at I percent per payment period, each payment having a value of P dollars.

This program calculates a table of:

Payment Number	Interest Paid	Payment to Principal	Balance of Principal	Accumulated Interest
1	175.00	25.00	29975.00	176.00
2	174.85	25.15	29949.90	349.85
3	174.71	25.29	29924.60	524.56
4	174.56	25.44	29899.10	699.12
.	.	.	.	.
.	.	.	.	.
.	.	.	.	.

The calculation stops when the Balance of Principal column becomes zero or negative, meaning of course that the loan has been paid in full.

PROGRAM RESTRICTIONS

None.

INPUT REQUIREMENTS

Real values of LØ, I, and P.

PROGRAM OUTPUT

Table above, with N rows of values, N being the number of time payments it takes to pay back the principal.

REFERENCES

Any standard business or accounting textbook.

SAMPLE PROGRAM

Calculations for a rate of interest of 7.5% per annum:

Year	Amount Owed, Amount Borrowed or Principal	Yearly Payment	Fraction of Yearly Payment to Pay Interest	Fraction of Yearly Payment to Pay Principal	Unpaid Balance	Accumulated Interest
0	15,000					
1		1,700	1,125	575	14,425	1,125
2		1,700	1,082	618	13,806	2,206
3		1,700	1,035	664	13,142	3,242
.		.	.	.	.	.
.		.	.	.	.	.
.		.	.	.	.	.
14		1,700	227	1,472	1,564	10,364
15		1,700	117	1,582	-18	10,482

Given:

Calculate:

```
RUN
LRAS
        DIRECT REDUCTION LOAN AMORTIZATION SCHEDULES
THIS PROGRAM CALCULATES A TABLE OF INTEREST PAID, PAYMENT TO
PRINCIPAL, AND PRESENT VALUE OF A MORTGAGE. IT ALSO CALCULATES THE
ACCUMULATED INTEREST.
THE DATA REQUIRED IS :
I=INTEREST RATE,PERCENT,FOR THE TIME PERIOD.
LO=AMOUNT OF LOAN.
P=PAYMENT AMOUNT.

ENTER VALUE OF I=
? 7.5
ENTER VALUE OF LO=
? 15000
ENTER VALUE OF P=
? 1700

PAYMENT NO.    INTEREST PAID PAYMENT      BALANCE      ACCUM INTEREST
1              1125          575          14425        1125
2              1081.88       618.125      13806.9      2206.88
3              1035.52       664.484      13142.4      3242.39
4              985.679       714.321      12428.1      4228.07
5              932.105       767.895      11660.2      5160.18
6              874.513       825.487      10834.7      6034.69
7              812.602       887.398      9947.29      6847.29
8              746.047       953.953      8993.34      7593.34
9              674.5         1025.5       7967.84      8267.84
10             597.588       1102.41      6865.43      8865.42
11             514.907       1185.09      5680.33      9380.33
12             426.025       1273.98      4406.36      9806.36
13             330.477       1369.52      3036.83      10136.8
14             227.763       1472.24      1564.6       10364.6
15             117.345       1582.66      -18.0579     10481.9
CALCULATIONS COMPLETED

Ready

LIST
LRAS
00100 PRINT"        DIRECT REDUCTION LOAN AMORTIZATION SCHEDULES"
00110 PRINT"THIS PROGRAM CALCULATES A TABLE OF INTEREST PAID, PAYMENT TO"
00120 PRINT"PRINCIPAL, AND PRESENT VALUE OF A MORTGAGE. IT ALSO CALCULATES THE"
00130 PRINT"ACCUMULATED INTEREST."
00140 PRINT"THE DATA REQUIRED IS :"
00150 PRINT"I=INTEREST RATE,PERCENT,FOR THE TIME PERIOD."
00160 PRINT"LO=AMOUNT OF LOAN."
00170 PRINT"P=PAYMENT AMOUNT."
00180 PRINT
00190 PRINT"ENTER VALUE OF I="     I
00191 INPUT I
00200PRINT"ENTER VALUE OF LO="      P
00201 INPUT LO
00210 PRINT"ENTER VALUE OF P="      AA
00211 INPUT P
00220 PRINT
00230 PRINT"PAYMENT NO.","INTEREST PAID","PAYMENT","BALANCE","ACCUM INTEREST"
00240 I=I/100
00250 K=K+1
00260 X=I*LO       → INTEREST
00270 Y=P-X
00280 L1=LO-Y      → PRINCIPLE - PAYMENT +
00290 X1=X1+X      → ACCUM INT
00300 PRINT K,X,Y,L1,X1
00310 LO=L1
00320 IF L1<0 THEN 330
00321 GO TO 250
00330 PRINT"CALCULATIONS COMPLETED"
00340 END

Ready
```

RUN#SFIR
SINKING FUND: INTEREST RATE

Consider a fund being built by N periodic payments of P dollars each. The desired future value at the end of the N periods is F dollars. This program calculates the rate of interest I percent one should invest this money at, in order to have the F dollars after N equal payments.

PROGRAM RESTRICTIONS

None.

INPUT REQUIREMENTS

Integer value of N. Real values of P and F.

PROGRAM OUTPUT

Value of I.

REFERENCES

Any standard business or accounting textbook.

SAMPLE PROGRAM

Year	Desired (Target) Amount of Money at the End of 10 Years	Yearly Payment into Sinking Fund
0		800
1		800
2		800
3		800
4		800
5		800
6		800
7		800
8		800
9		800
10	10,000	800

These yearly payments are invested immediately at 4.87% interest per annum (0.0487).

Given:

Calculate:

```
RUN
SFIR
          SINKING FUND INTEREST RATE
THIS PROGRAM CALCULATES THE INTEREST RATE ON A SAVINGS PROGRAM WHERE
PAYMENTS ARE ASSUMED TO BE MADE AT THE END OF THE COMPOUNDING PERIOD.
THE DATA REQUIRED IS :
F=FUTURE VALUE OR AMOUNT.
P=PAYMENT AMOUNT.
N=NUMBER OF TIME PERIODS.

ENTER VALUE OF F=
? 10000
ENTER VALUE OF P=
? 800
ENTER VALUE OF N=
? 10

THE INTEREST RATE = 4.86684 %
CALCULATIONS COMPLETED

Ready
```

```
Ready

LIST
SFIR
00100 PRINT"           SINKING FUND INTEREST RATE"
00110 PRINT"THIS PROGRAM CALCULATES THE INTEREST RATE ON A SAVINGS PROGRAM WHERE"
00120 PRINT"PAYMENTS ARE ASSUMED TO BE MADE AT THE END OF THE COMPOUNDING PERIOD."
00130 PRINT"THE DATA REQUIRED IS :"
00140 PRINT"F=FUTURE VALUE OR AMOUNT."
00150PRINT"P=PAYMENT AMOUNT."
00160 PRINT"N=NUMBER OF TIME PERIODS."
00170 PRINT
00180 PRINT"ENTER VALUE OF F="
00181 INPUT F
00190 PRINT"ENTER VALUE OF P="
00191 INPUT P
00200 PRINT"ENTER VALUE OF N="
00201 INPUT N
00210 PRINT
00220 M =F/P
00230 F1 =(((1+.004)**N-1)/.004)-M
00240 F2 =(((1+.003)**N-1)/.003)-M
00250 F3 =(F2-F1)/(.003-.004)
00260 I2 = .2
00270 I1 =I2-(F2/F3)
00280 F1 =F2
00290 FOR J=1 TO 100 STEP 1
00300 F2 = (((1+I1)**N-1)/I1)-M
00310 F3 = (F2-F1)/(I1-I2)
00320 I2=I1
00330 I1 = I1-(F2/F3)
00340 F1=F2
00350 IF F2<.0000001 THEN 380
00360 NEXT J
00370 PRINT
00380 I1=I1*100
00390 PRINT"THE INTEREST RATE =";I1;"%"
00400 PRINT"CALCULATIONS COMPLETED"
00410 END

Ready
```

RUN#SFP
SINKING FUND: PAYMENT

It is desired to have accumulated a future amount of F dollars at the end of N time periods. We can safely invest the N periodic payments at I percent per payment period as soon as they are received. This program calculates the required value P of such payments.

PROGRAM RESTRICTIONS

None.

INPUT REQUIREMENTS

Integer N. Real values of F and I.

PROGRAM OUTPUT

Value of P.

REFERENCES

Any standard business or accounting textbook.

SAMPLE PROGRAM

Year	Desired (Target) Amount of Money at the End of 10 Years	Yearly Payment into Sinking Fund
0		800
1		800
2		800
3		800
4		800
5		800
6		800
7		800
9		800
10	10,000	800

These yearly payments are invested immediately at 4.87% interest per annum (0.0487).

Given:

Calculated:

```
RUN
SFP
THIS PROGRAM CALCULATES THE PAYMENT AMOUNTS IN A SINKING FUND
GIVEN :
N=NUMBER OF TIME PERIODS
I=INTEREST RATE,PERCENT,FOR THE LENGTH OF THE PERIOD ABOVE
F=FUTURE VALUE OR AMOUNT

ENTER VALUE OF N=
? 10
ENTER VALUE OF I=
? 4.86681
ENTER VALUE OF F=
? 10000

THE PAYMENT AMOUNT IS = 800.001
CALCULATIONS COMPLETED

Ready
```

```
Ready

LIST
SFP
00100 PRINT "THIS PROGRAM CALCULATES THE PAYMENT AMOUNTS IN A SINKING FUND"
00110 PRINT"GIVEN :"
00120 PRINT "N=NUMBER OF TIME PERIODS"
00130PRINT"I=INTEREST RATE,PERCENT,FOR THE LENGTH OF THE PERIOD ABOVE"
00140 PRINT"F=FUTURE VALUE OR AMOUNT"
00150 PRINT
00160 PRINT"ENTER VALUE OF N="
00161 INPUT N
00170 PRINT"ENTER VALUE OF I="
00171 INPUT I
00180 I=I/100
00190 PRINT"ENTER VALUE OF F="
00191 INPUT F
00200 PRINT
00210 P= F*(I/((1+I)**N-1))
00220 PRINT"THE PAYMENT AMOUNT IS =";P
00230 PRINT"CALCULATIONS COMPLETED"
00240 END

Ready
```

RUN#SFFV
SINKING FUND: FUTURE VALUE

N periodic payments of A dollars each are made into a sinking fund, in which each payment immediately begins to accumulate interest of I percent per payment period. The future amount, F dollars, in the fund after the N payment periods is calculated by this program.

PROGRAM RESTRICTIONS

None.

INPUT REQUIREMENTS

Integer N. Real values of A and I.

PROGRAM OUTPUT

Value of F.

REFERENCES

Any standard business or accounting textbook.

SAMPLE PROGRAM

Year	Desired (Target) Amount of Money at the End of 10 Years	Yearly Payment into Sinking Fund
0		800
1		800
2		800
3		800
4		800
5		800
6		800
7		800
8		800
9		800
10	10,000	800

These yearly payments are invested immediately at 4.87% interest per annum (0.0487).

Given:

Calculate:

```
RUN
SFFV
THIS PROGRAM CALCULATES THE FUTURE AMOUNT IN A SINKING FUND
GIVEN :
N=NUMBER OF PAYMENT PERIODS
A=PAYMENT AMOUNT
I=INTEREST RATE,PERCENT,FOR THE LENGTH OF THE PERIOD ABOVE

ENTER VALUE OF N=
? 10
ENTER VALUE OF A=
? 800
ENTER VALUE OF I, PERCENT, I=
? 4.86681

THE FUTURE AMOUNT = 9999.99
CALCULATIONS COMPLETED

Ready
```

```
Ready

LIST
SFFV
00100 PRINT"THIS PROGRAM CALCULATES THE FUTURE AMOUNT IN A SINKING FUND"
00110 PRINT"GIVEN :"
00120 PRINT"N=NUMBER OF PAYMENT PERIODS"
00130 PRINT"A=PAYMENT AMOUNT"
00140 PRINT"I=INTEREST RATE,PERCENT,FOR THE LENGTH OF THE PERIOD ABOVE"
00150PRINT
00160 PRINT"ENTER VALUE OF N="
00161 INPUT N
00170 PRINT"ENTER VALUE OF A="
00171 INPUT A
00180 PRINT"ENTER VALUE OF I, PERCENT, I="
00181 INPUT I
00190 I=I/100
00200 F = A*(((1+I)**N-1)/I)
00210PRINT
00220 PRINT"THE FUTURE AMOUNT =";F
00230 PRINT"CALCULATIONS COMPLETED"
00240 END

Ready
```

RUN#SFNTP
SINKING FUND: NUMBER OF TIME PERIODS

The number of time periods N required for a sinking fund calculation to satisfy the following constraints:

Future amount   = F dollars

Periodic payment amount = A dollars

Periodic interest rate   = I percent

PROGRAM RESTRICTIONS

None.

INPUT REQUIREMENTS

Real values of F, A, and I.

PROGRAM OUTPUT

Value of N, the required number of time periods.

REFERENCES

Any standard business or accounting textbook.

SAMPLE PROGRAM

Year	Desired (Target) Amount of Money at the End of 10 Years	Yearly Payment into Sinking Fund	
0		800	
1		800	
2		800	
3		800	These yearly payments are
4		800	invested immediately at
5		800	4.87% interest per annum
6		800	(0.0487),
7		800	
8		800	
9		800	
10	10,000	800	

Given:

Calculate:

```
RUN
SFNTP
THIS PROGRAM CALCULATES THE NUMBER OF TIME PERIODS IN A SINKING FUND
GIVEN :
F=FUTURE AMOUNT
A=PAYMENT AMOUNT
I=INTEREST RATE,PERCENT,FOR THE LENGTH OF THE PERIOD ABOVE

ENTER VALUE OF F=? 10000
ENTER VALUE OF A=? 800
ENTER VALUE OF I IN PERCENT BUT PLEASE DO NOT USE THE '%' SYMBOL I=? 4.86681

THE NUMBER OF TIME PERIODS = 10
CALCULATIONS COMPLETED

Ready
```

```
Ready

LIST
SFNTP
100 PRINT"THIS PROGRAM CALCULATES THE NUMBER OF TIME PERIODS IN A SINKING FUND"
110 PRINT"GIVEN :"
120 PRINT"F=FUTURE AMOUNT
130 PRINT"A=PAYMENT AMOUNT"
140 PRINT"I=INTEREST RATE,PERCENT,FOR THE LENGTH OF THE PERIOD ABOVE"
150PRINT
160 INPUT"ENTER VALUE OF F=";F
170 INPUT"ENTER VALUE OF A=";A
180INPUT"ENTER VALUE OF I IN PERCENT BUT PLEASE DO NOT USE THE '%' SYMBOL I=";I
190 I=I/100
200 N=LOG(I*F/A+1)/LOG(1+I)
210PRINT
220 PRINT"THE NUMBER OF TIME PERIODS =";N
230 PRINT"CALCULATIONS COMPLETED"
240 END

Ready
```

RUN#DCF
DISCOUNTED CASH FLOW

This program calculates a chronological table:

Year	Cash Flow (given)	Present Value (Calculated)
1	15,000	83,000
2	30,000	48,000
.	.	.
.	.	.
.	.	.
N	5,000	0

given the original investment A dollars, and yearly cash flow data for N consecutive periods beginning the day of the original investment. The rate of interest, which makes the Present Value column equal to zero at the end of the Nth period, is calculated.

The calculation stops when the Present Value column becomes zero or positive at the end of the Nth period to a tolerance of 0.001A (one-tenth of one percent of the original investment). The Year column can be made to represent payment period--say, a month--provided the interest rate is expressed per payment period. DCF calculations are almost invariably performed annually; that is why the heading of Year, rather than payment period.

PROGRAM RESTRICTIONS

None.

INPUT REQUIREMENTS

N real values of yearly cash flows. Integer value N. Real value of original investment A. Initial guess for I, the interest rate.

PROGRAM OUTPUT

Value of interest rate I that makes present value equal to zero at year N.

REFERENCES

Any standard business or accounting textbook.

SAMPLE PROGRAM

The yearly cash flows in a given business have been:

Year	Cash Flow	Present Value
1	15,000	
2	30,000	
3	9,000	
4	21,000	
5	5,000	$0 \pm \dfrac{A}{1,000}$

The original investment was: 1,000,000.

An initial guess for i, the interest rate, must be given. The value of i (the interest rate for the 10-year period) that makes the present value equal to zero at the end of the 10th year is -7.92%.

```
RUN
DCF
THIS PROGRAM CALCULATES THE VALUE AT PERIOD K OF AN ORIGINAL INVESTMENT
AND THE ASSOCIATED DCF INTEREST RATE ASSOCIATED WITH A SET OF CASH FLOWS
AN INITIAL GUESS FOR THE INTEREST RATE AFTER TAXES MUST BE SUPPLIED TO START THE CALCULATION
ENTER ORIGINAL INVESTMENT, DOLLARS? 100000
ENTER NUMBER OF PERIODS FOR WHICH CASH FLOW DATA IS AVAILABLE? 5
ENTER THE CASH FLOW FOR PERIOD 1 =
? 15000
ENTER THE CASH FLOW FOR PERIOD 2 =
? 30000
ENTER THE CASH FLOW FOR PERIOD 3 =
? 9000
ENTER THE CASH FLOW FOR PERIOD 4 =
? 21000
ENTER THE CASH FLOW FOR PERIOD 5 =
? 5000
ENTER INITIAL GUESS FOR AFTER TAX INTEREST RATE PER PERIOD, AS PERCENT
THIS INTEREST RATE IS ASSUMED TO REMAIN CONSTANT THROUGHOUT THE
 5 PERIODS. ENTER PERCENT INTEREST RATE =
? 1
YEAR            CASH FLOW       PRESENT VALUE
  1             15000           -83709.8
  2             30000           -48327.1
  3             9000            -36799.3
  4             21000           -7587.51
  5             5000            -34.0806
THE CALCULATED INTEREST RATE IS-7.92002 %
TO A TOLERANCE OF + OR - .1% OF THE ORIGINAL INVESTMENT
CALCULATIONS COMPLETED

Ready


Ready

LIST
DCF
100 DIM C(100)
110 PRINT"THIS PROGRAM CALCULATES THE VALUE AT PERIOD K OF AN ORIGINAL INVESTMENT"
120 PRINT"AND THE ASSOCIATED DCF INTEREST RATE ASSOCIATED WITH A SET OF CASH FLOWS"
130 PRINT"AN INITIAL GUESS FOR THE INTEREST RATE AFTER TAXES MUST BE SUPPLIED TO START
    THE CALCULATION"
140 INPUT"ENTER ORIGINAL INVESTMENT, DOLLARS";IO
150 INPUT"ENTER NUMBER OF PERIODS FOR WHICH CASH FLOW DATA IS AVAILABLE";N
160 FOR I=1 TO N STEP 1
170 PRINT"ENTER THE CASH FLOW FOR PERIOD";I;"="
180 INPUT C(I)
190 NEXT I
200 PRINT"ENTER INITIAL GUESS FOR AFTER TAX INTEREST RATE PER PERIOD, AS PERCENT"
210 PRINT"THIS INTEREST RATE IS ASSUMED TO REMAIN CONSTANT THROUGHOUT THE"
220 PRINTN;"PERIODS. ENTER PERCENT INTEREST RATE ="
230 INPUT I2
240 L=IO/2000
250 I2=I2/100
260 M=0
270 P1=0
280 PRINT"YEAR            CASH FLOW       PRESENT VALUE"
290 V5=-IO
300 FOR I=1 TO N STEP 1
310 M=M+1
320 V5=V5+(C(I)/(1+I2)**I)
330 IF P1==1 THEN 340 ELSE 350
340 PRINT I,C(I),V5
350 NEXT I
360IF P1==1 THEN 490 ELSE 370
370 IF M>N*1000 THEN 470 ELSE 380
380 IF V5<-L THEN 390 ELSE 410
```

```
390 I2=I2-.0002
400 GO TO 290
410 IF V5>L THEN 420 ELSE 440
420 I2=I2+.0002
430 GO TO 290
440 IF V5>-L AND V5<+L THEN 450
450 P1=1
460 GO TO 290
470 PRINT"TOO MANY ITERATIONS. RERUN WITH NEW GUESS"
480 P1=1:GO TO 290
490 PRINT"THE CALCULATED INTEREST RATE IS";I2*100;"%"
500 PRINT"TO A TOLERANCE OF + OR - .1% OF THE ORIGINAL INVESTMENT"
510 PRINT"CALCULATIONS COMPLETED"
520 END
```

Ready

RUN#DSLBV
DEPRECIATION: STRAIGHT-LINE BOOK VALUE

This program calculates a table as follows:

Period K	Book Value	Depreciation
1	36,400	3,600
2	32,800	3,600
.	.	.
.	.	.
.	.	.
N		

given P = original value of an asset.

S = salvage value of asset at the end of K time periods.

N = number of time periods.

PROGRAM RESTRICTIONS

None.

INPUT REQUIREMENTS

Integer value of K, real values of P and S.

PROGRAM OUTPUT

Table of K, book value at end of time period K, depreciation allowed during time period K, for N values of K.

REFERENCES

Any standard business or accounting textbook.

SAMPLE PROGRAM

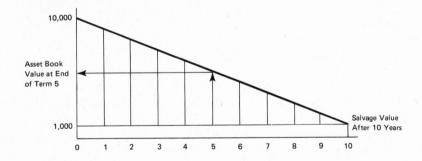

SAMPLE PROGRAM

```
RUN
DSLBV
THIS PROGRAM CALCULATES THE BOOK VALUE AT A TIME PERIOD K, USING THE
STRAIGHT LINE METHOD OF DEPRECIATION,
GIVEN :
P=ORIGINAL VALUE OF ASSET
S=SALVAGE VALUE OF ASSET AT THE END OF K TIME PERIODS
K=NUMBER OF TIME PERIODS

ENTER VALUE OF P=? 10000
ENTER SALVAGE VALUE, S=? 1000
ENTER VALUE OF K=? 10
TIME PERIOD    BOOK VALUE    DEPRECIATION
    1            9100           900
    2            8200           900
    3            7300           900
    4            6400           900
    5            5500           900
    6            4600           900
    7            3700           900
    8            2800           900
    9            1900           900
    10           1000           900
CALCULATIONS COMPLETED

Ready


Ready

LIST
DSLBV
100 PRINT"THIS PROGRAM CALCULATES THE BOOK VALUE AT A TIME PERIOD K, USING THE"
110 PRINT"STRAIGHT LINE METHOD OF DEPRECIATION,"
120 PRINT"GIVEN :"
130 PRINT"P=ORIGINAL VALUE OF ASSET"
140 PRINT"S=SALVAGE VALUE OF ASSET AT THE END OF K TIME PERIODS"
150 PRINT"K=NUMBER OF TIME PERIODS"
160 PRINT
170 INPUT"ENTER VALUE OF P=";P
180 INPUT"ENTER SALVAGE VALUE, S=";S
190 INPUT"ENTER VALUE OF K=";K
200 D=(P-S)/K
210 PRINT"TIME PERIOD    BOOK VALUE    DEPRECIATION"
220 FOR I=1 TO K STEP 1
230 B=P-I*D
240 PRINT I,B,D
250 NEXT I
260 PRINT"CALCULATIONS COMPLETED"
270 END

Ready
```

RUN#DSYDB
DEPRECIATION: SUM OF THE YEARS' DIGITS—BOOK VALUE

This program calculates a table as follows:

Period K	Book Value	Depreciation
1	33,454	6,545
2	27,563	5,890
.	.	.
.	.	.
.	.	.
N		

given P = original value of asset.

S = salvage value of asset.

N = number of time periods in asset life.

PROGRAM RESTRICTIONS

None.

INPUT REQUIREMENTS

Integer value of N, real values of P and S.

PROGRAM OUTPUT

Table of K, book value at the end of time period K, depreciation allowed during time period K, for N values of K.

REFERENCES

Any standard business or accounting textbook.

SAMPLE PROGRAM

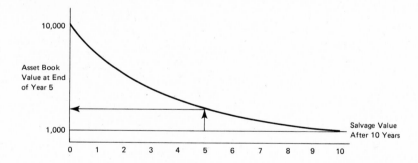

Ten yearly unequal payments, calculated according to the sum of the years' digits formulae.

```
RUN
DSYDB
THIS PROGRAM CALCULATES THE BOOK VALUE AT THE TIME PERIOD K
USING THE SUM-OF-THE-YEAR'S-DIGITS METHOD
GIVEN :
P=ORIGINAL VALUE OF ASSET
S=SALVAGE VALUE.
N=NUMBER OF PERIODS IN ASSET LIFE.

ENTER VALUE OF P=? 10000
ENTER VALUE OF S=? 1000
ENTER VALUE OF N=? 10
TIME PERIOD     BOOK VALUE     DEPRECIATION
   1             8363.64         1636.36
   2             6890.91         1472.73
   3             5581.82         1309.09
   4             4436.36         1145.45
   5             3454.55         981.818
   6             2636.36         818.182
   7             1981.82         654.545
   8             1490.91         490.909
   9             1163.64         327.273
   10            1000            163.636
CALCULATIONS COMPLETED

Ready



Ready

LIST
DSYDB
100 PRINT "THIS PROGRAM CALCULATES THE BOOK VALUE AT THE TIME PERIOD K"
110 PRINT"USING THE SUM-OF-THE-YEAR'S-DIGITS METHOD"
120 PRINT"GIVEN :"
130 PRINT"P=ORIGINAL VALUE OF ASSET"
140 PRINT"S=SALVAGE VALUE."
150 PRINT"N=NUMBER OF PERIODS IN ASSET LIFE."
160 PRINT
170 INPUT"ENTER VALUE OF P=";P
180 INPUT"ENTER VALUE OF S=";S
190 INPUT"ENTER VALUE OF N=";N
200 PRINT"TIME PERIOD    BOOK VALUE     DEPRECIATION"
210 FOR K=1 TO N STEP 1
220 D=2*(P-S)*(N-K+1)/(N*(N+1))
230 B = S+(N-K)*D/2
240 PRINT K,B,D
250 NEXT K
260 PRINT"CALCULATIONS COMPLETED"
270 END

Ready
```

RUN#DDBV
DEPRECIATION: DECLINING BALANCE BOOK VALUE

Given values of:

P = original value of asset,

N = number of periods in asset life,

R - depreciation rate, R = 1.0   simple declining balance method.

R = 1.5   150% declining balance method

R = 2.0   double declining balance method.

This program calculates a table as follows:

Period K	Book Value	Depreciation
1	32,400	3,600
2	29,168	3,248
.	.	.
.	.	.
.	.	.
.	.	.
N		

PROGRAM RESTRICTIONS

None, but R must be equal to 1 or 1.5 or 2.

INPUT REQUIREMENTS

Integer value of N, and real values of P and R.

PROGRAM OUTPUT

Table of K, book value at the end of time period K, depreciation allowed during time period K, for N values of K.

REFERENCES

Any standard business or accounting textbook.

SAMPLE PROGRAM

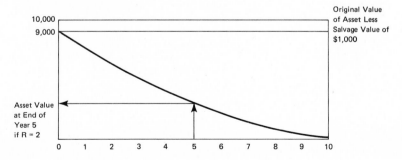

Ten yearly unequal payments, calculated according to chosen R sinking fund formulae.

```
RUN
DDBBV
THIS PROGRAM CALCULATES THE BOOK VALUE USING A VARIABLE RATE
DECLINING BALANCE FORMULA. THE DATA REQUIRED IS :
P=ORIGINAL VALUE OF ASSET (LESS SALVAGE VALUE).
N=NUMBER OF PERIODS IN ASSET LIFE.
R=DEPRECIATION RATE.
NOTE: IF R=2 THE PROGRAM GIVES THE DOUBLE DECLINING BALANCE METHOD.
      IF R=1.5 THE PROGRAM GIVES THE 150% DECLINING BALANCE METHOD.

ENTER VALUE OF P=? 9000
ENTER VALUE OF N=? 10
ENTER VALUE OF R=? 2
TIME PERIOD     BOOK VALUE      DEPRECIATION
    1           7200            1800
    2           5760            1440
    3           4608            1152
    4           3686.4          921.6
    5           2949.12         737.28
    6           2359.3          589.824
    7           1887.44         471.859
    8           1509.95         377.487
    9           1207.96         301.99
    10          966.367         241.592
CALCULATIONS COMPLETED

Ready



Ready

LIST
DDBBV
100 PRINT"THIS PROGRAM CALCULATES THE BOOK VALUE USING A VARIABLE RATE"
110 PRINT"DECLINING BALANCE FORMULA. THE DATA REQUIRED IS :"
120 PRINT"P=ORIGINAL VALUE OF ASSET (LESS SALVAGE VALUE)."
130 PRINT"N=NUMBER OF PERIODS IN ASSET LIFE."
140 PRINT"R=DEPRECIATION RATE."
150 PRINT"NOTE: IF R=2 THE PROGRAM GIVES THE DOUBLE DECLINING BALANCE METHOD."
160 PRINT"       IF R=1.5 THE PROGRAM GIVES THE 150% DECLINING BALANCE METHOD."
170 PRINT
180 INPUT"ENTER VALUE OF P=";P
190 INPUT"ENTER VALUE OF N=";N
200 INPUT"ENTER VALUE OF R=";R
210 PRINT"TIME PERIOD    BOOK VALUE     DEPRECIATION"
220 FOR K=1 TO N STEP 1
230 D=P*R/N*(1-(R/N))**(K-1)
240 B = P*(1-(R/N))**K
250 PRINT K,B,D
260   NEXT K
270 PRINT"CALCULATIONS COMPLETED"
280 END

Ready
```

RUN#CIIR
COMPOUND INTEREST: INTEREST RATE

This program calculates the required interest rate, as a percentage, for a compound interest calculation:

$$I = \left(\frac{F}{P}\right)^{1/N} - 1$$

given I = interest rate per time period.

           F = future value after N time periods.

           P = present value or principal at the beginning of the first time period.

           N = number of time periods.

Note: Where the number of time periods is given in months, and the periodic interest rate is given as a monthly percentage, then the calculated interest rate is per month and should be converted to a yearly rate by the user. This should be done, subsequent to execution of the program for greater ease of interpretation, by multiplying by 12.

INPUT REQUIREMENTS

Values of F, P, N.

PROGRAM OUTPUT

Value of I (as a percentage).

REFERENCES

Any standard business or accounting textbook.

SAMPLE PROGRAM

Year	Initial Value	Interest Accumulated During Year	Total Accumulated Value
0	15,000		
1		1,500	16,500
2		1,650	18,150
3		1,815	18,965
N=4		1,896	19,861=
.		.	.
.		.	.
.		.	.

Future value at the end of 4 years.

Going rate of interest, per annum, i = 7.25%

Given:

Calculate:

```
RUN
CIIR
THIS PROGRAM CALCULATES THE INTEREST RATE IN A COMPOUND
INTEREST CALCULATION GIVEN :
F=FUTURE VALUE OR AMOUNT
P=PRESENT VALUE OR PRINCIPAL
N=THE NUMBER OF TIME PERIODS
ENTER VALUE OF F=? 19861
ENTER VALUE OF P =? 15000
ENTER VALUE OF N =? 4
  THE INTEREST RATE = 7.26979
CALCULATIONS COMPLETED

Ready


Ready

LIST
CIIR
100PRINT"THIS PROGRAM CALCULATES THE INTEREST RATE IN A COMPOUND"
110 PRINT"INTEREST CALCULATION GIVEN :"
120 PRINT"F=FUTURE VALUE OR AMOUNT"
130 PRINT"P=PRESENT VALUE OR PRINCIPAL"
140 PRINT "N=THE NUMBER OF TIME PERIODS"
150 INPUT"ENTER VALUE OF F=";F
160 INPUT"ENTER VALUE OF P =";P
170 INPUT"ENTER VALUE OF N =";N
180 I=((F/P)**(1/N)-1)*100
190 PRINT" THE INTEREST RATE =";I
200 PRINT"CALCULATIONS COMPLETED"
210 END

Ready
```

RUN#CIPW
COMPOUND INTEREST: PRESENT WORTH

This program calculates the present worth in a compound interest calculation:

$$P = F(1 + I) - N$$

given   P = present value or principal at the beginning of the first time period.

F = future value after N time periods.

I = interest rate per time period.

N = number of time periods.

INPUT REQUIREMENTS

Values of F, I, N.

PROGRAM OUTPUT

Value of P.

REFERENCES

Any standard business or accounting textbook.

SAMPLE PROGRAM

Year	Initial Value	Interest Accumulated During Year	Total Accumulated Value
0	15,000		
1		1,500	16,500
2		1,650	18,150
3		1,815	18,965
N=4		1,896	19,861=
.		.	.
.		.	.
.		.	.

Future value
at the end of
of 4 years.

Going rate of interest, per annum, i = 7.25%

Given:

Calculate:

```
RUN
CIPW
THIS PROGRAM CALCULATES THE PRESENT VALUE IN A COMPOUND
INTEREST CALCULATION GIVEN :
N=NUMBER OF TIME PERIODS
I=INTEREST RATE,PERCENT,FOR THE LENGTH OF THE PERIOD ABOVE
F=FUTURE VALUE OR AMOUNT
ENTER VALUE OF N =? 4
ENTER VALUE OF I IN PERCENT BUT PLEASE DO NOT USE THE '%' SYMBOL I=? 7.25
ENTER VALUE OF F=? 19861
THE PRESENT VALUE = 15011.1
CALCULATIONS COMPLETED

Ready
```

```
Ready

LIST
CIPW
100 PRINT"THIS PROGRAM CALCULATES THE PRESENT VALUE IN A COMPOUND"
110 PRINT"INTEREST CALCULATION GIVEN :"
120 PRINT "N=NUMBER OF TIME PERIODS"
130PRINT"I=INTEREST RATE,PERCENT,FOR THE LENGTH OF THE PERIOD ABOVE"
140 PRINT"F=FUTURE VALUE OR AMOUNT"
150 INPUT"ENTER VALUE OF N =";N
160 INPUT"ENTER VALUE OF I IN PERCENT BUT PLEASE DO NOT USE THE '%' SYMBOL I=";I
170 I=I/100
180 INPUT"ENTER VALUE OF F=";F
190 P=F*(1+I)**-N
200 PRINT"THE PRESENT VALUE =";P
210 PRINT"CALCULATIONS COMPLETED"
220 END

Ready
```

RUN#CIFV
COMPOUND INTEREST: FUTURE VALUE

This program calculates the future value F in a compound interest calculation:

$$F = P(1 + I)N$$

given   F = future value after N time periods.

P = present value or principal at the beginning of the first time period.

I = interest rate per time period.

N = number of time periods.

INPUT REQUIREMENTS

Values of P, I, N.

PROGRAM OUTPUT

Value of F.

REFERENCES

Any standard business or accounting textbook.

SAMPLE PROGRAM

Year	Initial Value	Interest Accumulated During Year	Total Accumulated Value
0	15,000		
1		1,500	16,500
2		1,650	18,150
3		1,815	18,965
N=4		1,896	19,861=
.		.	.
.		.	.
.		.	.

Future value
at the end of
4 years.

Going rate of interest, per annum, i = 7.25%

Given:

Calculate:

```
RUN
CIFV
THIS PROGRAM CALCULATES THE FUTURE VALUE IN A COMPOUND
INTEREST CALCULATION GIVEN :
N=NUMBER OF TIME PERIODS
I=INTEREST RATE,PERCENT,FOR THE LENGTH OF THE PERIOD ABOVE
P=PRESENT VALUE OR PRINCIPAL
ENTER VALUE OF N =? 4
ENTER VALUE OF I IN PERCENT BUT PLEASE DO NOT USE THE '%' SYMBOL I=? 7.25
ENTER VALUE OF P=? 15000
THE FUTURE VALUE IS= 19846.3
CALCULATIONS COMPLETED

Ready
```

```
Ready

LIST
CIFV     11:02 AM        11-May-80
100 PRINT "THIS PROGRAM CALCULATES THE FUTURE VALUE IN A COMPOUND"
110 PRINT"INTEREST CALCULATION GIVEN :"
120 PRINT "N=NUMBER OF TIME PERIODS"
130PRINT"I=INTEREST RATE,PERCENT,FOR THE LENGTH OF THE PERIOD ABOVE"
140 PRINT"P=PRESENT VALUE OR PRINCIPAL"
150 INPUT"ENTER VALUE OF N =";N
160 INPUT"ENTER VALUE OF I IN PERCENT BUT PLEASE DO NOT USE THE '%' SYMBOL I=";I
170 I=I/100
180 INPUT"ENTER VALUE OF P=";P
190 F=P*(1+I)**N
200 PRINT"THE FUTURE VALUE IS=";F
210 PRINT"CALCULATIONS COMPLETED"
220END

Ready
```

RUN#CINTP
COMPOUND INTEREST: NUMBER OF TIME PERIODS

This program calculates the number of time periods N (years or months) in a compound interest calculation:

$$N = \frac{\ln\left(\frac{F}{P}\right)}{\ln(1 + I)}$$

given   N = number of time periods.

F = future value after N time periods.

P = present value or principal at the beginning of the first time period.

I = interest rate per time period.

INPUT REQUIREMENTS

Values of F, P, I.

PROGRAM OUTPUT

Value of N.

REFERENCES

Any standard business or accounting textbook.

SAMPLE PROGRAM

Year	Initial Value	Interest Accumulated During Year	Total Accumulated Value
0	15,000		
1		1,500	16,500
2		1,650	18,150
3		1,815	18,965
N=4		1,896	19,861=
.		.	.
.		.	.
.		.	.

Future value
at the end of
4 years.

Going rate of interest, per annum, i = 7.25%

Given:

Calculate:

```
RUN
CINTP
THIS PROGRAM CALCULATES THE NUMBER OF TIME PERIODS IN A COMPOUND
INTEREST CALCULATION GIVEN :
I=INTEREST RATE,PERCENT,FOR THE LENGTH OF THE PERIOD ABOVE
F=FUTURE VALUE OR AMOUNT
P=PRESENT VALUE OR PRINCIPAL
ENTER VALUE OF I IN PERCENT BUT PLEASE DO NOT USE THE '%' SYMBOL I=? 7.25
ENTER VALUE OF F=? 19861
ENTER VALUE OF P =? 15000
THE NUMBER OF TIME PERIODS = 4.01055
CALCULATIONS COMPLETED

Ready
```

```
Ready

LIST
CINTP
100 PRINT"THIS PROGRAM CALCULATES THE NUMBER OF TIME PERIODS IN A COMPOUND"
110 PRINT"INTEREST CALCULATION GIVEN :"
120PRINT"I=INTEREST RATE,PERCENT,FOR THE LENGTH OF THE PERIOD ABOVE"
130 PRINT"F=FUTURE VALUE OR AMOUNT"
140 PRINT"P=PRESENT VALUE OR PRINCIPAL"
150 INPUT"ENTER VALUE OF I IN PERCENT BUT PLEASE DO NOT USE THE '%' SYMBOL I=";I
160 I=I/100
170 INPUT"ENTER VALUE OF F=";F
180 INPUT"ENTER VALUE OF P =";P
190 N=LOG(F/P)/LOG(1+I)
200 PRINT"THE NUMBER OF TIME PERIODS =";N
210 PRINT"CALCULATIONS COMPLETED"
220 END

Ready
```

RUN#CIAPI
COMPOUND INTEREST: AMOUNT PAID AS INTEREST

This program calculates the amount paid as interest A in a compound interest calculation:

$$A = P\left[(1 + I)^N - 1\right]$$

given   A = amount paid as interest over N time periods.

P = present value or principal at the beginning of the first time period.

I = interest rate per time period.

N = number of time periods.

INPUT REQUIREMENTS

Values of P, I, N.

PROGRAM OUTPUT

Value of A.

REFERENCES

Any standard business or accounting textbook.

SAMPLE PROGRAM

Year	Initial Value	Interest Accumulated During Year	Total Accumulated Value	
0	15,000			
1		1,500	16,500	
2		1,650	18,150	
3		1,815	18.965	
N=4		1,896	19,861=	19,861 - 15,000 = 4,861

Future value at the end of 4 years.

(round-off error makes calculation 4846.)

Going rate of interest, per annum, i = 7.25%

Given:

Calculate:

```
RUN
CIAPI
THIS PROGRAM CALCULATES THE INTEREST AMOUNT IN A COMPOUND
INTEREST CALCULATION GIVEN :
N=NUMBER OF TIME PERIODS
I=INTEREST RATE,PERCENT,FOR THE LENGTH OF THE PERIOD ABOVE
P=PRESENT VALUE OR PRINCIPAL
ENTER VALUE OF N =? 4
ENTER VALUE OF I IN PERCENT BUT PLEASE DO NOT USE THE '%' SYMBOL I=? 7.25
ENTER VALUE OF P =? 15000
THE INTEREST AMOUNT = 4846.34
CALCULATIONS COMPLETED

Ready
```

```
Ready

LIST
CIAPI
100 PRINT"THIS PROGRAM CALCULATES THE INTEREST AMOUNT IN A COMPOUND"
110 PRINT"INTEREST CALCULATION GIVEN :"
120 PRINT "N=NUMBER OF TIME PERIODS"
130PRINT"I=INTEREST RATE,PERCENT,FOR THE LENGTH OF THE PERIOD ABOVE"
140 PRINT"P=PRESENT VALUE OR PRINCIPAL"
150 INPUT"ENTER VALUE OF N =";N
160 INPUT"ENTER VALUE OF I IN PERCENT BUT PLEASE DO NOT USE THE '%' SYMBOL I=";I
170 I=I/100
180INPUT"ENTER VALUE OF P =";P
190 A= P*((1+I)**N-1)
200 PRINT"THE INTEREST AMOUNT =";A
210 PRINT"CALCULATIONS COMPLETED"
220 END

Ready
```

RUN#CPM
CRITICAL PATH METHOD

This program calculates the expected time, early start time, slack time, and variance of individual activities. It is used in the program evaluation review technique (PERT), to determine the critical path of a prescribed job. The statistical approach to activity and project durations is a characteristic of PERT (Program Evaluation Review Technique). This approach is appropriate for unfamiliar or experimental projects. The equations used for calculating the variance and expected times are:

$$G = variance = \frac{(A(I) - (B(I))^2}{6}$$

$$F = expected\ time = \frac{A(I) + 4M(I) + B(I))}{6}$$

for $I = 2$ to $T9$ and $A(I) \leq M(I) \leq B(I)$

where $T9$ = number of tasks,

   $A(I)$ = optimistic time,

   $B(I)$ = pessimistic time,

   $M(I)$ = most likely time.

Note: The range of values of $A(I)$ and $B(I)$ follows a Beta distribution.

PROGRAM RESTRICTIONS

Maximum number of tasks = 25.
Maximum number of predecessors = 25.

INPUT REQUIREMENTS

Data cards should be inserted commencing from line number 2,000 and incremented by 1.
The first data card contains the total number of tasks.
The second data card must read as follows: 0,0,0, BEGIN,0.
Next are the operators' data cards, and each task must be set out as follows: optimistic time, pessimistic time, most likely time, name of task, number of predecessors, predecessors names, separated by commas.
The last data card must be read as follows: 0,0,0, END, number of predecessors, predecessors' names.

PROGRAM OUTPUT

The program prints out the following:

1. Table of tasks with respective--optimistic, pessimistic, most likely, and expected times and variances.

2. Table of tasks with respective--expected time, early start time, and slack time.

A bar chart allowing a visual check of the network tasks against a time scale indicating the critical path of the project.

Time of completion.

REFERENCES

Riggs, J. L., Production Systems, 1st ed. J. Wiley and Sons, Inc., New York, 1970.

Kemeny, J. G., Kurtz, T. E., Basic Programming, 2nd ed., John Wiley and Sons, Inc., New York, 1971.

Bennet, W. R., Introduction to Computer Applications for Nonscience Students (BASIC), 1st ed., Prentice-Hall, Englewood Cliffs, N.J., 1976.

SAMPLE PROGRAM

A simple, but typical, multistage project is shown below, of which the relevant data has been entered into:

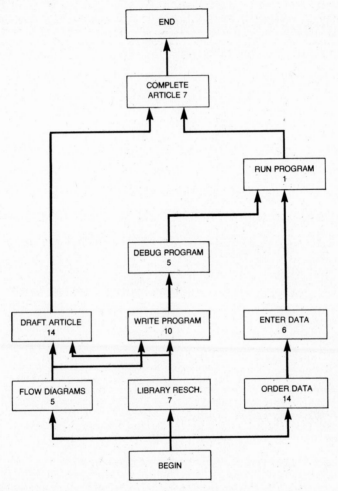

Example problem taken from Kemeny, J. G. and Kurtz, T. E., ob. cit.

```
RUN SIMPLE:CPM

THIS PROGRAM CALCULATES THE EXPECTED TIME AND THE
VARIANCE OF INDIVIDUAL ACTIVITIES AND IS USED IN
THE PROGRAM EVALUATION REVIEW TECHNIQUE (PERT), TO
DETERMINE THE CRITICAL PATH OF A PRESCRIBED JOB.


A SAMPLE PERT PROGRAM PRINT OUT WILL BE SHOWN BELOW

 IN ORDER TO EVALUATE THE USER'S PROGRAM, THE FOLLOWING STEPS MUST BE CARRIED OUT.
1.   DATA CARDS SHOULD BE INSERTED STARTING FROM LINE NO. 2000 AND INCREMENTED BY 1.
2.   THE FIRST DATA CARD CONTAINS THE TOTAL NO. OF TASKS.
3.   THE SECOND DATA CARD MUST READ AS FOLLOWS: 0,0,0, BEGIN,0
4.   INSERT USER'S DATA CARDS, AND EACH TASK MUST BE SET OUT AS FOLLOWS.
OPTIMISTIC TIME, PESSIMISTIC TIME, MOST LIKELY TIME,
NAME OF TASK, NUMBER OF PREDECESSORS, PREDECESSOR NAME(S)
SEPERATED BY COMMAS
5.   THE LAST DATA CARD MUST READ AS FOLLOWS: 0,0,0, END, NO. OF PREDECESSORS,
PREDECESSOR NAME(S).


WHEN USING CPM. METHOD, THE PESSIMISTIC AND OPTIMISTIC TIMES ARE EQUAL TO MOST LIKELY
TIMES AND MUST BE SHOWN ON THE DATA CARDS ACCORDINGLY.
```

THE MOST LIKELY TIME IS THE DURATION THAT WOULD OCCUR MOST OFTEN
IF THE ACTIVITY WAS REPEATED MANY TIMES UNDER THE SAME CONDITIONS.
THE OPTIMISTIC AND PESSIMISTIC TIME ESTIMATES ARE THE OUTSIDE LIMITS
OF COMPLETION TIME WHEN EVERYTHING GOES EITHER ALL RIGHT OR ALL WRONG

TASK	OPTIMISTIC TIME	PESSIMISTIC TIME	MOST LIKELY TIME	EXPECTED TIME	VARIANCE
DIAGRAMS	4	6	5	5	.111
LIBRARY	6	8	7	7	.111
ORDER	13	15	14	14	.111
DRAFT	13	15	14	14	.111
PROGRAM	9	11	10	10	.111
ENTER	5	7	6	6	.111
DEBUG	4	6	5	5	.111
RUN	.5	1.5	1	1	.027
ARTICLE	6	8	7	7	.111

TASK	EXPECTED TIME	EARLY START	SLACK
DIAGRAMS	5	0	2
LIBRARY	7	0	0
ORDER	14	0	2
DRAFT	14	7	2
PROGRAM	10	7	0
ENTER	6	14	2
DEBUG	5	17	0
RUN	1	22	0
ARTICLE	7	23	0

TIME OF COMPLETION = 30

CRITICAL PATH CHART, BASED ON EARLIEST START INFORMATION.

```
                              TIME SCALE
          TASK     0
------------!-------------!-------------!-------------!-------------!-------------!-------------!
DIAGRAMS         + + + + +

LIBRARY          * * * * * *

ORDER            + + + + + + + + + + + + + +

DRAFT                      + + + + + + + + + + + + + +

PROGRAM                    * * * * * * * * * *

ENTER                                  + + + + + +

DEBUG                                        * * * * *

RUN                                                *

ARTICLE                                              * * * * * * *
------------!-------------!-------------!-------------!-------------!-------------!-------------!
```

TIME SCALE = !------------! = 5 TIME UNITS.

  *** INDICATES THOSE TASKS THAT ARE ON THE CRITICAL PATH.

```
CALCULATIONS COMPLETED.
THIS PROGRAM WAS COMPILED BY FOURTH YEAR PRODUCTION
ENGINEERING STUDENTS 1978;
G.CLANCEY, W.GRIMSTON, H.VAN DER BIJL, A.ZUCCON.

Ready

LIST 2000-2110
CPM
2000    DATA    11
2010    DATA    0,0,0, BEGIN, 0
2020    DATA    4,6,5, DIAGRAMS, 1 , BEGIN
2030    DATA    6,8,7, LIBRARY,1, BEGIN
2040    DATA    13,15,14,ORDER ,1, BEGIN
2050    DATA    13,15,14, DRAFT, 2, DIAGRAMS, LIBRARY
2060    DATA    9,11,10, PROGRAM,2, DIAGRAMS , LIBRARY
2070    DATA    5,7,6, ENTER , 1, ORDER
2080    DATA    4,6,5, DEBUG, 1, PROGRAM
2090    DATA    .5,1.5,1, RUN, 2, DEBUG, ENTER
2100    DATA    6,8,7, ARTICLE, 2, DRAFT, RUN
2110    DATA    0,0,0, END, 1, ARTICLE

Ready

RUN


1000 REM PROGRAM EVALUATION REVIEW TECHNIQUE
1005    DIM N$(25), P%(25,25), T(25,4), A(25), B(25), M(25)
1010    PRINT
1015    PRINT "THIS PROGRAM CALCULATES THE EXPECTED TIME AND THE"
1020    PRINT "VARIANCE OF INDIVIDUAL ACTIVITIES AND IS USED IN"
1025    PRINT "THE PROGRAM EVALUATION REVIEW TECHNIQUE (PERT), TO"
1030    PRINT "DETERMINE THE CRITICAL PATH OF A PRESCRIBED JOB."
1035    PRINT
1040    PRINT
1041    PRINT"A SAMPLE PERT PROGRAM PRINT OUT WILL BE SHOWN BELOW"
1042    PRINT
1043     PRINT" IN ORDER TO EVALUATE THE USER'S PROGRAM, THE FOLLOWING STEPS MUST
        BE CARRIED OUT."
1044    PRINT"1.   DATA CARDS SHOULD BE INSERTED STARTING FROM LINE NO. 2000 AND
        INCREMENTED BY 1."
1045    PRINT    "2.   THE FIRST DATA CARD CONTAINS THE TOTAL NO. OF TASKS."
1046    PRINT    "3.   THE SECOND DATA CARD MUST READ AS FOLLOWS; 0,0,0, BEGIN,0"
1047    PRINT    "4.   INSERT USER'S DATA CARDS, AND EACH TASK MUST BE SET OUT AS FOLLOWS."
1048    PRINT    "OPTIMISTIC TIME, PESSIMISTIC TIME, MOST LIKELY TIME, "
1049    PRINT    "NAME OF TASK, NUMBER OF PREDECESSORS, PREDECESSOR NAME(S)"
1050    PRINT    "SEPERATED BY COMMAS"
1051    PRINT    "5.   THE LAST DATA CARD MUST READ AS FOLLOWS; 0,0,0, END, NO. OF
        PREDECESSORS,PREDECESSOR NAME(S)."
1055    PRINT
1056    PRINT
1057    PRINT"WHEN USING CPM. METHOD, THE PESSIMISTIC AND OPTIMISTIC TIMES ARE EQUAL TO
        MOST LIKELY"
1058    PRINT    "TIMES AND MUST BE SHOWN ON THE DATA CARDS ACCORDINGLY."
1060    PRINT
1065    PRINT
1070 PRINT"THE MOST LIKELY TIME IS THE DURATION THAT WOULD OCCUR MOST OFTEN"
1075    PRINT "IF THE ACTIVITY WAS REPEATED MANY TIMES UNDER THE SAME CONDITIONS."
1080    PRINT "THE OPTIMISTIC AND PESSIMISTIC TIME ESTIMATES ARE THE OUTSIDE LIMITS"
1085    PRINT "OF COMPLETION TIME WHEN EVERYTHING GOES EITHER ALL RIGHT OR ALL WRONG"
1090    PRINT
1095    PRINT
1100    READ T9
1105    MAT P% = ZER (T9,T9)
1110    Z = INT (T9)
1115    Y = Z - T9
1120    IF Y = 0 GO TO 1145
1125    MAT T = ZER (T9,4)
1130    PRINT "INCORRECT NUMBER FOR DATA SET"
```

```
1135    PRINT "SHOULD BE INTEGER NUMBER ONLY"
1140    STOP
1145    FOR I = 1 TO T9 STEP 1
1150    READ A(I), B(I), M(I)
1155    READ N$(I), N
1160    FOR J = 1 TO N STEP 1
1165    READ P$
1170    FOR I1 = 1 TO I -1 STEP 1
1175    IF P$ = N$(I1) THEN 1195
1180    NEXT I1
1185    PRINT "DATA OUT OF ORDER"
1190    STOP
1195    LET P%(I,I1) = 1
1200    NEXT J
1205    NEXT I
1210    IF N$(T9) = "END" THEN 1235
1215    PRINT "NO END TASK"
1220    STOP
1225    PRINT
1230    PRINT
1235    PRINT " TASK            OPTIMISTIC    PESSIMISTIC   MOST LIKELY   EXPECTED        VARIANCE"
1240    PRINT "                 TIME          TIME          TIME          TIME "
1245    PRINT "----------------------------------------------------------------------------------------"
1250    FOR I = 2 TO T9 - 1 STEP 1
1255    IF A(I) <= 0 GO TO 1305
1260    IF M(I) < A(I) GO TO 1305
1265    IF M(I) > B(I) GO TO 1305
1270    LET D = B(I) - A(I)
1275    IF D< 0 GO TO 1305
1280    LET G = INT ((( D/6 ) **2 ) *1000)
1281    LET G = G/1000
1285    LET F = ( A(I) + 4*M(I) + B(I) )/6
1290    IF F < 0 GO TO 1305
1295    LET T(I,0) = F
1300    GO TO 1315
1305    PRINT N$(I), A(I), B(I), M(I), "INCORRECT DATA"
1310    GO TO 1320
1315    PRINT N$(I), A(I), B(I), M(I), F,G
1320    NEXT I
1325    REM EARLY TIMES
1330    FOR I = 1 TO T9 STEP 1
1335    LET E = 0
1340    FOR J = 1 TO T9 STEP 1
1345    IF P%(I,J) = 0 THEN 1360
1350    IF E >= T(J,2) THEN 1360
1355    LET E = T(J,2)
1360    NEXT J
1365    LET T(I,1) = E
1370    LET T(I,2) = E + T(I,0)
1375    NEXT I
1380    REM LATE TIMES
1385    LET T = T(T9,1)
1390    FOR I = T9 TO 1 STEP -1
1395    LET E = T
1400    FOR J = 1 TO T9 STEP 1
1405    IF P%(J,I) =0 THEN 1420
1410    IF E <= T(J,3) THEN 1420
1415    LET E = T(J,3)
1420    NEXT J
1425    LET T(I,4) = E
1430    LET T(I,3) = E - T(I,0)
1435    NEXT I
1440    REM PRINT RESULTS
1445    PRINT
1450    PRINT
1455    PRINT
1460    PRINT
1465     PRINT" TASK","EXPECTED","EARLY","SLACK"
1470     PRINT ,"TIME","START"
1475    PRINT "-----------------------------------------------------"
```

```
1480    PRINT
1485    FOR I = 2 TO T9 - 1 STEP 1
1490    PRINT N$(I), T(I,0), T(I,1), T(I,3)-T(I,1)
1495    NEXT I
1500    PRINT
1505    PRINT "TIME OF COMPLETION = " T
1510    PRINT
1515    PRINT
1520    PRINT "CRITICAL PATH CHART, BASED ON EARLIEST START INFORMATION."
1525    PRINT "————————————————————————————————————————————————————————"
1530    PRINT
1535    PRINT
1539    PRINT TAB (35); " TIME SCALE"
1540    PRINT "        TASK        0"
1545    PRINT "——————————————————!" ;
1546    FOR I = 1 TO T STEP 5
1547    PRINT "—————————!";
1548    NEXT I
1549    PRINT
1550    IF T <= 10 THEN K = 4
1551    IF T > 10 GO TO 1553
1552    GO TO 1561
1553    IF T > 40 GO TO 1556
1554    LET K = 2
1555    GO TO 1561
1556    LET K = 1
1559    PRINT
1561    FOR I = 2 TO T9 - 1 STEP 1
1562    IF T(I,3) - T(I,1) = 0 GO TO 1605
1563    PRINT N$(I), ;
1565    FOR J = 0 TO K*T(I,0) - K STEP K
1570    LET X = 16 + K * T(I,1) + J
1575    PRINT TAB (X) ; "+" ;
1580    NEXT J
1585    PRINT
1590    PRINT
1595    NEXT I
1600    GO TO 1650
1605    PRINT N$(I),;
1610    FOR J = 0 TO 2 *T(I,0) - 2 STEP 2
1615    LET X = 16 + 2 * T(I,1) + J
1620    PRINT TAB (X) ; "*" ;
1625    NEXT J
1630    PRINT
1635    PRINT
1640    GO TO 1595
1645    IF T(I,3)-T(I,1) =0 GO TO 1605
1650    PRINT "——————————————————!" ;
1651    FOR I = 1 TO T STEP 5
1652    PRINT "—————————!" ;
1653    NEXT I
1654    PRINT
1655    PRINT
1656    LET X = 10 / K
1657    PRINT "TIME SCALE = !—————————! =";  X ; "TIME UNITS."
1658    PRINT
1660    PRINT    " *** INDICATES THOSE TASKS THAT ARE ON THE CRITICAL PATH."
1665    PRINT
1670    PRINT
1675    PRINT "CALCULATIONS COMPLETED."
2000    DATA    11
2010    DATA    0,0,0, BEGIN, 0
2020    DATA    4,6,5, DIAGRAMS, 1 , BEGIN
2030    DATA    6,8,7, LIBRARY,1, BEGIN
2040    DATA    13,15,14,ORDER ,1, BEGIN
2050    DATA    13,15,14, DRAFT, 2, DIAGRAMS, LIBRARY
2060    DATA    9,11,10, PROGRAM,2, DIAGRAMS , LIBRARY
2070    DATA    5,7,6, ENTER , 1, ORDER
2080    DATA    4,6,5, DEBUG, 1, PROGRAM
2090    DATA    .5,1.5,1, RUN, 2, DEBUG, ENTER
2100    DATA    6,8,7, ARTICLE, 2, DRAFT, RUN
2110    DATA    0,0,0, END, 1, ARTICLE
3000    PRINT    "THIS PROGRAM WAS COMPILED BY FOURTH YEAR PRODUCTION"
3001    PRINT"ENGINEERING STUDENTS 1978;"
3002    PRINT "G.CLANCEY, W.GRIMSTON, H.VAN DER BIJL, A.ZUCCON."
4000    END
```

SECTION

APPLYING SIMPLE

MOST COMMON
BASIC INSTRUCTIONS

RADIO SHACK'S TRS-80

Special Characters and Abbreviatons

Command Mode

ENTER	Return carriage and interpret command
◄	Cursor backspace and delete last character typed
SHIFT ◄	Cursor to beginning of logical line; erase line
▼	Linefeed
:	Statement delimiter; use between statements on same logical line
►	Move cursor to next tab stop. Tab stops are at positions 0, 8, 16, 24, 32, 40, 48, and 56.
SHIFT ►	Convert display to 32 characters per line
CLEAR	Clear Display and convert to 64 characters per line

Execute Mode

SHIFT @	Pause in execution; freeze display during LIST
BREAK	Stop execution
ENTER	Interpret data entered from Keyboard with INPUT statement

Abbreviations

?	Use in place of PRINT.
'	Use in place of :REM
.	"Current line"; use in place of line number with LIST, EDIT, etc.

Type Declaration Characters

Character	Type	Examples
$	String	A$, ZZ$
%	Integer	A1%, SUM%
!	Single-Precision	B!, NI!
#	Double-Precision	A#, 1/3#
D	Double-Precision (exponential notation)	1.23456789D-12
E	Single-Precision (exponential notation)	1.23456E+30

Arithmetic Operators

+ add   – subtract   * multiply   / divide
↑ exponentiate (e.g., 2 ↑ 3 = 8)

String Operator

+ concatenate (string together)   "2" + "2" = "22"

Relational Operators

Symbol	meaning in numeric expressions	in string expressions
<	is less than	precedes
>	is greater than	follows
=	is equal to	equals
< = or = <	is less than or equal to	precedes or equals
> = or = >	is greater than or equal to	follows or equals
<> or ><	does not equal	does not equal

Order of Operations (operators on same line have same precedence)

↑ (Exponentiation)
– (Negation)
*, /
+, –
Relational operators
NOT
AND
OR

Commands

Command	Function	Examples
AUTO *mm,nn*	Turn on automatic line numbering beginning with *mm*, using increment of *nn*.	AUTO AUTO 10 AUTO 5,5 AUTO .,10
CLEAR	Set numeric variables to zero, strings to null.	CLEAR
CLEAR *n*	Same as CLEAR but also sets aside *n* bytes for strings.	CLEAR 500 CLEAR MEM/4

CONT	Continue after BREAK or STOP in execution.	**CONT**
DELETE *mm-nn*	Delete program lines from line *mm* to line *nn*.	**DELETE 100** **DELETE 10-50** **DELETE .**
EDIT *mm*	Enter Edit Mode for line *mm*. See Edit Mode Sub-commands below.	**EDIT 100** **EDIT .**
LIST *mm-nn*	List all program lines from *mm* to *nn*.	**LIST** **LIST 30-60** **LIST 30-** **LIST -90** **LIST .**
NEW	Delete entire pro-gram and reset all variables, pointers etc.	**NEW**
RUN *mm*	Execute program beginning at lowest numbered line or *mm* if specified.	**RUN** **RUN 55**
SYSTEM	Enter Monitor Mode for loading of machine-language file from cassette.	See Chapter 2
TROFF	Turn off Trace	**TROFF**
TRON	Turn on Trace	**TRON**

Edit Mode Subcommands and Function Keys

Subcommand/Function Key	Function
ENTER	End editing and return to Command Mode.
SHIFT ↑	Escape from subcommand and remain in Edit Mode.
*n*Space-Bar	Move cursor *n* spaces to right.
n ←	Move cursor *n* spaces to left.
L	List remainder of program line and return to beginning of line.
X	List remainder of program line, move cursor to end of line, and start Insert subcommand.
I	Insert the following sequence of characters at current cursor position; use Escape to exit this subcommand.

A	Cancel changes and return cursor to beginning of line.
E	End editing, save all changes and return to Command Mode.
Q	End editing, cancel all changes made and return to Command Mode.
H	Delete remainder of line and insert following sequence of characters; use Escape to exit this subcommand.
nD	Delete specified number of characters n beginning at current cursor position.
nC	Change (or replace) the specified number of characters n using the next n characters entered.
nSc	Move cursor to nth occurrence of character c, counting from current cursor position.
nKc	Delete all characters from current cursor position up to nth occurrence of character c, counting from current cursor position.

Input/Output Statements

Statement*	Function	Examples

PRINT exp	Output to Display the value of exp. Exp may be a numeric or string expression or constant, or a list of such items.	`PRINT A$`
		`PRINT X+3`
		`PRINT "D=" D`

	Comma serves as a PRINT modifier. Causes cursor to advance to next print zone.	`PRINT 1,2,3,4`
		`PRINT "1","2"`
		`PRINT 1,,2`

	Semi-colon serves as a PRINT modifier. Inserts a space after a numeric item in PRINT list. Inserts no space after a string item. At end of PRINT list, suppresses the automatic carriage return.	`PRINT X;"=ANSWER"`
		`PRINT X;Y;Z`
		`PRINT "ANSWER IS";`

*exp may be a string or numeric constant or variable, or a list of such items.

PRINT @ *n*	PRINT modifier; begin PRINTing at specified display position *n*.	**PRINT @ 540,"CENTER"** **PRINT @ N+3,X*3**
TAB *n*	Print modifier: moves cursor to specified Display position *n* (expression).	**PRINT TAB(N) N**
PRINT USING *string;exp*	PRINT format specifier: output *exp* in form specified by *string* field (see below).	**PRINT USING A\$;X** **PRINT USING "#.#";Y+Z**
INPUT *"message";variable*	Print message (if any) and await input from Keyboard.	**INPUT"ENTER NAME";A\$** **INPUT"VALUE"; X** **INPUT"ENTER NUMBERS" ;X,Y** **INPUT A,B,C,D\$**
PRINT #−1	Output to Cassette #1.	**PRINT #−1,A,B,C,D\$**
INPUT #−1	Input from Cassette #1.	**INPUT #−1,A,B,C,D\$**
DATA *item list*	Hold data for access by READ statement.	**DATA 22,33,11,1.2345** **DATA "HALL","SMITH","DOE"**
READ *variable list*	Assign value(s) to the specified variable(s), starting with current DATA element.	**READ A,A1,A2,A3** **READ A\$,B\$,C\$,D**
RESTORE	Reset DATA pointer to first item in first DATA statement.	**RESTORE**

Field Specifiers for PRINT USING statements

Numeric Character	Function	Example
#	Numeric field (one digit per #).	###
.	Decimal point position.	##.###
+	Print leading or trailing sign (plus for positive numbers, minus for negative numbers).	+#.### #.###+ −#.### #.###−

—	Print trailing sign only if value printed is negative.	###.## —
**	Fill leading blanks with asterisk.	**###.##
$$	Place dollar sign immediately to left of leading digit.	$$####.##
**$	Dollars sign to left of leading digit and fill leading blanks with asterisks.	**$####.##
↑↑↑↑	Exponential format, with one significant digit to left of decimal.	#.######↑↑↑↑

String Character	Function	Example
!	Single character.	!
%spaces%	String with length equal to 2 plus number of spaces between % symbols.	% %

Program Statements

Statement	Function	Examples
(Type Definition)		
DEFDBL *letter list or range*	Define as double-precision all variables beginning with specified letter, letters or range of letters.	DEFDBL J DEFDBL X,Y,A DEFDBL A-E,J
DEFINT *letter list or range*	Define as integer all variables beginning with specified letter, letters or range of letters.	DEFINT A DEFINT C,E,G DEFINT A-K
DEFSNG *letter list or range*	Define as single-precision all variables beginning with specified letter, letters or range of letters.	DEFSNG L DEFSNG A-L, Z DEFSNG P,R,A-K

DEFSTR *letter list or range*	Define as string all variables beginning with specified letter, letters or range of letters.	**DEFSTR A,B,C** **DEFSTR S,X-Z** **DEFSTR M**

(Assignment and Allocation)

CLEAR *n*	Set aside specified number of bytes *n* for string storage.	**CLEAR 750** **CLEAR MEM/10** **CLEAR 0**
DIM *array(dim#1, . . . ,dim#k)*	Allocate storage for *k*-dimensional *array* with the specified size per dimension: dim#1, dim#2,. . ., etc. DIM may be followed by a list of arrays separated by commas.	**DIM A(2,3)** **DIM A1(15), A2(15)** **DIM B(X+2),C(J,K)** **DIM T(3,3,5)**

Statement	**Function**	**Examples**
LET *variable=expression*	Assign value of *expression* to *variable*. LET is optional in LEVEL II BASIC.	**LET A$="CHARLIE"** **LET B1=C1** **LET A%=I#**

(Sequence of Execution)

END	End execution, return to Command Mode.	**99 END**
STOP	Stop execution, print Break message with current line number. User may continue with CONT.	**100 STOP**
GOTO *line-number*	Branch to specified *line-number*.	**GOTO 100**
GOSUB *line-number*	Branch to sub-routine beginning at *line-number*.	**GOSUB 3000**
RETURN	Branch to statement following last--executed GOSUB.	**RETURN**

Statement	Function	Examples
ON *exp* GOTO *line#1*, . . . ,*line#k*	Evaluate expression; if INT(exp) equals one of the numbers 1 through *k*, branch to the appropriate line number. Otherwise go to next statement.	**ON K+1 GOTO 100,200,300**
ON *exp* GOSUB *line#1*,. . . ,*line#k*	Same as ON . . . GOTO except branch is to subroutine beginning at *line#1*, *line#2*, . . ., or *line#k*, depending on *exp*.	**ON J GOSUB 330,7000**
FOR *var=exp* TO *exp* STEP *exp*	Open a FOR-NEXT loop. STEP is optional; if not used, increment of one is used. See Chapter 4.	**FOR I=1 TO 50 STEP 1.5** **FOR M%=J% TO K—1%**
NEXT *variable*	Close FOR-NEXT loop. *Variable* may be omitted. To close nested loops, a variable list may be used. See Chapter 4.	**NEXT** **NEXT I** **NEXT I,J,K**
ERROR *(code)*	Simulate the error specified by *code* (see Error Code Table).	**ERROR (14)**
ON ERROR GOTO *line-number*	If an error occurs in subsequent program lines, branch to error routine beginning at *line-number*.	**ON ERROR GOTO 999**
RESUME *n*	Return from error routine to line specified by *n*. If *n* is zero or not specified, return to statement containing error. If *n* is "NEXT", return to statement following error-statement.	**RESUME** **RESUME 0** **RESUME 100** **RESUME NEXT**
RANDOM	Reseeds random number generator	**RANDOM**

Statement	Function	Examples
REM	REMark indicator; ignore rest of line	REM A IS ALTITUDE

(Tests — Conditional Statements)

Statement	Function	Examples
IF *exp–1* THEN *statement–1* ELSE *statement–2*	Tests *exp–1:* If True, execute *statement–1* then jump to next program line (unless statement–1 was a GOTO).	IF A=0 THEN PRINT ''ZERO'' ELSE PRINT ''NOT ZERO''
	If *exp–1* is False, jump directly to ELSE statement and execute subsequent statements.	

(Graphics Statements)

Statement	Function	Examples
CLS	Clear Video Display.	CLS
RESET(*x,y*)	Turn off the graphics block with horizontal coordinate *x* and vertical coordinate *y*. 0<=X<128 and 0<=Y<48	RESET(8+B,11)
SET (*x,y*)	Turn on the graphics block specified by coordinates *x* and *y*. Same argument limits as RESET.	SET(A*2,B+C)

(Special Statements)

Statement	Function	Examples
POKE *location,value*	Load *value* into memory *location* (both arguments in decimal form) 0<= *value* <=255.	POKE 15635,34 POKE 17770,A+N
OUT *port,value*	Send *value* to *port* (both arguments between 0 and 255 inclusive)	OUT 255,10 OUT 55,A

String Functions

Function	Operation	Examples
ASC(*string*)	Returns ASCII code of first character in string argument.	ASC(B$) ASC("H")
CHR$(*code exp*)	Returns a one-character string defined by *code*. If *code* specifies a control function, that function is activated.	CHR$(34) CHR$(I)
FRE(*string*)	Returns amount of memory available for string storage Argument is a dummy variable.	FRE(A$)
INKEY$	Strobes Keyboard and returns a one-character string corresponding to key pressed during strobe (null string if no key is pressed).	INKEY$
LEN(*string*)	Returns length of *string* (zero for null string).	LEN(A$+B$) LEN("HOURS")
LEFT$(*string,n*)	Returns first *n* characters of *string*.	LEFT$(A$,1) LEFT$(L1$+C$,8) LEFT$(A$,M+L)
MID$(*string,p,n,*)	Returns substring of *string* with length *n* and starting at position *p* in *string*.	MID$(M$,5,2) MID$(M$+B$,P,L—1)
RIGHT$(*string,n*)	Returns last *n* characters of *string*.	RIGHT$(NA$,7) RIGHT$(AB$,M2)
STR$(*numeric exp*)	Returns a string representation of the evaluated argument.	STR$(1.2345) STR$(A+B*2)
STRING$(*n,char*)	Returns a sequence of *n char* symbols using first character of *char*.	STRING$(30, ".") STRING$(25, "A") STRING$(5,C$)
VAL(*string*)	Returns a numeric value corresponding to a numeric-valued string.	VAL("1"+A$+"."+C$) VAL(A$+B$) VAL(G1$)

string may be a string variable, expression, or constant.

Arithmetic Functions*

Function	Operation (unless noted otherwise, $-1.7E+38 <= exp <= 1.7E+38$)	Examples
ABS(*exp*)	Returns absolute value.	ABS(L*.7) ABS(SIN(X))
ATN(*exp*)	Returns arctangent in radians.	ATN(2.7) ATN(A*3)
CDBL(*exp*)	Returns double-precision representation of *exp*.	CDBL(A) CDBL(A+1/3#)
CINT(*exp*)	Returns largest integer not greater than *exp*. Limits: $-32768 <= exp < +32768$.	CINT(A#+B)
COS(*exp*)	Returns the cosine of *exp*; assumes *exp* is in radians.	COS(2*A) COS(A/57.29578)
CSNG(*exp*)	Returns single-precision representation, with 5/4 rounding in least significant decimal when *exp* is double-precision.	CSNG(A#) CSNG(.33*B#)
EXP(*exp*)	Returns the natural exponential, $e^{exp} = EXP(exp)$.	EXP(34.5) EXP(A*B*C−1)
FIX(*exp*)	Returns the integer equivalent to truncated *exp* (fractional part of *exp* is chopped off).	FIX(A−B)
INT(*exp*)	Returns largest integer not greater than *exp*.	INT(A+B*C)
LOG(*exp*)	Returns natural logarithm (base e) of *exp*. Limits: *exp* must be positive.	LOG(12.33) LOG(A↑B+B)
RND(0)	Returns a pseudo-random number between 0.000001 and 0.999999 inclusive.	RND(0)
RND(*exp*)	Returns a pseudo-random number between 1 and INT(*exp*) inclusive. Limits: $1 <= exp < 32768$.	RND(40) RND(A+B)
SGN(*exp*)	Returns −1 for negative *exp*; 0 for zero *exp*; +1 for positive *exp*.	SGN(A*B+3) SGN(COS(X))
SIN(*exp*)	Returns the sine of *exp*; assumes *exp* is in radians.	SIN(A/B) SIN(90/57.29578)
SQR(*exp*)	Returns square root of *exp*. Limits: *exp* must be non-negative.	SQR(A*A−B*B)
TAN(*exp*)	Returns the tangent of *exp*; assumes *exp* is in radians.	TAN(X) TAN(X*.0174533)

*exp is any numeric-valued expression or constant.

Special Functions

Function	Operation and Limits	Examples
ERL	Returns line number of current error.	ERL
ERR	Returns a value related to current error code (if error has occurred). ERR = (error code−1)*2. Also: (ERR/2)+1 = error code.	ERR/2+1
INP(*port*)	Inputs and returns the current value from the specified *port*. Both argument and result are in the range 0 to 255 inclusive.	INP(55)
MEM	Returns total unused and unprotected bytes in memory.	MEM
PEEK(*location*)	Returns value stored in the specified memory byte. *location* must be a valid memory address in decimal form (see Memory Map in Appendix D).	PEEK(15370)
POINT (*x,y*)	Checks the graphics block specified by horizontal coordinate *x* and vertical coordinate *y*. If block is "on". returns a True (−1); if block is "off", returns a False (0). Limits: $0 <= x < 128; 0 <= y < 48$.	
POS(0)	Returns a number indicating the current cursor position. The argument "0" is a dummy variable.	POS(0)
USR(*n*)	Branches to machine language subroutine. For LEVEL II BASIC, *n* must equal 0. See Chapter 8.	USR(0)
VARPTR(*var*)	Returns the address where the specified variable's name, value, and pointer are stored. *var* must be a valid variable name. Returns 0 if *var* has not been assigned a value.	VARPTR(A$) VARPTR(N1)

LEVEL II Reserved Words*

@	FIX	OUT
ABS	FOR	PEEK
AND	FRE	POINT
ASC	GET	POKE
ATN	GOSUB	POS
CDBL	GOTO	PRINT
CHR$	IF	PUT

* Many of these words have no function in LEVEL II BASIC; they are reserved for use in LEVEL II DISK BASIC. None of these words can be used inside a variable name.

CINT	INKEY$	RANDOM
CLEAR	INP	READ
CLOSE	INPUT	REM
CLS	INSTR	RESET
CMD	INT	RESTORE
CONT	KILL	RESUME
COS	LEFT$	RETURN
CSNG	LET	RIGHT$
CVD	LSET	RND
CVI	LEN	SAVE
CVS	LINE	SET
DATA	LIST	SGN
DEFDBL	LOAD	SIN
DEFFN	LOC	SQR
DEFINT	LOF	STEP
DEFSNG	LOG	STOP
DEFUSR	MEM	STRING$
DEFSTR	MERGE	STR$
DELETE	MID$	TAB
DIM	MKD$	TAN
EDIT	MKI$	THEN
ELSE	MKS$	TIME$
END	NAME	TROFF
ERL	NEW	TRON
ERR	NEXT	USING
ERROR	NOT	USR
EXP	ON	VAL
FIELD	OPEN	VARPTR

HEWLETT-PACKARD'S HP-85

The HP-85 BASIC language consists of **statements, functions, operators,** and **commands**. Operators and functions are used with variables, numbers, and strings to create numeric and string **expressions**. Expressions and functions can be included in statements and executed from the keyboard. Each statement can be preceded by a statement number and stored as a program statement. Most functions, statements, and commands can also be separately executed from the keyboard; exceptions are noted.

Operators

Arithmetic

+	Add
−	Subtract
✱	Multiply
∕	Divide
^	Exponentiate
MOD	Modulo: $A \ MOD \ B = A - B ✱ INT(A/B)$
∖ or DIV	Integer divide: $A \ DIV \ B = IP(A/B)$

Logical Evaluation

Logical expressions return the values 0 for false and 1 for true. Non-zero values are considered true; zero values are false.

Relational

=	Equal to
>	Greater than
<	Less than
>=	Greater than or equal to
<=	Less than or equal to
<> or #	Not equal to

Non-numeric values can also be compared with relational operators. Strings are compared, character by character, from left to right until a difference is found. If one string ends before a difference is found, the shorter string is considered the lesser.

Logical

AND
OR
EXOR
NOT

String

    &   String concatenation

Math Hierarchy

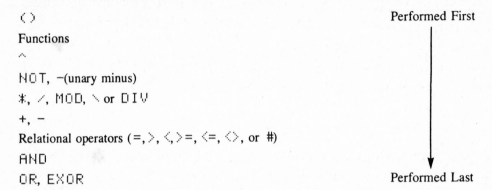

( )   Performed First

Functions

^

NOT, −(unary minus)

*, /, MOD, \ or DIV

+, −

Relational operators (=, >, <, >=, <=, <>, or #)

AND

OR, EXOR   Performed Last

Expressions are evaluated from left to right for operators at the same level. Operations within parentheses are performed first. Nested parentheses are evaluated inward out.

Data Precision

Precision	Accuracy	Range	Maximum array size with standard memory and no program.
REAL	12 Digits	±9.99999999999E±499	1800
SHORT	5 Digits	±9.9999E±99	3600
INTEGER	5 Digits	−99999 through 99999	4800

Special Characters

@   Enables multi-statement lines.

                         100 CLEAR @ KEY LABEL

!   Remarks follows.

                         110 DISP C ! Display cost.

?   INPUT prompt. Input items are expected.

Variables

Simple Numeric Variables: A1, B, C3.

The name consists of a letter or a letter and one digit. Real precision is assumed unless SHORT or INTEGER type is declared.

Arrays: A1(50,5), B(20,20), C3(10).

The name consists of a letter or a letter and one digit. An array name can be the same as a simple variable name used elsewhere in the program, but a one-dimensional array cannot have the same name as a two-dimensional array.

Arrays contain numeric elements only. Subscripts dimension the row or row and column in `DIM`, `COM`, or type (`REAL`, `INTEGER`, `SHORT`) declaration statements. The lower bound of an array subscript is 0 unless `OPTION BASE 1` is specified before all array references. The default upper bound for row and column subscripts is 10.

Subscripts reference a particular array element in non-declaratory statements with three exceptions. Entire arrays (either one- or two-dimensional) may be referenced in `TRACE VAR`, `PRINT#`, or `READ#` statements by specifying the array name followed by a pair of parentheses and no subscripts (e.g., `C3( )`). A comma may be enclosed within the parentheses for documentation purposes to specify a two-dimensional array (e.g., `A1( , )`). This notation enables you to trace, write onto tape, or read from tape all elements of the specified array.

String Variables: `A1$, B$, C3$`.

The name consists of a letter or a letter and one digit followed by a dollar sign. The default length is 18 characters unless otherwise specified in a `COM` or `DIM` statement. The maximum length of a string is limited only by available memory. Dimension strings in a `DIM` or `COM` statement by specifying the variable name followed by the length enclosed within brackets: `A1$[25]`, `B$[415]`, `C3$[5]`.

Substrings: `A1$[2,25]`, `B$[5]`, `C3$[3,3]`.

Substrings are specified by one or two numbers (or expressions) enclosed within *brackets*. One number specifies a beginning character; the substring extends to the end of the string. Two numbers separated by a comma specify beginning and ending character positions, respectively.

Strings can be compared with the relational operators and can be concatenated by `&` operator. (Refer to Operators.)

Syntax Guidelines to Commands and BASIC Statements

These terms and conventions are used in the following list of statements and commands.

`dot matrix`	All items in dot matrix denote system commands or BASIC statements that must appear exactly as shown. Either small or capital letters may be used to spell keywords.
[ ]	All items enclosed within square brackets are optional unless the brackets are in dot matrix.
...	Three dots indicate that the previous item can be repeated.
statement number	An integer from 1 through 9999.
numeric expression	A logical combination of variables, constants, operators, and functions (including user-defined functions), grouped within parentheses as necessary.
string expression	A logical combination of text within quotes, string variables, substrings, string concatenations, and string functions.

file name
or
program name
	A program or file name can be any string expression. Any letter, number, symbol, or character except quotes or the null string may be used. Only the first six letters of the string expression are used for the name.
	    LOAD "PROG1*"
	    LOAD T$

buffer number	The number assigned to a tape data file by an ASSIGN# statement, and referenced by the PRINT# and READ# statements. Its range is 1 through 10.

Commands

Non-Programmable

AUTO [beginning line number [, increment value]]
CONT [statement number]
DELETE first statement number [, last statement number]
INIT
LOAD program name
REN [first statement number [, increment value]]
RUN [statement number]
SCRATCH
STORE program name
UNSECURE file name , security code , secure type

Programmable

CAT
COPY
CTAPE
ERASETAPE
FLIP
LIST [beginning statement number [, ending statement number]]
PLIST [beginning statement number [, ending statement number]]
PRINT ALL
REWIND
SECURE file name , security code , secure type

BASIC Statements

ASSIGN# buffer number TO file name
ASSIGN# buffer number TO *
BEEP [tone , duration]

CHAIN file name

CLEAR

COM common variable list

CRT IS output code number

CREATE file name , number of records [, number of bytes per record]

DATA data list

DEFAULT OFF

DEFAULT ON

DEF FN numeric variable name [(parameter)][= numeric expression]

DEF FN string variable name [(parameter)][= string expression]

DEG

DIM dimension list

DISP display list

DISP USING image format string [; disp using list]

DISP USING statement number [; disp using list]

END

FN END

FOR loop counter = initial value TO final value [STEP increment value]

GOSUB statement number

GOTO statement number

GRAD

IF numeric expression THEN statement number [ELSE statement number

or   or

executable statement   executable statement]

IMAGE image format string

INPUT variable name₁ [, variable name₂ ...]

INTEGER numeric variable [(subscripts)][, numeric variable] (subscripts)] ...]

KEY LABEL

[LET] numeric variable₁ [, numeric variable₂ ...] = numeric expression

[LET] string variable₁ [, string variable₂ ...] = string expression

[LET] FN variable name = expression

LOAD BIN file name

NEXT loop counter

NORMAL

OFF ERROR

OFF KEY# key number

OFF TIMER# timer number

ON ERROR GOSUB statement number

ON ERROR GOTO statement number

ON numeric expression GOSUB statement number list

ON numeric expression GOTO statement number list

ON KEY# key number [, key label] GOSUB statement number

ON KEY# key number [, key label] GOTO statement number

ON TIMER# timer number , milliseconds GOSUB statement number

ON TIMER# timer number , milliseconds GOTO statement number

OPTION BASE 1 or 0

PAUSE

PRINT [print list]

PRINT# buffer number ; [print# list]

PRINT# buffer number , record number [; print# list]]

PRINT USING image format string [; print using list]

PRINT USING statement number [; print using list]

PRINTER IS output code number

PURGE file name [, purge code number]

RAD

RANDOMIZE [numeric expression]

READ variable name$_1$ [, variable name$_2$ ...]

READ# buffer number ; variable list

READ# buffer number , record number [; variable list]

REAL numeric variable [(subscripts)][, numeric variable [(subscripts)] ...]

REM [any combination of characters]

RENAME old file name TO new file name

RESTORE [statement number]

RETURN

SHORT numeric variable [(subscripts)][, numeric variable [(subscripts)] ...]

STOP

STORE BIN file name

TRACE

TRACE ALL

TRACE VAR variable$_1$ [, variable$_2$ ...]

SETTIME seconds since midnight , Julian day in form yyddd

WAIT number of milliseconds

Graphics Statements

ALPHA

BPLOT character string, number of characters per line

DRAW x-coordinate , y-coordinate

GCLEAR [y]

GRAPH

IDRAW x-increment , y-increment

IMOVE x-increment , y-increment

LABEL character string

LDIR numeric expression

MOVE x-coordinate , y-coordinate

PEN numeric expression

PENUP

PLOT x-coordinate , y-coordinate

SCALE xmin , xmax , ymin , ymax

XAXIS y-intercept [, tic length [, xmin , xmax]]

YAXIS x-intercept [, tic length [, ymin , ymax]]

BASIC Predefined Functions

ABS(X)	Absolute value of X.
ACS(X)	Arcosine of X, in 1st or 2nd quadrant.
ASN(X)	Arcsine of X, in 1st or 4th quadrant.
ATN(X)	Arctangent of X, in 1st or 4th quadrant.
ATN2(Y,X)	Arctangent of Y/X, in proper quadrant.
CEIL(X)	Smallest integer $>=$X.
CHR$(X)	Character whose decimal character code is X, $0<=X<=255$.
COS(X)	Cosine of X.
COT(X)	Cotangent of X.
CSC(X)	Cosecant of X.
DATE	Julian date in format yyddd (assumes system timer has been set properly).
DTR(X)	Degree to radian conversion.
EPS	Smallest positive machine number (1E-499).
ERRL	Line number of latest error.
ERRN	Number of latest error.
EXP(X)	e^x
FLOOR(X)	Same as INT(X) (relates to CEIL).
FP(X)	Fractional part of X.
INF	Largest machine number (9.99999999999E499).
INT(X)	Largest integer $<=$X.
IP(X)	Integer part of X.
LEN(S$)	Length of string S$.
LGT(X)	Log to the base 10 of X, X>0.
LOG(X)	Natural logaritm, X>0.
MAX(X,Y)	If X>Y then X, else Y.
MIN(X,Y)	If X<Y then X, else Y.
NUM(S$)	Decimal character code of first character of S$.
PI	3.14159265359

POS(S1$, S2$)	Searches string S1$ for the first occurence of string S2$. Returns starting index if found, otherwise returns 0.
RMD(X,Y)	Remainder of X/Y: X − Y * IP(X/Y).
RND	Next number, X, in a sequence of pseudo-random numbers, $0 < = X < 1$.
RTD(X)	Radian to degree conversion.
SEC(X)	Secant of X.
SGN(X)	The sign of X, −1 if X<0, 0 if X=0, and +1 if X>0.
SIN(X)	Sine of X.
SQR(X)	Positive square root of X.
TAB(N)	Skips to specified column.
TAN(X)	Tangent of X.
TIME	Time in seconds since midnight (assumes system timer has been set properly).
UPC$(S$)	Returns string with all lower-case alphabetic characters converted to upper-case.
VAL(S$)	Returns the numeric equivalent of the string S$.
VAL$(X)	String equivalent of X.

APPLE II

The following commands and statements are for the Apple II Microcomputer System. Copyrighted Apple Computer Inc. Reproduced by permission.

BASIC COMMANDS

Commands are executed immediately; they do not require line numbers.Most Statements (see Basic Statements Section) may also be used as commands. Remember to press Return key after each command so that Apple knows that you have finished that line. Multiple commands (as opposed to statements) on same line separated by a " : " are NOT allowed.

COMMAND NAME

AUTO *num*

Sets automatic line numbering mode. Starts at line number *num* and increments line numbers by 10. To exit AUTO mode, type a control X*, then type the letters "MAN" and press the return key.

AUTO *num1, num2*

Same as above execpt increments line numbers by number *num2*.

CLR

Clears current BASIC variables; undimensions arrays. Program is unchanged.

CON

Continues program execution after a stop from a control C*. Does not change variables.

DEL *num1*

Deletes line number *num1*.

DEL *num1, num2*

Deletes program from line number *num1* through line number *num2*.

DSP *var*

Sets debug mode that will display variable *var* everytime that it is changed along with the line number that caused the change. (NOTE: RUN command clears DSP mode so that DSP command is effective only if program is continued by a CON or GOTO command.)

HIMEM: *expr*

Sets highest memory location for use by BASIC at location specified by expression *expr* in decimal. HIMEM: may not be increased without destroying program. HIMEM: is automatically set at maximum RAM memory when BASIC is entered by a control B*.

GOTO *expr*

Causes immediate jump to line number specified by expression *expr*.

GR

Sets mixed color graphics display mode. Clears screen to black. Resets scrolling window. Displays 40x40 squares in 15 colors on top of screen and 4 lines of text at bottom.

LIST

Lists entire program on screen.

LIST *num1*

Lists program line number *num1*.

LIST *num1, num2*

Lists program line number *num1* through line number *num2*.

LOAD *expr.*

Reads (Loads) a BASIC program from cassette tape. Start tape recorder before hitting return key. Two beeps and a " > " indicate a good load. "ERR" or "MEM FULL ERR" message indicates a bad tape or poor recorder performance.

LOMEM: *expr*   Similar to HIMEM: except sets lowest memory location available to BASIC. Automatically set at 2048 when BASIC is entered with a control B*. Moving LOMEM: destroys current variable values.

MAN   Clears AUTO line numbering mode to all manual line numbering after a control C* or control X*.

NEW   Clears (Scratches) current BASIC program.

NO DSP *var*   Clears DSP mode for variable *var*.

NO TRACE   Clears TRACE mode.

RUN   Clears variables to zero, undimensions all arrays and executes program starting at lowest statement line number.

RUN *expr*   Clears variables and executes program starting at line number specified by expression *expr*.

SAVE   Stores (saves) a BASIC program on a cassette tape. Start tape recorder in record mode prior to hitting return key.

TEXT   Sets all text mode. Screen is formated to display alpha-numeric characters on 24 lines of 40 characters each. TEXT resets scrolling window to maximum.

TRACE   Sets debug mode that displays line number of each statement as it is executed.

BASIC Operators

Symbol	Sample Statement	Explanation
Prefix Operators		
( )	10 X= 4*(5 + X)	Expressions within parenthesis ( ) are always evaluated first.
+	20 X= 1+4*5	Optional; +1 times following expression.
-	30 ALPHA = -(BETA +2)	Negation of following expression.
NOT	40 IF A NOT B THEN 200	Logical Negation of following expression; 0 if expression is true (non-zero), 1 if expression is false (zero).
Arithmetic Operators		
↑	60 Y = X↑3	Exponentiate as in X^3. NOTE: ↑ is shifted letter N.
*	70 LET DOTS=A*B*N2	Multiplication. NOTE: Implied multiplication such as (2 + 3)(4) is not allowed thus N2 in example is a variable not N * 2.

* Control characters such as control X or control C are typed by holding down the CTRL key while typing the specified letter. This is similiar to how one holds down the shift key to type capital letters. Control characters are NOT displayed on the screen but are accepted by the computer. For example, type several control G's. We will also use a superscript C to indicate a control character as in X^C.

/	80 PRINT GAMMA/S	Divide
MOD	90 X = 12 MOD 7 100 X = X MOD(Y+2)	Modulo: Remainder after division of first expression by second expression.
+	110 P = L + G	Add
-	120 XY4 = H-D	Substract
=	130 HEIGHT=15 140 LET SIZE=7*5 150 A(8) = 2 155 ALPHA$ = "PLEASE"	Assignment operator; assigns a value to a variable. LET is optional

Relational and Logical Operators

The numeric values used in logical evaluation are "true" if non-zero,
"false" if zero.

Symbol	Sample Statement	Explanation
=	160 IF D = E THEN 500	Expression "equals" expression.
=	170 IF A$(1,1)= "Y" THEN 500	String variable "equals" string variable.
# or < >	180 IF ALPHA #X*Y THEN 500	Expression "does not equal" expression.
#	190 IF A$ # "NO" THEN 500	String variable "does not equal" string variable. NOTE: If strings are not the same length, they are considered un-equal. < > not allowed with strings.
>	200 IF A>B THEN GO TO 50	Expression "is greater than" expression.
<	210 IF A+1<B-5 THEN 100	Expression "is less than" expression.
>=	220 IF A>=B THEN 100	Expression "is greater than or equal to" expression.
<=	230 IF A+1<=B-6 THEN 200	Expression "is less than or equal to" expression.
AND	240 IF A>B AND C<D THEN 200	Expression 1 "and" expression 2 must both be "true" for statements to be true.
OR	250 IF ALPHA OR BETA+1 THEN 200	If either expression 1 or expression 2 is "true", statement is "true".

BASIC FUNCTIONS

Functions return a numeric result. They may be used as expressions or as part
of expressions. PRINT is used for examples only, other statements may
be used. Expressions following function name must be enclosed between two
parenthesis signs.
FUNCTION NAME

ABS *(expr)*	300 PRINT ABS(X)	Gives absolute value of the expression *expr*.
ASC *(str$)*	310 PRINT ASC("BACK") 320 PRINT ASC(B$) 330 PRINT ASC(B$(4,4)) 335 PRINT ASC(B$(Y))	Gives decimal ASCII value of designated string variable *str$*. If more than one character is in designated string or sub-string, it gives decimal ASCII value of first character.

LEN *(str$)*	340 PRINT LEN(B$)	Gives current length of designated string variable *str$*; i.e., number of characters.
PDL *(expr)*	350 PRINT PDL(X)	Gives number between 0 and 255 corresponding to paddle position on game paddle number designated by expression *expr* and must be legal paddle (0,1,2,or 3) or else 255 is returned.
PEEK *(expr)*	360 PRINT PEEK(X)	Gives the decimal value of number stored of decimal memory location specified by expression *expr*. For MEMORY locations above 32676, use negative number; i.e., HEX location FFF0 is -16
RND *(expr)*	370 PRINT RND(X)	Gives random number between 0 and (expression *expr* -1) if expression *expr* is positive; if minus, it gives random number between 0 and (expression *expr* +1).
SCRN(*expr1,* *expr2)*	380 PRINT SCRN (X1,Y1)	Gives color (number between 0 and 15) of screen at horizontal location designated by expression *expr1* and vertical location designated by expression *expr2* Range of expression *expr1* is 0 to 39. Range of expression *expr2* is 0 to 39 if in standard mixed colorgraphics display mode as set by GR command or 0 to 47 if in all color mode set by POKE -16304 ,0: POKE - 16302,0.
SGN *(expr)*	390 PRINT SGN(X)	Gives sign (not sine) of expression *expr* i.e., -1 if expression *expr* is negative, zero if zero and +1 if *expr* is positive.

BASIC STATEMENTS

Each BASIC statement must have a line number between 0 and 32767. Variable names must start with an alpha character and may be any number of alpha-numeric characters up to 100.   Variable names may not contain buried any of the following words: AND, AT, MOD, OR, STEP, or THEN. Variable names may not begin with the letters END, LET, or REM. String variables names must end with a $ (dollar sign). Multiple statements may appear under the same line number if separated by a : (colon) as long as the total number of characters in the line (including spaces) is less than approximately 150 characters
Most statements may also be used as commands. BASIC statements are executed by RUN or GOTO commands.

NAME	EXAMPLE	DESCRIPTION
CALL *expr*	10 CALL-936	Causes execution of a machine level language subroutine at <u>decimal</u> memory location specified by expression *expr* Locations above 32767 are specified using negative numbers; i.e., location in example 10 is hexidecimal number $FC53
COLOR=*expr*	30 COLOR=12	In standard resolution color (GR) graphics mode, this command sets screen TV color to value in expression *expr* in the range 0 to 15 as described in Table A. Actually expression *expr* may be in the range 0 to 255 without error message since it is implemented as if it were expression *expr* MOD 16.

DIM *var1 (expr1)* *str$ (expr2)* *var2 (expr3)*	50 DIM A(20),B(10) 60 DIM B$(30) 70 DIM C (2) Illegal: 80 DIM A(30) Legal: 85 DIM C(1000)	The DIM statement causes APPLE II to reserve memory for the specified variables. For number arrays APPLE reserves approximately 2 times *expr* bytes of memory limited by available memory. For string arrays - *str$ (expr)* must be in the range of 1 to 255. Last defined variable may be redimensioned at any time; thus, example in line is illegal but 85 is allowed.
DSP *var*	Legal: 90 DSP AX: DSP L Illegal: 100 DSP AX,B 102 DSP AB$ 104 DSP A(5) Legal: 105 A=A(5): DSP A	Sets debug mode that DSP variable *var* each time it changes and the line number where the change occured.
END	110 END	Stops program execution. Sends carriage return and "> " BASIC prompt) to screen.
FOR *var=* *expr1* TO *expr2* STEP *expr3*	110 FOR L=0 to 39 120 FOR X=Y1 TO Y3 130 FOR I=39 TO 1 150 GOSUB 100 *J2	Begins FOR...NEXT loop, initializes variable *var* to value of expression *expr1* then increments it by amount in expression *expr3* each time the corresponding "NEXT" statement is encountered, until value of expression *expr2* is reached. If STEP *expr3* is omitted, a STEP of +1 is assumed. Negative numbers are allowed.
GOSUB *expr*	140 GOSUB 500	Causes branch to BASIC subroutine starting at legal line number specified by expression *expr* Subroutines may be nested up to 16 levels.
GOTO *expr*	160 GOTO 200 170 GOTO ALPHA+100	Causes immediate jump to legal line number specified by expression *expr*.
GR	180 GR 190 GR: POKE -16302,0	Sets mixed standard resolution color graphics mode. Initializes COLOR = 0 (Black) for top 40x40 of screen and sets scrolling window to lines 21 through 24 by 40 characters for four lines of text at bottom of screen. Example 190 sets all color mode (40x48 field) with no text at bottom of screen.
HLIN *expr1,* *expr2* AT *expr3*	200 HLIN 0,39 AT 20 210 HLIN Z,Z+6 AT I	In standard resolution color graphics mode, this command draws a horizontal line of a predefined color (set by COLOR=) starting at horizontal position defined by expression *expr1* and ending at position *expr2* at vertical position defined by expression *expr3* . *expr1* and *expr2* must be in the range of 0 to 39 and *expr1* < = *expr2* . *expr3* be in the range of 0 to 39 (or 0 to 47 if not in mixed mode).

Note: HLIN 0, 19 AT 0 is a horizontal line at the top of the screen extending from left corner to center of screen and HLIN 20,39 AT 39 is a horizontal line at the bottom of the screen extending from center to right corner.

<u>IF</u> *expression* <u>THEN</u> *statement*	220 IF A > B THEN
	    PRINT A
	230 IF X=Ø THEN C=1
	240 IF A#1Ø THEN
	    GOSUB 2ØØ
	250 IF A$(1,1)# "Y"
	    THEN 1ØØ
	Illegal:
	260 IF L > 5 THEN 5Ø:
	    ELSE 6Ø
	Legal:
	270 IF L > 5 THEN 5Ø
	    GO TO 6Ø
		If *expression* is true (non-zero) then execute *statement*; if false do not execute *statement*. If *statement* is an expression, then a GOTO *expr* type of statement is assumed to be implied. The "ELSE" in example 26Ø is illegal but may be implemented as shown in example 27Ø.

<u>INPUT</u> *var1*,
   var2, *str$*
	28Ø INPUT X,Y,Z(3)
	29Ø INPUT "AMT",
	   DLLR
	3ØØ INPUT "Y or N?", A$
		Enters data into memory from I/O device. If number input is expected, APPLE wil output "?"; if string input is expected no "?" will be outputed. Multiple numeric inputs to same statement may be separated by a comma or a carriage return. String inputs must be separated by a carriage return only. One pair of " " may be used immediately after INPUT to output prompting text enclosed within the quotation marks to the screen.

<u>IN#</u> *expr*	31Ø IN# 6 32Ø IN# Y+2 33Ø IN# Ø	Transfers source of data for subsequent INPUT statements to peripheral I/O slot (1-7) as specified as by expression *expr*. Slot Ø is not addressable from BASIC. IN#Ø (Example 33Ø) is used to return data source from peripherial I/O to keyboard connector.
<u>LET</u>	34Ø LET X=5	Assignment operator. "LET" is optional

<u>LIST</u> *num1*,
   num2
	35Ø IF X > 6 THEN
	   LIST 5Ø
		Causes program from line number *num1* through line number *num2* to be displayed on screen.

<u>NEXT</u> *var1*, *var2*	36Ø NEXT I 37Ø NEXT J,K	Increments corresponding "FOR" variable and loops back to statement following "FOR" until variable exceeds limit.
<u>NO DSP</u> *var*	38Ø NO DSP I	Turns-off DSP debug mode for variable
<u>NO TRACE</u>	39Ø NO TRACE	Turns-off TRACE debug mode
<u>PLOT</u> *expr1*, *expr2*	4ØØ PLOT 15, 25 4ØØ PLT XV,YV	In standard resolution color graphics, this command plots a small square of a predefined color (set by COLOR=) at horizontal location specified by expression *expr1* in range Ø to 39 and vertical location specified by expression *expr2* in range Ø to 39 (or Ø to 47 if in all graphics mode) NOTE: PLOT Ø Ø is upper left and PLOT 39, 39 (or PLOT 39, 47) is lower right corner.
<u>POKE</u> *expr1*, *expr2*	42Ø POKE 2Ø, 4Ø 43Ø POKE 7*256, XMOD255	Stores decimal number defined by expression *expr2* in range of Ø 255 at decimal memory location specified by expression *expr1* Locations above 32767 are specified by negative numbers.
<u>POP</u>	44Ø POP	"POPS" nested GOSUB return stack address by one.

PRINT *var1, var, str$*	45Ø PRINT L1 46Ø PRINT L1, X2 47Ø PRINT "AMT=";DX 48Ø PRINT A$;B$; 49Ø PRINT 492 PRINT "HELLO" 494 PRINT 2+3	Outputs data specified by variable *var* or string variable *str$* starting at current cursor location. If there is not trailing "," or ";" (Ex 45Ø) a carriage return will be generated. Commas (Ex. 46Ø) outputs data in 5 left justified columns. Semi-colon (Ex. 47Ø) inhibits print of any spaces. Text imbedded in " " will be printed and may appear multiple times.
PR# *expr*	5ØØ PR# 7	Like IN#, transfers output to I/O slot defined by expression *expr* PR# Ø is video output not I/O slot Ø.
REM	51Ø REM REMARK	No action. All characters after REM are treated as a remark until terminated by a carriage return.
RETURN	52Ø RETURN 53Ø IFX= 5 THEN RETURN	Causes branch to statement following last GOSUB; i.e., RETURN ends a subroutine. Do not confuse "RETURN" <u>statement</u> with Return <u>key</u> on keyboard.
TAB *expr*	53Ø TAB 24 54Ø TAB I+24 55Ø IF A#B THEN TAB 2Ø	Moves cursor to absolute horizontal position specified by expression *expr* in the range of 1 to 4Ø. Position is left to right
TEXT	55Ø TEXT 56Ø TEXT: CALL-936	Sets all text mode. Resets scrolling window to 24 lines by 4Ø characters. Example 56Ø also clears screen and homes cursor to upper left corner
TRACE	57Ø TRACE 58Ø IFN > 32ØØØ THEN TRACE	Sets debug mode that displays each line number as it is executed.
VLIN *expr1, expr2* AT *expr3*	59Ø VLIN Ø, 39AT15 6ØØ VLIN Z,Z+6ATY	Similar to HLIN except draws vertical line starting at *expr1* and ending at *expr2* at horizontal position *expr3*.
VTAB *expr*	61Ø VTAB 18 62Ø VTAB Z+2	Similar to TAB. Moves cursor to absolute vertical position specified by expression *expr* in the range 1 to 24. VTAB 1 is top line on screen; VTAB24 is bottom.

SPECIAL CONTROL AND EDITING CHARACTERS

"Control" characters are indicated by a super-scripted "C" such as G^C. They are obtained by holding down the CTRL key while typing the specified letter. Control characters are NOT displayed on the TV screen. B^C and C^C must be followed by a carriage return. Screen editing characters are indicated by a sub-scripted "E" such as D$_E$. They are obtained by pressing <u>and releasing</u> the ESC key then typing specified letter. Edit characters send information only to display screen and does not send data to memory. For example, U^C moves to cursor to right and copies text while A$_E$ moves cursor to right but does not copy text.

CHARACTER	DESCRIPTION OF ACTION
RESET key	Immediately interrupts any program execution and resets computer. Also sets all text mode with scrolling window at maximum. Control is transferred to System Monitor and Apple prompts with a "*" (asterisk) and a bell. Hitting RESET key does NOT destroy existing BASIC or machine language program.

Control B	If in System Monitor (as indicated by a "*"), a control B and a carriage return will transfer control to BASIC, scratching (killing) any existing BASIC program and set HIMEM: to maximum installed user memory and LOMEM: to 2048.
Control C	If in BASIC, halts program and displays line number where stop occurred*. Program may be continued with a CON command. If in System Monitor, (as indicated by "*"), control C and a carraige return will enter BASIC without killing current program.
Control G	Sounds bell (beeps speaker)
Control H	Backspaces cursor and deletes any overwritten characters from computer but not from screen. Apply supplied keyboards have special key "←" on right side of keyboard that provides this functions without using control button.
Control J	Issues line feed only
Control V	Compliment to H^C. Forward spaces cursor and copies over written characters. Apple keyboards have "→" key on right side which also performs this function.
Control X	Immediately deletes current line.

CHARACTER	DESCRIPTION OF ACTION
A_E	Move cursor to right
B_E	Move cursor to left
C_E	Move cursor down
D_E	Move cursor up
E_E	Clear text from cursor to end of line
F_E	Clear text from cursor to end of page
$@_E$	Home cursor to top of page, clear text to end of page.

Table A: APPLE II COLORS AS SET BY COLOR =

Note: Colors may vary depending on TV tint (hue) setting and may also be changed by adjusting trimmer capacitor C3 on APPLE II P.C. Board.

0 = Black		8 = Brown	
1 - Magenta		9 = Orange	
2 = Dark Blue		10 = Grey	
3 = Light Purple		11 = Pink	
4 = Dark Green		12 = Green	
5 = Grey		13 = Yellow	
6 = Medium Blue		14 = Blue/Green	
7 = Light Blue		15 = White	

* If BASIC program is expecting keyboard input, you will have to hit carriage return key after typing control C.

COMMODORE PET (CBM INSTRUCTIONS)

BASIC STATEMENTS

DEF FN
DIM
END
FOR-TO-STEP-NEXT
GET
GOSUB-RETURN
GOTO
IF-THEN
INPUT
LET
ON-(GOSUB-GOTO)
POKE-PEEK
PRINT
READ-DATA-RESTORE
REM
STOP-CONT
WAIT

In the following description of statements, an argument of V or W denotes a numeric variable. X denotes a numeric expression, X$ denotes a string expression and an I or J denotes an expression that is truncated to an integer before the statement is executed. Truncation means that any fractional part of the number is lost, e.g. 3.9 becomes 3, 4.01 becomes 4.

DEF   100 DEF FNA (V) = V/B + C   The user can define functions like the built-in functions (SQR, SGN, ABS, etc) through the use of the DEF statement. The name of the function is 'FN' followed by any legal variable name, for example: FNX, FNJ7, FNKO, FNR2. User-furnished functions are restructed to one line. A function may be defined to be any expression, but may only have one argument. In the example, B & C are variables that are used in the program. Executing the DEF statement defines the function. User-defined functions can be redefined by executing another DEF statement for the same function. User-defined string functions are not allowed. 'V' is called the dummy variable. Execution of this statement following the above would cause Z to be set to 3/B + C, but the value of V would be unchanged.

110 Z = FNA(3)

A function definition may be recursive. A DEF statement may be written in terms of other functions, however.

200 DEF FNA(V) = FNB(V)

DIM

113 DIM A(3),B(10)

Allocates space for matrices. All matrix examples are set to zero by the DIM statement.

114 DIM R3(5,5), D$(2,2,2)

Matrices can have more than one dimension. Up to 255 elements

115 DIM Q1(N),Z(2*1)

Matrices can be dimensioned dynamically during program execution. If a matrix is not explicitly dimensioned with a DIM statement, it is assumed to have as many subscripts as implied in its first use and whose subscripts may range from 0 to 10 (eleven elements).

117 A(8) = 4

If this statement was encountered before a DIM statement for A was found in the program, it would be as if a DIM A(10) had been executed previous to the execution of line 117. All subscripts start at zero (0), which means that DIM x (100) really allocates 101 matrix elements.

END   999 END

Terminates program execution without printing a BREAK message. (See STOP) CONT after an END statement causes execution to resume at the statement after the END statement. END can be used anywhere in the program, and is optional.

FOR

300 FOR V = 1 TO 9.3 STEP .6

V is set equal to the value of the expression following the equal sign, in this case 1. This value is called the initial value. Then the statements between FOR and NEXT are executed. The final value is the value of the expression following the TO. The step is the value for the expression following STEP. When the NEXT statement is encountered, the step is added to the variable.

310 FOR V = 1 TO 9.3

If no STEP was specified, it is assumed to be one. If the step is positive and the new value of the variable is < = to the final value (9.3 in this example), or the step value is negative and the new value of the variable is = >the final value, then the first statement following the FOR statement is executed. Otherwise, the statement following the NEXT statement is executed. All FOR loops execute the statements between the FOR and the NEXT at least once, even in the case like FOR V = 1 TO 0.

315 FOR V = 10*N TO 3.4/Q STEP SQR(R)

Note that expressions (formulas) may be used for the initial, final and step values in the FOR loop. The variables of the expressions are computed only once, before the body of the FOR...NEXT loop to terminate. The statement between the FOR and its corresponding NEXT in both example above (310) would be executed 9 times.

340 NEXT V

Marks the end of a FOR loop.

345 NEXT

If no variable is given, matches the most recent FOR loop.

350 NEXT V,W

A single NEXT may be used to match multiple FOR statements. Equivalent to NEXT V: NEXT W. Specification the former way saves 1 byte of BASIC text storage.

GET | GET A | Works like INPUT or INPUT# on a single character basis. Unlike INPUT though, this function scans the keyboard and does not wait for carriage return to be pressed. If no key has been pressed, A$ = " "(null string) and A = 0 after executing this statement.

GET A$

10 GET A$: 1FA$ = " "THEN 10

This example stays in a loop until a key has been
pressed.

GOSUB | 10 GOSUB 910 | Branches to the specified statement (910) until a RETURN is encountered; when a branch is then made to the statement after the GOSUB. GOSUB nesting is limited to 23 levels.

Subroutines line numbers are searched for from the beginning of text. To increase execution speed, define subroutines first with low line numbers. Fewer digits in line numbers will also save storage space.

50 RETURN

Causes a subroutine to return to the statement after the most recently executed GOSUB.

GOTO | 50 GOTO 100 | Branches to the statement specified. Keeping line numbers low will save space on GOTO statements.

IF...GOTO | 32 IF x< = Y + 23x4 GOTO 92 | Equivalent to IF...THEN, except that IF...GOTO must be followed by a line number, while IF...THEN can be followed by either a line number or another statement.

IF...THEN | 15 IF x<0 THEN 5 | Branches to specified statement if the relation is True.

25 IF X = 5 THEN 50:Z = A

WARNING. The "Z = A" will never be executed because if the relation is true, BASIC will branch to line 50. If the relation is a false, BASIC will proceed to the line after line 25.

26 IF X<0 THEN PRINT "ERROR X NEGATIVE": GOTO 350

In this example, if X is less than 0, the PRINT statement will be executed and then the GOTO statement will branch to line 350. If the X was 0 or positive, BASIC will proceed to execute the lines after line 26. Binary floating point representations of decimal fractions may not always be exact. sometimes a comparison will fail because of this. In this case, compare the number to a ± range.

INPUT

Request information character by character until carriage return from the keyboard, turning the characters into numbers or strings of a maximum length of 79 characters.

3 INPUT V,W,W2

Requests data from the terminal (to be typed in). Each value must be separated from the preceeding value by a comma (,). The last value typed should be followed by a carriage return. A "?" is typed as a prompt character. However, only constants may be typed in as a response to an INPUT statement, such as 4.5E-3 or "CAT". If more data was requested in an INPUT statement than was typed in, a "??" is printed (if INPUT is from terminal) and the rest of the data should be typed in. If more data was typed in than requested, the extra data will be ignored and a warning "EXTRA IGNORED" will be printed when this happens. String must be input in the same format as they are specified in DATA statements.

5 INPUT "VALUE";V

Optionally types a prompt string ("VALUE") before requesting data from the terminal. Typing CONT after an INPUT command has been interrupted will cause execution to resume at the INPUT statement. An INPUT command is interrupted if a carriage return is the only character entered.

LET

300 LET W = X
310 V = 5.1

Assigns a value to a variable. "LET" is optional. The type of variable (numeric or string) must be the same as the evaluated expression.

ON...GOTO	100 ON I GOTO 10,20,30,40	Branches to the line indicated by the I'th number after the GOTO. That is :

If I = 1, THEN GOTO LINE 10
If I = 2, THEN GOTO LINE 20
If I = 3, THEN GOTO LINE 30
If I = 4, THEN GOTO LINE 40.
If I = 0 or I attempts to select a nonexistent line (> =) in this case, the statement after the ON statement is executed. However, if I is <255 or >0, an "ILLEGAL QUANTITY" error message will result. As many line numbers as will fit on a 79-byte line can follow an ON...GOTO.

105 ON SGN (X) + 2 GOTO
40,50,60

This statement will branch to line 40 if the expression X is less than zero, to line 50 if it equals zero, and to line 60 if it is equal to one.

ON...GOSUB 110 ON 1 GOSUB 50,60

Identical to "ON...GOTO", except that a subroutine called (GOSUB), is executed instead of a GOTO. RETURN from the GOSUB branches to the statement after the ON...GOSUB.

POKE 357 POKE I,J

The POKE statement stores the byte specified by its second argument (J) into the location given by its first argument (I). The byte to be stored must be =>0 and < = 255, or an "ILLEGAL QUANTITY" error will occur. The address (I) must be =>0 and < = 65535, or an "ILLEGAL QUANTITY" error will result. POKE works only on RAM and I/O POKEing. Certain locations will disturb normal CBM operation unless reset. It is not possible to POKE the PEEK of a location into a location in CBM ROM.

PEEK 10A = PEEK(I)

PEEK is a function of an address and returns a byte value contained in that location.

PRINT

Sends the data to CBM TV display. BASIC software calls a subroutine in the system software and loads the character in the accumulator.

```
360 PRINT X,Y,Z
370 PRINT
380 PRINT X,Y
390 PRINT "VALUE" IS";A
400 PRINT A2,B,
```

Prints the value of expressions on the terminal. If the list of values to be printed out does not end with a comma (,) or a semicolon (;), then a carriage return/line feed is executed after all the values have been printed. Strings enclosed in quotes (") may also be printed. If a semicolon separates two expressions in the list, their values are printed next to each other. If a comma appears after an expression in the list, then spaces are printed until the carriage is at the beginning of the next N column field (until the carriage is at column N,2N,3N,4N...). If there is no list of expressions to be printed, then a carriage return is executed.

```
410 PRINT MID$(A$,2);
```

String expressions may be printed. A semicolon is not needed between string expressions such as PRINT AB "HELLO" that are to be concatenated.

READ   `490 READ V,W`

Reads data into specified variable from a DATA statement. The first piece of data read will be the first piece of data listed in the first data statement of the program. The second piece of data read will be the second piece listed in the first DATA statement, and so on. When all of the data have been read from the first DATA statement, the next piece of data to be read will be the first piece listed in the second DATA statement of the program. Attempting to read more data then there is in all the DATA statements in a program will cause an "OUT OF DATA" error. The line number given in the "SYNTAX ERROR" will refer to the line number where the error actually is located.

DATA   `10DATA1,3, − 1E3,.04`

Specifies data, read from left to right. Information appears in data statements in

		the same order as it will be read in the program.
	20 DATA "CBM,INC" 30 DATA PET	Strings may be read from DATA statements. If you want the string to contain a colon (:) or commas (,), or leading blanks, you must enclose the string in double quotes. It is impossible to have a double quote within string data or a string literal. (" "ANYTHING" ") is illegal.
RESTORE	510 RESTORE	Allows the rereading of DATA statements. After a RESTORE, the next piece of data read will be the first piece listed in the first DATA statement, and so on as in a normal READ operation.
REM	500 REM NOW SET V = 0	Allows the programmer to put comments in his program. REM statements are not executed, but can be branched to. A REM statement is terminated by end of line, but not by a ":".
	505REM SET V = 0: V = 0	In this case, the V = 0 will never be executed by BASIC.
	506 V = 0: REM SET V = 0	In this case V = 0 will be executed.
STOP	9000 STOP	Causes a program to stop execution and to enter command mode. Prints BREAK IN LINE 9000 (as per this example). CONT after a STOP branches to the statement following the STOP.
CONT		A command that can be executed only in direct mode. Resumes program execution after STOP, END, or use of STOP key. A program cannot be resumed after error condition, editing, CLR, or NEW.
WAIT	WAIT I,J,K	This statement reads the status of memory location I, exclusive OR's K with status, then AND's the result with J until a non-zero result is obtained. Execution of the program continues at the statement following the WAIT. If the WAIT statement only has two arguments, K is assumed to be zero. If you are waiting for a bit to become zero, there

should be a one in the corresponding
position of K. 0 < = I < = 65536 J,K must be
< = 0 and > = 255.
The STOP key cannot interrupt a WAIT.

BASIC COMMANDS

CLR
LIST
LOAD
NEW
RUN
SAVE
VERIFY

A command is usually given after BASIC has typed READY. This is called the "Command Level".
Commands may be used as program statements. Certain commands, such as LIST and NEW will
terminate program execution when they finish.

CLR		Deletes all stored references to variables, arrays, functions, GOSUB and FOR-NEXT context.
LIST	LIST X	Lists line "X" if there is one.
	LIST or LIST-	Lists the entire program.
	LIST X-	Lists all lines in a program with a line number equal to, or greater than, "X".
	LIST -X	Lists all of the lines in a program with a line number less than, or equal to, "X".
	LIST Y-X	Lists all of the lines within a program with line numbers equal to, or greater than, "Y", and less than or equal to "X". If LIST is used as a program statement, the program will terminate after it is executed.
LOAD	LOAD	Load first program found on cassette #1 into memory.

	LOAD "HURKLE"	Search for named file on cassette #1 and then load it into memory.
	LOAD "HURKLE", 2	Same as previous, except from device #2.
	10 LOAD "HURKLE"	When LOAD is specified as a program statement, execution of the current program in memory stops at this point. A normal load of program proceeds. The new program begins execution from its lowest line number. Variables and their values are passed from the load to the new program. Strings and function definitions cannot be relied upon because BASIC maintains pointers into the old text where they used to be. Strings can be forced to exist in permanent string variable storage by performing an operation on them prior to LOAD, e.g. A$ = A$ + " ". WARNING: On an overlay LOAD, the overlaying program must have a text storage requirement less than or equal to the previous program. If this is not true, then the variables will be overwritten because they are stored immediately after text in memory.
NEW		Deletes current program and all variables.
RUN	RUN	Starts execution of the program currently in memory at the lowest numbered statementment. RUN deletes all variables (like CLR) and restores DATA. If you have stopped your program and wish to continue execution at some point in the program, use a direct GOTO statement to start execution of your program at the desired line.
	RUN 200	Optionally starts RUN at the specified line number.
SAVE	SAVE	Save BASIC text on cassette #1.
	SAVE "HURKLE"	Save and name the file on cassette #1.
	SAVE "HURKLE", 2	Save on 2nd cassette unit.
	SAVE "HURKLE", 2,1	Save and write end of tape block.
VERIFY	VERIFY "HURKLE"	Same parameters as LOAD. Compares contents of memory with file and reports success/failure of compare.

String Functions

FUNCTION	EXAMPLE	PURPOSE
ASC	10 A=ASC("XYZ")	Returns integer value corresponding to ASCII code of first character in string.
CHR$	10 A$=CHR$(N)	Returns character corresponding to ASCII code number
LEFT$	10 ?LEFT$(X$,A)	Returns leftmost A characters from string.
LEN	10 ?LEN(X$)	Returns length of string.
MID$	10 ?MID$(X$,A,B)	Returns B characters from string, starting with the Ath character.
RIGHT$	10 ?RIGHT$(X$,A)	Returns rightmost A characters from string.
STR$	10 A$=STR$(A)	Returns string representation of number.
VAL	10 A=VAL(A$)	Returns numeric representation of string.
	20 A=VAL("A")	If string not numeric, returns "0".

ASC, LEN and VAL functions return numerical results. They may be used as part of an expression. Assignment statements are used here for examples only; other statement types may be used.

Arithmetic Functions

FUNCTION	EXAMPLE	PURPOSE
ABS	10 C=ABS(A)	Returns magnitude of argument without regard to sign.
ATN	10 C=ATN(A)	Returns arctangent of argument. C will be expressed in radians.
COS	10 C=COS(A)	Returns cosine of argument. A must be expressed in radians.
DEF FN	10 DEF FNA(B)=C*D	Allows user to define a function. Function label A must be a single letter; argument B is a dummy.

Arithmetic Functions

SYMBOL	EXAMPLE	PURPOSE
EXP	10 C=EXP(A)	Returns constant 'e' raised to power of the argument. In this example, eA.
INT	10 C=INT(A)	Returns largest integer less than or equal to argument.
LOG	10 C=LOG(A)	Returns natural logarithm of argument. Argument must be greater than or equal to zero.
RND	10 C=RND(A)	Generates a random number between zero and one. If A is less than 0, the same random number is produced in each call to RND. If A=0, the same sequence of random numbers is generated each time RND is called. If A is greater than 0, a new sequence is produced for each call to RND.
SGN	10 C=SGN(A)	Returns –1 if argument is negative, returns 0 if argument is zero, and returns +1 if argument is positive.
SIN	10 C=SIN(A)	Returns sine or argument. A must be expressed in radians.
SQR	10 C=SQR(A)	Returns square root of argument.
TAN	10 C=TAN(A)	Returns tangent of argument. A must be expressed in radians.

EXPRESSIONS AND OPERATORS

RELATIONAL OPERATORS

=	equal
<	less than
>	greater than
< =	L.E.
> =	G.E.
<>	not equal

BOOLEAN OPERATORS

AND
OR
NOT

ARITHMETIC OPERATORS

+	add
–	subtract
*	multiply
/	divide
↑	exponentiation
–	(negation)

STRING OPERATOR

+	(concatenation)

ARITHMETIC OPERATORS

SYMBOL	SAMPLE STATEMENT	PURPOSE/USE
=	A = 100	Assigns a value to a variable,
	LET Z = 2.5	the LET is optional.
–	B = – A	Negation. Note that $0 - A$ is subtraction, while $- A$ is negation.
↑	130 PRINT X↑3	Exponentation (equal to X*X*X in the sample statement). $0↑0 = 1$. 0 to any other power $= 0$. A↑B, with A negative and B not an integer gives an FC error.
*	140 X = R*(B*D)	Multiplication.
/	150 PRINT x/1.3	Division.
+	160.Z = R + T + Q	Addition.
–	170 J = 100 – I	Subtraction.

RELATIONAL OPERATORS

Relational operators can be used as part of any expression.

Relational operator expressions will always have a value of True (– 1) or a value of False (0). Therefore, $(5 = 4) = 0$, $(5 = 5) = - 1$, etc.

The THEN clause of an IF statement is executed whenever the formula after the IF is not equal to 0. That is to say, IF X THEN...is equivalent to IF X < > 0 THEN....

SYMBOL	SAMPLE STATEMENT	PURPOSE/USE
=	10 IF A = 15 THEN 40	Expression Equals Expression.
< >	70 IF A < > 0 THEN 5	Expression Does Not Equal Expression.
>	30 IF B >100 THEN 8	Expression Greater Than Expression.
<	160 IF B <2 THEN 10	Expression Less Than Expression.
< = , =<	180 IF 100 < = B + C THEN 10	Expression Less Than Or Equal To Expression.
> = , =>	190 IF Q > = R THEN 50	Expression Greater Than Or Equal To Expression.

BOOLEAN OPERATORS

AND	2 IF A <5 AND B <2 THEN 7	If expression 1 (A <5) AND expression 2 (B <2) are both true, then branch to line 7.
OR	IF A <1 OR B <2 THEN 2	If either expression 1 (A <1) OR expression 2 (B <2) is true, then branch to line 2.
NOT	IF NOT Q3 THEN 4	If expression "NOT Q3" is true (because Q3 is false), then branch to line 4. NOT $- 1 = 0$ (NOT true = false).

AND, OR and NOT can be used for bit manipulation, and for performing boolean operations.

These three operators convert their arguments to sixteen bit, signed two's, complement integers in the range −32768 to +32767. They then perform the specified logical operation on them and return a result within the same range. If the arguments are not in this range, an ?ILLEGAL QUANTITY ERROR results. The operations are performed in bitwise fashion, this means that each bit of the result is obtained by examining the bit in the same position for each argument.

The following truth table shows the logical relationship between bits:

OPERATOR	ARG. 1	ARG. 2	RESULT
AND	1	1	1
	0	1	0
	1	0	0
	0	0	0
OR	1	1	1
	1	0	1
	0	1	1
	0	0	0
NOT	1	-	0
	0	-	1

EXAMPLES OF BOOLEAN EXPRESSIONS

63 AND 16 = 16 — Since 63 equals binary 111111 and 16 equals binary 10000, the result of the AND is binary 10000 or 16.

15 AND 14 = 14 — 15 equals binary 1111 and 14 equals binary 1110, so 15 and 14 equals binary 1110 or 14.

−1 AND 8 = 8 — −1 equals binary 1111111111111111 and 8 equals binary 1000, so the result is binary 1000 or 8 decimal.

4 AND 2 = 0 — 4 equals binary 100 and 2 equals binary 10, so the result is binary 0 because none of the bits in either argument match to give a 1 bit in the result.

10 OR 10 = 10 — Binary 1010 OR'd with binary 1010, or 10 decimal.

−1 OR −2 = −1 — Binary 1111111111111111 (−1) OR'd with binary 1111111111111110 (−2) equals binary 1111111111111111, or −1.

NOT 0 = −1 — The bit complement of binary 0 to 16 places is sixteen ones (1111111111111111) or −1. Also NOT −1 = 0.

NOT X — NOT X is equal to −(X + 1). This is because to form the sixteen bit two's complement of the binary, you take the bit (one's) complement and add one.

NOT 1 = −2 — The sixteen bit complement of 1 is 1111111111111110, which is equal to −(1 + 1) or −2.

RULES FOR EVALUATING EXPRESSIONS

Rules for Evaluating Expressions:

1. Operations of higher precedence are performed before operations of lower precedence. This means the multiplications and divisions are performed before additions and subtracions. As an example, 2 + 10/5 equals 4, not 2.4. When operations of equal precedence are found in a formula, the left-hand one is executed first: 6 − 3 + 5 = 8, not − 2.

2. The order in which operations are performed can always be specified explicitly through the use of parentheses. For instance, to add 5 to 3 and then divide that by 4, we would use (5 + 3)/4, which eqals 2. If, instead, we had used 5 + 3/4, we would get 5.75 as a result (5 plus 3/4).

The precedence of operators used in evaluating expressions is as follows, in order beginning with the highest precedence: (Note: Operators listed on the same line have the same precedence).

1) FORMULAS ENCLOSED IN PARENTHESIS ARE ALWAYS EVALUATED FIRST

2) ↑   EXPONENTATION

3) NEGATION   − X WHERE X MAY BE A FORMULA

4) * /   MULTIPLICATION AND DIVISION

5) + −   ADDITION AND SUBTRACTION

6) RELATIONAL OPERATORS: = EQUAL

<> NOT EQUAL

(equal precedence   < LESS THAN

for all six).   > GREATER THAN

< = LESS THAN OR EQUAL

> = GREATER THAN OR EQUAL

7) NOT   LOGICAL AND BITWISE "NOT" LIKE NEGATION, NOT TAKES ONLY THE FORMULA TO ITS RIGHT AS AN ARGUMENT

8) AND   LOGICAL AND BITWISE "AND"

9) OR   LOGICAL AND BITWISE "OR"

SPACE HINTS

In order to make your program smaller and save space, the following hints may be useful.

1) Use multiple statements per line. There is a small amount of overhead. (5 bytes) associated with each line in the program. Two of these five bytes contain the line number of the line in binary. This means that no matter how many digits you have in your line number (minimum line number is 0, maximum is 63999), it takes the same number of bytes. Putting as many statements as possible in a line will cut down on the number of bytes used by your program.

2) Delete all unnecessary spaces from your program. For instance:

10 PRINT X, Y, Z

uses three more bytes than

10 PRINTX,Y,Z

   Note: All spaces between the line number and the first non-blank character are ignored.

3) Delete all REM statements. Each REM statement uses at least one byte plus the number of bytes in the text. For instance, the statement 130 REM THIS IS A COMMENT uses up 24 bytes of memory.

In the statement 140 X = X + Y:REM UPDATE SUM, the REM uses 14 bytes of memory including the colon before the REM.

4) Use variables instead of constants. Suppose you use the constant 1.02369 ten times in your program. If you insert a statement

10Q = 1.02369

in the program, and use Q instead of 1.02369 each time it is needed, you will save 40 bytes. This will also result in a speed improvement.

5) A program need not end with an END; so, an END statement at the end of a program may be deleted.

6) Re-use the same variables. If you have a variable T which is used to hold a temporary result in one part of the program and you need a temporary variable later in your program, use it again. Or, if you are asking the terminal user to give a YES or NO answer to two different questions at two different times during the execution of the program, use the same temporary variable A$ to store the reply.

7) Use GOSUB's to execute sections of program statemnts that perform identical actions.

8) Use the zero elements of matrices; for instance, A(O), B(O,X)

SPEED HINTS

The hints below should improve the execution time of your BASIC program. Note that some of these hints are the same as those used to decrease the space used by your programs. This means that in many cases you can increase the efficiency of both the speed and size of your programs at the same time.

1) Delete all unnecessary spaces and REM's from the program. This may cause a small decrease in execution time because BASIC would otherwise have to ignore or skip over spaces and REM statements.

2) THIS IS PROBABLY THE MOST IMPORTANT SPEED HINT BY A FACTOR OF 10. Use variables instead of constants. It takes more time to convert a constant to its floating point representation than it does to fetch the value of a simple or matrix variable. This is especially important within FOR...NEXT loops or other code that is executed repeatedly.

3) Order your definitions of variables carefully. Variables which are encountered first during the execution of a BASIC program are allocated at the start of the variable table. This means that a statement such as 5 A = O:B = A:C = A, will place A first, B second, and C third in the symbol table (assuming line 5 is the first statement executed in the program). Later in the program, when BASIC finds a reference to the variable A, it will search only one entry in the symbol table to find A, two entries to find B and three entries to find C, etc.

4) Use NEXT statements without the index variable. NEXT is somewhat faster than NEXT I because no check is made to see if the variable specified in the NEXT is the same variable in the most recent FOR statement.

FORTRAN-BASIC
CONVERSION TABLES

The BASIC computer language is designed for usage in a time-sharing system. Its simplicity also makes it an ideal language for the beginning programmer. The FORTRAN (*Formula Trans*lation) language, however, was the first popular high level or computer language and is still widely used today for scientific applications.

Many similarities exist between the structure of the BASIC and FORTRAN languages. Some of these similarities are listed here with examples as to the differences which exist in most systems.

BASIC	FORTRAN
↑	**
*	*
/	/
+	+
—	—

BASIC	FORTRAN
( ),[ ]	( ),[ ]
= (assignment)	=
= (comparison)	.EQ.
<	.LT.
>	.GT.
#, < >	.NE.
< =	.LE.
> =	.GE.

For comparing variables of the same type (see below)

BASIC	FORTRAN
A, B1 (integers)	Any one- to six-letter combination of alphabetic or numerical characters, with the first character either I, J, K, L, M, or N.
C, D3 (having, having a decimal point)	Any one- to six-letter combination of alphabetic or numerical characters, with the first being any alphabetic character other than I, J, K, L, M, or N.
SIN(X)	SIN(X) Argument must be a real variable.
COS(X)	COS(X) Real argument
TAN(X)	TAN(X) Real argument
ATN(X)	ATAN(X) Real argument
SQR (X)	SQRT(X) Non-negative real argument
ABS(X)	ABS(X) Real or IABS(K) Integer argument
INT(X)	INT(X) Real argument with integer output
LOG(X)	ALOG(X) Real argument
EXP(X)	EXP(X) Real argument
OR	.OR.
AND	.AND.
NOT	.NOT.
n REM ..	C ...
n DATA	(Data on "data cards," placed in specified sequence in program deck.)
n READ	READ (a,b) A,B The a,b specify which input device is to be accessed and which FORMAT statement describes the data's form.

n PRINT	WRITE (a,b) A,B The a,b specify which ouput device is to be accessed and which FORMAT statement describes the form of the output.
n INPUT	(no batch-load equivalent)
n GOTO *m*	GOTO *m*
n GOTO A OF $s_1, s_2, \ldots, s_r$	GOTO $(s_1, s_2, \ldots, s_r)$, A
n GOSUB	CALL ... Subroutine must be named and previously identified as being in system library or in present compilation.
IF ... THEN ...	IF (A) *n,m,p* Transfers control to:

$$n \text{ if } A < 0$$
$$m \text{ if } A = 0$$
$$p \text{ if } A > 0$$

IF (A .LT. 0) *n*, etc., is also possible. This format can also reassign variables:

IF (A.LT.0) M = 3

n FOR A = *m* TO *p* STEP *r*	
q NEXT A	DO 10 A = *m, p, r* Where all statements after DO ... and including statement 10 are to be executed for a number of times given as A is incremented from *m* to *p* by a step with size *r*.
n DIM A[20,20]	DIMENSION A[20,20]

FORTRAN was the first "high-level" language of any consequence (1954-55, IBM); it quickly became a standard, and every scientist of any status, who wanted to use a computer, learned the language. Now, even though a myriad of other languages are available, FORTRAN still ranks as one of the major languages, especially FORTRAN IV. Our present pursuit will be to delve into a few intricacies of the language and observe a few examples. One precaution: as with any language, there are constant revisions to FORTRAN; a recent commission has proposed new standards for the language, and those standards have been adopted by the American Standards Institute. The text of the proposals is readily available in SIGPLAN *Notices* of ACM (Volume 11, No. 3, 1976 March) and subsequent draft revisions.

Considering the many texts available, of considerable page count, which deal with the many complexities of FORTRAN, we can hardly be expected to cover the language in any depth in such a brief section. We suggest, however, that the interested student pursue (now or later) a more exhaustive study of this very widely-used language.

Exercise

Write BASIC and FORTRAN statements for each of the following assignment statements. Note: "*ln*" means "$\log_e$."

(1) $G = \dfrac{1}{2} ln \dfrac{1 \pm \sin x}{1 - \sin x}$

(2) $R = \dfrac{\sin^3 x \cos^2 x}{5} + \dfrac{2}{15}\sin^2 x$

(3) $D = ln \left| \cos x + \tan x \right|$

(4) $P = x^2 - x - \sin x$

(5) $P = x^3 - 4.73\,x^2 + 2.393\,x + 4.336$

(6) $P = x^3 - 0.25\,x^2 + 0.75\,x - 2.5$

(7) $P = 0.3\,x - \tan x$

(8) $P = \sin x - \dfrac{1}{x}$

(9) $P = x^5 + 11\,x^4 + 12\,x^3 - 109\,x^2 - 119\,x - 120$

(10) $P = \sin \left[\tan^{-1} \dfrac{\sqrt{x^2 + v^2}}{|z|} \right] + 1$

(11) $C = \sqrt{a^2 + b^2 - 2\,a \cdot b \cdot \cos \nu}$

(12) $C = 2\,r \sin \dfrac{\nu}{2}$

(13) $Y = \dfrac{1}{1 + |\tan x|}$

(14) $S = a \cdot \sin kw - b \cdot \cos kw$

(15) $F = \csc^2 x + 1$

(16) $R = e^{-x} \sin 2x$

(17) $Y = \dfrac{e^{\tan^{-1} x}}{1 + x^2}$

(18) $C = \ln\left(x + \sqrt{x^2 + 1}\right)$

(19) $Z = \ln \dfrac{e^x}{1 + e^x}$

(20) $T = \tan^{-1}\left(\dfrac{1}{2} \ln \dfrac{1 + x}{1 - x}\right)$

(21) $S = \dfrac{1}{2} r^2 \left(v - \sin v\right)$

(22) $Y = \sqrt{\sqrt{x^2 + 1} - \sqrt{x^2 - 1}}$

(23) $P = 1 - \dfrac{\sqrt{s}}{1 - \dfrac{\sqrt{s}}{1 - \sqrt{s}}}$

(24) $W = [\![u]\!] \cdot \sqrt{\dfrac{1}{u}}$

(25) $M = \Big|\, \big|\, |x - 1| \cdot x + 1\,\big| \cdot x - 1 \,\Big|$

Still More Exercises

In these exercises, concentrate on making the programs easy to use and foolproof for *somebody else* who does not know BASIC. Have somebody else *use* the programs to see how good your prompting statements are.

1. Write a FORTRAN or BASIC program that will read 50 cards, each with two integers of 6 digits each, sum the two numbers separately, and then average the two sets separately. The output should echo the numbers on the cards, as well as show the two averages. Use comments inside the program to describe program activities.

2. Write a FORTRAN or BASIC program that will read input for the appropriate variables and that will then output the monthly payment amount using the following formula for payment amount for a direct reduction loan:

$$A = P \frac{I}{1 - (1 + I)^{-N}}$$

where A = amount of payment at the end of each payment period;
    P = present value or amount of principal;
    I = interest rate per time period (expressed as a decimal; must be expressed in rate for a month);
    N = number of payment periods (number of months)

Carefully identify input requirements and output information.
Extra: provide an additional output showing total of payments for the life of the loan, and the difference between the total of payments and the principal.

Program LRP in SIMPLE shows one way of tackling this problem. In fact, programs LRIR, LRP, LRPW, LRNTP, LRAI, LRRB, and LRAS all show different ways of attacking the same formula.

3. Write a FORTRAN or BASIC program that will read input for the appropriate variables and provide the required output from the formula given below for compound interest. Assume we wish to know what amount we should invest at a given rate of interest in order to achieve a particular future amount. Also assume that we compound monthly, and that the interest rate is given as a *yearly* decimal rate.

$$P = F \cdot (1 + I)^{-N}$$

where P = present value, that is, amount to be invested;
    F = future value, that is, the desired amount;
    I = interest rate *per period* (per month in this case);
    N = number of compounding periods (number of months, in this case;

Properly identify all requested input and describe the output, echoing the input information.

Program CIPW shows one way of tackling this problem. In fact, programs CIIR, CIPW, CIFV, CINTP, CIAPI are all different ways of attacking the same formula.

At this point it is a good idea to look back at the set of problems used in the BASIC discussions. Convert to FORTRAN as many (working) BASIC programs created there as there is time for. Pick one or two for special analysis; obtain as much information as you can on the times involved in running the same program in a BASIC environment and in a FORTRAN environment—both CPU time and elapsed time. Compare the relative storage requirements for the different executable forms (object code for FORTRAN). On your system, then, which seems to be more efficient in time? In storage? Overall (in your opinion)? What about preparation time (writing and inputting the source code)?

After doing this exercise, you should see quite clearly that converting a BASIC program to a FORTRAN program is simple. The wisdom of hindsight that the orginators of BASIC built into the language makes BASIC an unquestionably easier-to-use and more powerful program development tool than FORTRAN. The fact that usually a *compiled* FORTRAN program executes faster in most computer systems than an *interpreted* BASIC program does not outweigh the fact that it is faster and more cost-effective to develop a program in BASIC. Perhaps soon a truly interactive noncard-oriented, nonbatch-oriented FORTRAN system will be developed, and perhaps greater flexibility may be built into FORTRAN to bring it up to BASIC's standard ease of use and preprogrammed functional availability. Until then, however, it is safe to say that BASIC is a better language for the interdisciplinary practitioner, who views the computer as a tool and not as an ultimate object.

While on this subject, you might look at the work by Lykos, *Minicomputers and Large-Scale Calculations* (Washington, D.C.: A.C.S. Symposium Series #57, American Chemical Society, 1977). This work looks very carefully at the cost-benefit analysis of program development in a minicomputer (BASIC and APL) environment versus a large computer (usually FORTRAN) environment.

REFERENCES

Stern, Robert and Stern, Nancy. *FORTRAN Supplement to Arranging Principles of Data Processing*, New York: John Wiley & Sons, Inc., 1974.

Gately, W. U., and Bitter, G. G. *BASIC for Beginners*. New York: McGraw-Hill, 1970.

Hare, V. C. *BASIC Programming*. New York: Harcourt, Brace & World, 1970.

Kemeny, J. G., and Kurtz, T. E. *BASIC Programming*. New York: Wiley, 1970.

McCracken, Daniel D. *A Guide to FORTRAN IV Programming*. New York: Wiley, 1972. Especially note pp. 47-48, "A Checklist for Program Checkout."

Nolan, Richard L. *Introduction to Computing through the BASIC Language*. New York: Holt, Rinehart and Winston, 1969. Especially note chaps. 2-6, and Appendix A, "Time-sharing BASIC and Batch-mode BASIC."

Pavlovich, J. P., and Tahan, T. E. *Computer Programming in BASIC*. San Francisco: Holden-Day, 1971.

Smith, R. E. *Discovering BASIC: A Problem Solving Approach*. Rochelle Park, N.J.: Hayden, 1970.

Spencer, Donald D. *A Guide to BASIC Programming: A Time-sharing Language*. Reading, Mass.: Addison-Wesley, 1970.

———. *Computers in Action: How Computers Work*. Rochelle Park, N.J.: Hayden, 1974. Especially note chap. 7, "The Language of the Computer," and chap. 8, "Introduction to Computer Programming."

———. *Computers in Society: The Wheres, Whys, and Hows of Computer Usage*. Rochelle Park, N.J.: Hayden, 1974.

Draft Proposed ANS FORTRAN, Notices of the Special Interest Group on Programming Languages, ACM, Vol. 11, No. 3, March, 1976.

Weiss, Eric A., ed. *Computer Usage: Fundamentals*. New York: McGraw-Hill, 1969. Especially note chap. 12, "FORTRAN, COBOL, and other Programming Languages," chap. 15, "Techniques for Computing Scientific Problems," and chap. 19, "Specifying and Documenting Computers Programs."

Lykos, P. ed., *Minicomputers and Large-Scale Calculations*, A.C.S. Symposium Series #57. Washington, D.C.: American Chemical Society, 1977.

SUGGESTED SOURCES FOR ADDITIONAL MATERIAL

Coan, J. S. *Basic BASIC: An Introduction to Computer Programming in BASIC Language*. Rochelle Park, N.J.: Hayden, 1970.

DeRossi, Claude J. *Learning BASIC Fast*. Reston, Virginia: Reston, 1974.

Estes, James W., and Estes, B. Robert. *Elements of Computer Science*. San Francisco: Canfield Press, 1973. Especially note chap. 8, "Programming Languages."

Farina, Mario V. *Elementary BASIC with Applications*. Englewood Cliffs, N.J.: Prentice-Hall, 1970.

———. *FORTRAN IV Self-taught*. Englewood Cliffs, N.J.: Prentice-Hall, 1966.

CROSS-REFERENCES TO
LEADING STATISTICS TEXTBOOKS

This table correlates each of the programs in this book with specific sections of the leading statistics and business statistics textbooks. For example, the factorial (F) program is treated in Chapter 2, and questions 1 through 14 on page 90 represent applications for the factorial program.

HAMBURG

Factorial (F)   2   Means "Chapter 2"
                                 p.90,#1-14 Means "See questions 1 through 14
                                                   on page 90 of Hamburg."

The following textbooks are referred to in the table:

Neter, J., W. Wasserman, and G. A. Whitmore
    APPLIED STATISTICS
    Allyn and Bacon, Inc.
    Second Printing, 1978
    ISBN: 0-205-05982-1

Mendenhall, W. and J. E. Reinmuth
    STATISTICS FOR MANAGEMENT AND ECONOMICS
    Duxbury Press
    1978
    ISBN: 0-87872-142-8

Hamburg, Morris
    STATISTICAL ANALYSIS FOR DECISION MAKING
    Harcourt, Brace, Jovanovich, Inc.
    Second Edition, 1977
    ISBN: 0-15-583747-8

Berenson, Mark L. and David M. Levine
    BASIC BUSINESS STATISTICS--CONCEPTS AND APPLICATIONS
    Prentice-Hall, Inc.
    1979
    ISBN: 0-13-057596-8

Freund, John E. and Frank J. Williams
    ELEMENTARY BUSINESS STATISTICS--THE MODERN APPROACH
    Prentice-Hall, Inc.
    1977
    ISBN: 0-13-253062-7

Levin, Richard L.
    STATISTICS FOR MANAGEMENT
    Prentice-Hall, Inc.
    1978
    ISBN: 0-13-845305-5

Horngren, Charles T.
    COST ACCOUNTING--A MANAGERIAL EMPHASIS
    4th Edition
    Prentice-Hall, Inc.
    1977
    ISBN: 0-13-179739-5

Fertig, Paul E., Donald F. Istvan, and Homer J. Mottle
    USING ACCOUNTING INFORMATION
    Second Edition, 1971
    Harcourt, Brace, Jovanovich, Inc.
    ISBN: 0-15-594454-1

Dopuch, Nicholas, Jacob G. Birnberg, and Joel Demski
    COST ACCOUNTING--ACCOUNTING DATA FOR MANAGEMENT DECISIONS
    Harcourt, Brace, Jovanovich, Inc.
    1974
    ISBN: 0-15-514198-8

	NETER, WASSERMAN, WHITMORE	MENDENHALL, REINMUTH	HAMBURG	FREUND, WILLIAMS	LEVINE, BERENSON	LEVIN
PROBABILITY CALCULATIONS	4,5,6,7					
Factorial (F)	6	4	2	5	5 5.30-5.39	5
Permutations (P)		4	2 p.90,#1-14	5 p.93,#1-28	5.30-5.39	5
Combinations (C)		4	2 p.90,#1-14	6,9 p.93,#1-28	5.30-5.39	5
Bayes Formula (BF)	22,23 Chaps. 22, 23 problems (modified)	4 4.21-4.24	2 p.82,#1-5	5 p.138,#1-14 p.209,#1-10	5.23-5.29 11.1-11.12	5 Chap. 5 #33-38
Prob. of No Repetition (PNR)			p.90,#1-14		5 5.30-5.39	5
ONE INDEPENDENT VARIABLE STAT'S.	1,2,3					
Single Variable Statistics (SVS)	1,2,3 3.2,3.3,3.5 3.6,3.7, 3.15	3 3.8,3.13, 3.17,3.20 3.44	1 p.25,#1-5, p.35,#1-6 p.46,#1-5	3 p.31,#3,5,6, 7-17 p.42,#1-16 p.54,#1-6	4 4.1-4.33	3 Chap. 3 #5-14 15-36, Chap. 4, #1-32
Moving Average (MA)	24 24.1,24.4, 24.5,24.6, 24.7, 24.8	14 14.6-14.8	p.489,#1-5	19 p.438,#1-10		
Standardized Scores (SS)	5				3.1-3.28	
Generalized Mean						
Frequency Histogram (FH)	2 2.9,2.10, 2.11,2.14, 2.17	3 3.1,3.2,3.3 3.4,3.5,3.6 3.7,3.23	1 p.17,#1-16	14 p.16,#1-15 p.50,#1-10	3 3.1-3.28 4.1-4.28	2 Chap. 2 #22-32
DISCRETE DISTRIBUTION FUNCTIONS						
Binomial Distribution (BD)	6,10 6.1,6.2,6.3 6.4,10.6	6 6.3-6.8 6.9-6.12	3 p.115,#1-16	8 p.192,#1-29	6 6.1-6.44	6 Chap. 6 #11-17
Poisson Distribution (PD)	6,10 6.5,6.6,6.7 6.8,6.9 6.21,17.13	6 6.13-6.17	3 p.139,#1-11	8 p.192,#1-29	6 6.1-6.44	6 Chap. 6 #18-25

CONTINUOUS DISTRIBUTION FUNCTIONS

Khrgian & Mazin Distribution (KMD)	16 7.5					
Exponential Distribution (ED)	6 6.19,6.20 6.18	5		10	6 6.1-6.44	6 Chap. 6 #26-36
Normal Distribution (ND)	6,7 6.14,6.12 7.8	7 7.3-7.9 7.10-7.14	p.209,#1-16	10 p.230,#1-9 p.237,#1-15	10	10 Chap. 10 #1-19
Inverse Normal Distribution (IND)						
Chi-Squared Distribution (CSD)	7 7.3,7.4 7.5,7.16 9.24-9.26	9	8 p.327,#1-5	13 p.309,#1-17		10 Chap. 10 #20-31
F-Distribution (FD)	7 7.11,7.12, 7.13,7.14 7.15,7.16	9 9.27-9.30	8 p.354,#1-4	13 p.352,#1-8	12 12.1-12.24	
T-Distribution (TD)	7 7.9,7.10 7.15,7.16	9.1-9.10	6 p.219,#1-12	12 p.271,#1-25	8 8.1-8.47 7.1-7.18	8 Chap. 8 #36-39
Random Number Generator (RNG)	8 Chap. 8 problems		p.186			Chap. 7 #7-14

SURVEY DATA & CONTINGENCY TABLES — 16

Contingency Tables (CT)	17 17.9,17.10 17.11	16,17 17.5-17.12	8	14 p.120,#1-8 p.128,#1-12 p.340,#1-12	10 5.1-5.19 10.1-10.80	10
Mann-Whitney Statistic (MWS)	15 15.1-15.25	18 18.6-18.8	12 p.531,#1-4	16 p.371,#1-11	13 13.1-13.33	12 Chap. 12 #11-16
Spearman's Rank Correlation Coefficient (SRCC)	15 15.1-15.25	18 18.17-18.19	12 p.542,#1-3	18 p.412,#1-6		Chap. 12 #23-28

REGRESSION AND CORRELATION

One Independent Variable Regression (OIVR)	18,20 18.2,18.4, 18.11,18.12 18.27,19.14 19.18,19.21 20.21,24.4 24.5,24.6	11 11.4,11.5 11.10,11.16 11.19,11.24 11.27,11.32 11.34,11.41 11.44,11.46 11.50,11.54 11.59,14.4 14.8,14.11	9 p.372,#1-6 p.407,#1-8	17 p.386,#1-8 p.393,#1-8 p.406,#1-14 p.430,#1-14	14 14.1-14.20 17.1-17.22	11 Chap. 11 #1-33 Chap. 13 #1-39

	NETER, WASSERMAN, WHITMORE	MENDENHALL, REINMUTH	HAMBURG	FREUND, WILLIAMS	LEVINE, BERENSON	LEVIN
Polynomial Regression (PR)	18 20.20	11,12 12.27,12.28	9 p.465,#7	17 p.430,#1-14	14,15 p.529,15.1- 15.46	11 Chap. 11 #34-37
Multiple Linear Regression (MLR)	20 20.3,20.6 20.25	12 12.1,12.29 12.30	9 p.431,#1-6	17 p.397,#1-4 p.412	15 p.506,15.1- 15-14	11 Chap. 11 #34-37
ANALYSIS OF VARIANCE						
Analysis of Variance--One Independent Variable (AV1)	21 18.15,18.17 18.18,18.19 18.22,18.23 19.14,19.18 19.21,20.20	13 13.1-13.7 13.8-13.11	8 p.354,#1-4	15 p.352,#1-8	12 12.1-12.24	10 Chap. 10 #1-19,20-31
Analysis of Variance--Two Independent Variables (AV2)	20.6			15 p.359,#1-4		
Analysis of Variance--Three Independent Variables (AV3)	20.3,20.25					
FACTORIAL INFORMATION MATRICES						
Principal Component Analysis (PCA)						
ANALYSIS OF TIME SERIES	24,25,18,20	14,15,11	10	17,19	16,17	11,13,14
Forecasting: Monthly Data, Decomposition (FCAST)	24.1,24.4 24.5,24.6 24.7,24.8 24.13,24.15 24.16,24.17 24.20	14 14.4,14.8 14.11,14.20	9,10,11 p.463,#1-11	p.70,#1-15 p.80,#1-14 p.430,#1-14 p.451,#1-11	16.1-16.10 17.1-17.22	Chap. 13 #1-39 Chap. 14
MISCELLANEOUS BUSINESS CAL'NS.						
Loan Repayment: Interest Rate (LRIR)						
Loan Repayment: Payments (LRP)						
Loan Repayment: Present Worth (LRPW)						
Loan Repayment: Number of Time Periods (LRNTP)						

Loan Repayment: Accumulated Interest (LRAI)

Loan Repayment: Remaining Balance (LRRB)

Loan Repayment: Amortization Schedule (LRAS)

Sinking Fund: Interest Rate (SFIR)

Sinking Fund: Payment (SFP)

Sinking Fund: Future Value (SFFV)

Sinking Fund: Number of Time Periods (SFNTP)

Discounted Cash Flow (DCF)

Depreciation: Straight-Line Book Value (DSLBV)

Depreciation: Sum of the Year's Digits--Book Value (DSYDB)

Depreciation: Declining Balance-- Book Value (DDBBV)

Compound Interest: Interest Rate (CIIR)

Compound Interest: Present Worth (CIPW)

Compound Interest: Future Value (CIFV)

Compound Interest: Number of Time Periods (CINTP)

Compound Interest: Amound Paid as Interest (CIAPI)